RAND NATIONAL SECURITY RESEARCH DIVISION

Countering Sectarianism in the Middle East

Volume Editors: Jeffrey Martini, Dalia Dassa Kaye, Becca Wasser
Contributing Authors: Amanda Rizkallah, Justin Gengler,
Kathleen Reedy, Ami Carpenter

Sponsored by the Henry Luce Foundation

For more information on this publication, visit www.rand.org/t/RR2799

Library of Congress Cataloging-in-Publication Data is available for this publication.
ISBN: 978-1-9774-0191-5

Published by the RAND Corporation, Santa Monica, Calif.
© Copyright 2019 RAND Corporation
RAND® is a registered trademark.

Cover image: Mohamed Azakir/Reuters

Limited Print and Electronic Distribution Rights

This document and trademark(s) contained herein are protected by law. This representation of RAND intellectual property is provided for noncommercial use only. Unauthorized posting of this publication online is prohibited. Permission is given to duplicate this document for personal use only, as long as it is unaltered and complete. Permission is required from RAND to reproduce, or reuse in another form, any of its research documents for commercial use. For information on reprint and linking permissions, please visit www.rand.org/pubs/permissions.

The RAND Corporation is a research organization that develops solutions to public policy challenges to help make communities throughout the world safer and more secure, healthier and more prosperous. RAND is nonprofit, nonpartisan, and committed to the public interest.

RAND's publications do not necessarily reflect the opinions of its research clients and sponsors.

Support RAND
Make a tax-deductible charitable contribution at
www.rand.org/giving/contribute

www.rand.org

Preface

Scholars and policymakers alike have sought to understand what drives sectarianism in the Middle East and its relationship to multiple conflicts. But far less attention has been focused on what factors make a community more resilient to sectarianism. This report seeks to address this gap by providing a better understanding of how communities inoculate themselves from sectarianism or recover from it and draws lessons on how to promote resilience and cross-sectarian cooperation.

To carry out this study, RAND researchers collaborated with a group of scholars with extensive regional and subject-matter expertise on sectarianism in the Middle East. This report begins with a treatment of conceptual issues, covers four case studies in countries with sectarian divisions, and concludes with key findings and recommendations for countering sectarianism and promoting resilience in the Middle East.

This research was sponsored by the Henry Luce Foundation under the foundation's Religion in International Affairs program. The program supports projects that promote a deeper understanding of the role of religion in international affairs and that foster dialogue between the academic community and policymakers. The research was conducted within the International Security and Defense Policy Center of the RAND National Security Research Division (NSRD). NSRD conducts research and analysis for the Office of the Secretary of Defense, the Joint Staff, the Unified Combatant Commands, the defense agencies, the Navy, the Marine Corps, the U.S. Coast Guard, the U.S. Intelligence Community, allied foreign governments, and foundations.

For more information on the RAND International Security and Defense Policy Center, see www.rand.org/nsrd/ndri/centers/isdp or contact the director (contact information is provided on the webpage).

Contents

Preface iii
Figures and Tables vii
Summary ix
Acknowledgments xiii
Abbreviations xv

CHAPTER ONE
Identifying Resilience and Cross-Sectarian Cooperation 1
Literature on Sectarianism 2
Policymaker Views on Sectarianism 4
Knowledge Gaps 6
Conceptual Issues 7
Research Approach and Organization of This Report 9

CHAPTER TWO
Transcending Sectarian Politics: The Case of Beirut Madinati 15
Lebanese Political Institutions and Elections 16
Formation: What Is Beirut Madinati? 18
Anatomy of a Campaign 21
From Campaign to Political Movement 26
Why Now? 27
Sustainability and Continuity 32
Implications and Conclusions 39

CHAPTER THREE
Segregation and Sectarianism: Geography, Economic Distribution, and Sectarian Resilience in Bahrain 41
A Tale of Two Bahraini Cities: 'Isa Town and Hamad Town 43
Segregation and Distribution in Bahrain 50
Local Integration and Sectarian Relations During the 2011 Uprising 57
Conclusion 61

CHAPTER FOUR
Resilience and Sectarianism in Syria: The Role of Foreign Support 65
Experiences in the Civil War 69
Variables in Sectarianism 71
Discussion 87

CHAPTER FIVE
Resilience to Sectarianism in Baghdad and Dohuk 91
Resilience, Conflict Escalation, and Social Capital 92
Background 93
Neighborhood Versus City Resilience 95
Social Capital 98
Translating Trust to Action 106
Discussion 112
Conclusion 114

CHAPTER SIX
Lessons and Policy Recommendations for Countering Sectarianism 115
Summary of Case Study Findings 116

References 125

Figures

Figures

1.1.	Levels of Sectarian Division and Conflict in the Middle East, 2018	11
3.1.	'Isa Town	46
3.2.	Hamad Town	47
3.3.	Sectarian Segregation in Bahrain	51
3.4.	Public-Sector Employment and Local Sectarian Segregation	54
3.5.	Household Income and Local Sectarian Segregation	55
3.6.	Self-Assessed Economic Satisfaction and Local Sectarian Segregation	56
4.1.	Political Map of Syria	67
4.2.	Reported Ideology of Respondents According to a Survey on Sectarianism, 2016	73
4.3.	Perceived Origins of Sectarianism in Syria	74
4.4.	Attacks in Syria, 2011–2016	75

Tables

2.1.	Beirut Municipal Election Results	25
4.1.	Active and Supporting Members in the Ba'th Party	80
4.2.	Service Provision in Syria, 2009	81
5.1.	Research Site Selection	96

Summary

Sectarianism has become a destructive feature of the modern Middle East. Whether it is driven by political elites as a regime-survival strategy, by major powers as part of a strategy for building regional influence, or by religious leaders and believers who are unwilling to accept the equal status of other religious groups, sectarianism is likely to remain part of the regional landscape for years to come. This does not mean, however, that sectarianism defines all facets of the Middle East or that the violence that stems from this strand of identity politics is irreversible in all cases. Although sectarian conflicts have led to horrific bloodshed, sectarian violence in the region is still the exception rather than the norm. Middle Eastern communities are generally resilient to the worst sectarian impulses, and even communities that experience sectarian strife can recover from it. Indeed, the research described in this report demonstrates that, at least at the local level, communities can resist the slide toward sectarianism.

This report takes a multidisciplinary approach to explore resilience to sectarianism in four Middle Eastern case studies: Lebanon, Bahrain, Syria, and Iraq. The case study authors—who have backgrounds in political science, anthropology, and conflict resolution—analyze what accounts for the ability of some communities to remain resilient in the face of sectarianism. Despite the different disciplinary lenses, all cases apply a similar methodological approach. First, the authors employ an in-country comparison (cross-sectional or temporal) to explore what makes one community more resilient to sectarianism than another. Second, the authors consider common factors across cases, including political and social mechanisms for mediating among sectarian communities, the nature of the physical environment, and the proximity and access of outside forces that might have an interest in instrumentalizing sectarian identity. This allows for more-generalizable conclusions, particularly because the four cases represent a large share of the total universe of Middle Eastern cases where there is significant sectarian diversity and some history of sectarian tension or violence.

From the case studies, several findings emerge about which factors better insulate communities from sectarianism and promote resilience, highlighting a complex interplay of external and domestic factors. Border management was a critical factor in several communities' vulnerability to sectarian actors. In the Syrian case, for example, the ability of sectarian actors to cross the border from Turkey into Idlib was a key driver for higher levels of sectarian violence there than in communities on the Jordanian border, like Dara'a. Similarly, in Iraq, the ability to prevent the physical entry of sectarian militias into some neighborhoods helped explain the variation in the levels of sectarian violence in different communities.

The role of political leaders also proved critical in all cases, in both positive and negative ways. Political elites with patronage systems, particularly from external sources, tended to foster sectarianism and stymie cross-sectarian cooperation. But when such elites lose legitimacy and are unable to deliver to their constituencies, as we saw in the Lebanon case, windows of opportunity can emerge for leaders and movements with nonsectarian agendas. However, it is difficult to capitalize on windows of opportunity if there are no alternative political leaders or movements with nonsectarian agendas who can seize the moment. This requires some opening of political space, at least at the local level, for movements to form around issues that transcend sectarian politics, such as economic development, education reform, female empowerment, or environmental challenges.

Communities with higher levels of existing cross-sectarian interaction can further boost resilience, even in the face of sectarian-driven armed conflict, as occurred during the height of the civil war in Iraq. The stronger the level of trust and social connection among community members across sectarian lines, the better equipped communities are to avoid sliding into sectarianism when conflict emerges. Conversely, when communities are built to segregate citizens along sectarian lines, as occurred in the Bahrain case, the prospects for division and conflict increase. And finally, less pronounced socioeconomic gaps improve a community's ability to resist sectarianism.

Several policy recommendations emerge from the case study analysis and findings. Beyond the long-term goal of reducing the salience of sectarianism by ending conflicts or narrowing socioeconomic gaps that make populations more susceptible to sectarianism, this research offers the following more-achievable recommendations in the short term:

- *Improve the control of borders.* Cutting off the resources, supplies, and fighters coming from foreign sources is critical, as is pressing border countries to stop these flows, particularly in conflict zones like Syria and Iraq. Communities that are better walled off from external sectarian influence exhibit higher levels of resilience and lower levels of violence.
- *Limit foreign funding of sectarian leaders and parties.* One of the most significant drivers of sectarian tension and violence in the region is the fueling of sectarian conflict from external sources and the patronage systems that sustain it. Exerting leverage on regional governments (in particular, Iran and Saudi Arabia) to curtail such activities is critical. Preventing sectarian conflicts that have negative spillover effects across the region should create a common incentive among external

powers to limit the influence of sectarian actors, even if the external powers are at odds on broader policy goals.
- *Encourage civil-society development.* Pressing for freedom of expression and association in bilateral dialogues with regional partners is crucial. This does not mean insisting on elections or backing specific opposition leaders or parties. Rather, the focus should be on opening up space at the local level for civic engagement as a peaceful channel for expressing grievances and discussing policy challenges that cut across sectarian agendas. Civil-society movements can help cultivate new cadres of leaders and form an important alternative to sectarian-driven elites.
- *Focus on governance.* Like encouraging civil-society development, supporting regional leaders with domestic governance agendas is critical, particularly in terms of the ability to better deliver public services through institutional capacity-building and skills development among their youthful populations. Highlighting leaders who are dependent on patronage and corrupt practices and who are not delivering basic services to their people can open up opportunities for alternative leaders. Cultivating leaders who support domestic reform programs aimed to benefit the broader public—not just a particular group or tribe—will be critical for reducing sectarianism and solving day-to-day public policy challenges.
- *Take urban planning seriously.* How cities are designed in the Middle East matters, not only for sustainable development but also for social and political stability. Urban areas designed to better integrate different sectors of society and increase opportunities for interaction through public spaces are more likely to remain stable and peaceful when societal tensions increase. Although it will be difficult to redesign villages and urban areas already based on segregated models where interaction across tribal or sectarian affiliations is limited, post-conflict areas provide an opportunity to rebuild in ways that could foster greater integration and reduce intercommunal tension in the future.
- *Promote local media.* Regional media outlets on both sides of the sectarian divide are increasingly promoting sectarian agendas. Sectarian framing by the media reinforces the narratives of sectarian leaders and movements and increases the prospects for conflict in communities with high levels of socioeconomic grievance and low levels of cross-sectarian interaction and trust. More support for local media could help counter such trends, increasing coverage of technocratic municipal issues that transcend sectarian differences, such as water challenges, trash collection, youth unemployment, and education gaps.

The premise of this research effort is not that Western governments are required to save the Middle East from sectarian prejudice; rather, the premises are that the international community should be cognizant of factors that act as antibodies against sectarianism and that its involvement in regional affairs should be calibrated to strengthen—or, at a minimum, not to undermine—these resiliencies. This research seeks to fill important gaps in our understanding of how resilience might already be at work and the factors that might boost or undermine it. Although research has already illuminated what might be driving sectarianism in the region, we have far less understanding about how we might counter it. Identifying resilience at the community level in divided societies in the Middle East is a step in that direction.

Acknowledgments

This project was made possible by the generous support of the Henry Luce Foundation, and the authors would like to thank Toby Volkman, Director of Policy Initiatives at the foundation, for her support and guidance throughout this study.

We are grateful to our contributing authors from academia for their willingness to channel their expertise into this study. We would also like to thank the participants of a two-day workshop RAND convened at its headquarters in Santa Monica, California, in September 2017 to discuss this study and the initial drafts of the case studies.

At RAND, we would like to thank Leah Hershey for her coordination and support throughout this research effort. Finally, we are grateful to Andrew Parasiliti, Stephen Flanagan, and Geneive Abdo for their thoughtful and constructive reviews.

Abbreviations

AQI	Al-Qaeda in Iraq
AUB	American University of Beirut
BHD	Bahraini dinar
BICI	Bahrain Independent Commission of Inquiry
HTS	Hay'at Tahrir al-Sham
IDP	internally displaced person
IS	Islamic State
ISIL	Islamic State of Iraq and the Levant
ISIS	Islamic State of Iraq and Syria
JCC	Joint Crisis Coordination Center
KDP	Kurdistan Democratic Party
KRI	Kurdistan region of Iraq
KRG	Kurdistan Regional Government
NGO	nongovernmental organization
NIF	Network of Iraqi Facilitators
PUK	Patriotic Union of Kurdistan
START	National Consortium for the Study of Terrorism and Responses to Terrorism
UNHCR	United Nations High Commissioner for Refugees
USD	U.S. dollar

CHAPTER ONE

Identifying Resilience and Cross-Sectarian Cooperation

Jeffrey Martini, Dalia Dassa Kaye, and Becca Wasser
RAND Corporation

Spurred by the shock of multiple regional conflicts, the challenge of sectarianism in the Middle East has generated significant research.[1] Whether the focus is the Lebanese civil war (1975–1990), the insurgency that followed the 2003 invasion of Iraq, the 2011 uprising in Bahrain, or Saudi-Iranian rivalry, scholars have sought to better understand how sectarianism fuels conflict, contributes to regime-survival strategies, and is reproduced at different levels of society.

Although the literature is diverse, some common themes have emerged. The first is an emphasis on sectarianism as instrumental in understanding poor state-society relations or regional instability. The second theme is a fierce internal debate among scholars of the salience of sectarianism as a cause of conflict, whether as the principal or a secondary factor to regional-power competition and regime survival. What is missing from these debates, however, is an expansion beyond what makes a society *susceptible* to sectarianism to what makes a community *more resilient* in the face of sectarianism.

More practically, if sectarianism undermines the outcomes (e.g., stability, peace) and values (e.g., tolerance) that the international community seeks to advance, what can be done to mitigate those effects and enhance societies' resilience? This study aims to address these gaps. Readers will come away with a better understanding of what makes a community resist the descent into sectarianism or recover from it, as well as

---

[1] For excellent studies of different manifestations of sectarianism in Lebanon, Bahrain, Syria, and Iraq, see Justin Gengler, *Group Conflict and Political Mobilization in Bahrain and the Arab Gulf: Rethinking the Rentier State*, Bloomington, Ind.: Indiana University Press, 2015; Fanar Haddad, "Sectarian Relations in Arab Iraq: Contextualising the Civil War of 2006–2007," *British Journal of Middle Eastern Studies*, Vol. 40, No. 2, 2013; Steven Heydemann, "Syria's Uprising: Sectarianism, Regionalization, and State Order in the Levant," FRIDE Working Paper, No. 119, 2013; Christopher Phillips, "Sectarianism and Conflict in Syria," *Third World Quarterly*, Vol. 36, No. 2, March 2015; Melani Cammett, *Compassionate Communalism: Welfare and Sectarianism in Lebanon*, Ithaca, N.Y.: Cornell University Press, 2014; and Paul W. T. Kingston, *Reproducing Sectarianism: Advocacy Networks and the Politics of Civil Society in Post-War Lebanon*, Albany, N.Y.: State University of New York Press, 2014. For a study on sectarianism seeking to inform U.S. policy in Syria and Iraq, see Heather M. Robinson, Ben Connable, David E. Thaler, and Ali G. Scotten, *Sectarianism in the Middle East: Implications for the United States*, Santa Monica, Calif.: RAND Corporation, RR-1681-A, 2018.

how regional actors and the international community can best support resilience and cross-sectarian cooperation.

Literature on Sectarianism

Many analysts are quick to cite identity politics—and sectarianism in particular—as feeding the multiple conflicts raging across the Middle East in recent years. As noted by Vali Nasr, "Since the Iraq War, sectarian conflict between Shiites and Sunnis has emerged as a major fissure in Middle East politics. . . . From country to country, across the region, sectarian conflict is the thread that runs through each crisis, tying them into a strategic Gordian knot."[2] It was Nasr's influential book, *The Shia Revival*, that helped ignite more general interest in sectarianism and provoked a debate on whether sect was the appropriate lens through which to understand regional developments.[3] The 2003 Iraq War is a frequent point of departure for the study of sectarianism, because of the horrific intercommunal violence it featured and for shifting the regional balance of power in ways that some argue have motivated Saudi Arabia to more aggressively confront Iran and Shi'a movements.[4]

The contemporary literature on sectarianism in the Middle East can be grouped into three principle units of analysis: single-country case studies, regional or sub-regional treatments, and in-depth studies of "sectarian entrepreneurs." Among the case studies that explain how sectarianism manifests in a particular society, Lebanon is one of the most oft-studied countries, with its clientelism and consociational political system serving as entry points for exploring sectarian loyalties. More recently, Bahrain has emerged as a focal point for this research, with scholars seeking to solve the riddle of how the Sunni Al Khalifa monarchy perpetuates its rule in a Shi'a-majority country.

In this branch of the literature, a common argument is that sectarian mobilization is an instrument for regime survival.[5] Specifically, states with a history of sectarian politics and division, such as Bahrain and Lebanon, mobilize support around sects to reinforce the existing power structure. The regimes not only are derelict in supporting cross-sectarian cooperation but also actively work against it to head off the emergence

---

[2] Vali Nasr, "The War for Islam," *Foreign Policy*, January 22, 2016.

[3] Vali Nasr, *The Shia Revival*, New York: Norton, 2006.

[4] F. Gregory Gause III, *Beyond Sectarianism: The New Middle East Cold War*, Washington, D.C.: Brookings Institution, Doha Center, Analysis Paper No. 11, July 2014; and Laurence Louër, *Shiism and Politics in the Middle East*, New York: Columbia University Press, 2012.

[5] See, for example, Toby Matthiesen, "Sectarianization as Securitization: Identity Politics and Counter Revolution in Bahrain," in Nader Hashemi and Danny Postel, eds., *Sectarianization: Mapping the New Politics of the Middle East*, New York: Oxford University Press, 2017.

of political challengers that could construct a broader, more inclusive coalition.[6] As noted by Justin Gengler, "That decades have passed without the emergence of a successful cross-sectarian political movement in Bahrain, is, of course, no accident. The state has a direct interest—and a direct hand—in preventing such an emergence, as cross-societal coordination alone represents a viable political threat to the regime."[7]

The second branch of the literature looks across cases—focusing on the Middle East as a whole or on a subregion, such as the Arab Gulf—to identify common themes that drive sectarian behavior.[8] Because this literature treats multiple cases and often takes the form of edited volumes in which contributing authors may differ in their arguments, these studies vary considerably in their conclusions. That said, regional-power rivalry between Saudi Arabia and Iran features heavily in these works. Frederic Wehrey flags "the long shadow of the Iranian Revolution" and Ayatollah Khomeini's threats to export the revolution as motivating the Arab Gulf's sectarian mobilization.[9] Like single-country case studies, these treatments also delve into governing strategies that seek to divide publics into in-groups and out-groups to strengthen regime control.

In addition, both sets of literature (i.e., single-country case studies and regionally focused treatments) feature historians who often trace cycles of sectarianism to colonial strategies. For instance, Ussama Makdisi points to the legacies of both Ottoman rule and Western imperialism in the post-Ottoman period as cultivating sectarianism, either purposely—in a divide-and-rule strategy—or inadvertently, because of foreign powers' ignorance of societies' histories of communal coexistence.[10] Among single-country treatments, "Greater Lebanon" has generated enormous scholarly interest, with French cultivation of the Maronites and British cultivation of the Druze as a way

---

[6] Laurence Louër, "Sectarianism and Coup-Proofing Strategies in Bahrain," *Journal of Strategic Studies*, Vol. 36, No. 2, 2013.

[7] Gengler, 2015, p. 143. Madawi Rashid makes a similar argument as it relates to Saudi Arabia, contending that the Saudi "strategy to depict protests as a Shia conspiracy was successful in pushing the Sunnis to renew their allegiance to the regime." Madawi Rashid, "Sectarianism as Counter-Revolution: Saudi Responses to the Arab Spring," *Studies in Ethnicity and Nationalism*, Vol. 11, No. 3, 2011, p. 522.

[8] See Matthiesen, 2017; Geneive Abdo, "The New Sectarianism: The Arab Uprisings and the Rebirth of the Shi'a–Sunni Divide," Washington, D.C.: Brookings Institution, Saban Center for Middle East Policy, Analysis Paper No. 29, April 2013; Frederic Wehrey, *Sectarian Politics in the Gulf*, New York: Columbia University Press, 2014; Toby Matthiesen, *Sectarian Gulf: Bahrain, Saudi Arabia, and the Arab Spring That Wasn't*, Stanford, Calif.: Stanford University Press, 2013; and Laurence Potter, ed., *Sectarianism in the Persian Gulf*, New York: Oxford University Press, 2014.

[9] Wehrey, 2014.

[10] Ussama Makdisi, "The Problem of Sectarianism in the Middle East in an Age of Western Hegemony," in Nader Hashemi and Danny Postel, eds., *Sectarianization: Mapping the New Politics of the Middle East*, New York: Oxford University Press, 2017.

of understanding European competition with Ottoman rule and fostering of specific communities as conduits for their ambitions.[11]

The third branch of the literature on sectarianism shifts the unit of analysis from states to individuals, focusing on the "sectarian entrepreneurs" who awake and amplify religious identities. Muhammad Baqr al-Sadr and Musa al-Sadr, two individuals central to the emergence of Shi'a political mobilization in Iraq and Lebanon, respectively, are among the most studied.[12] Accounts of Muhammad Baqr al-Sadr typically focus on his appeal to religious authenticity, effectively offsetting the inroads communism was making in the Iraqi Shi'a community in the mid-20th century, as both al-Sadr's al-Da'wa Party and communist groups were seeking to mobilize around similar grievances. More recently, violent Salafi jihadists, such as Abu Mus'ab al-Zarqawi, have become the subject of attention, although their views are fringe and their followings are small.[13]

Taken together, this research provides an important foundation for understanding one of the more destructive variants of Middle East identity politics. Debates remain, but scholars have generally reached consensus on the following key points:

- Middle Easterners possess multiple identities (nation, gender, class, religion, etc.), and the hierarchy among them varies based on circumstance.
- Identities are created, nurtured, and stifled; they are not a given or primordial.
- Rulers, foreign powers, and sectarian entrepreneurs seek to mobilize religious identities in service of their interests.
- Sectarian identities might be real, but they are not the only factor explaining regional dynamics. Other key drivers include geostrategic rivalry, domestic political considerations, economic pressures, geography, and other social identities.

Policymaker Views on Sectarianism

In contrast to the scholarly treatment of sectarianism, political leaders are typically coarser in their discussion of the issue. The Middle Eastern leaders who reference sects are often doing so to cast aspersions at rivals. For example, King Abdullah II of Jordan famously warned of a rising "Shi'a crescent," and the Crown Prince of Saudi Arabia, Mohammed bin Salman, has rejected dialogue with Iran so long as the Islamic Republic is dedicated to spreading Shi'ism "in all areas of the Islamic world until the Awaited

---

[11] Samir Khalaf, *Civil and Uncivil Violence in Lebanon: A History of the Internationalization of Communal Conflict*, New York: Columbia University Press, 2002.

[12] Ali Rahnema, ed., *Pioneers of Islamic Revival*, London: Zed Books, 1994.

[13] Al-Zarqawi was killed in 2006.

Mahdi returns."[14] Not to be outdone, Iranian policymakers and their local partners (e.g., Hizbullah) are prone to dismissing their Sunni rivals as "takfiris."[15]

Regional powers are quick to blame their adversaries for the spread of sectarian prejudice while glossing over their own roles. In an obvious shot at Saudi Arabia, Iranian Foreign Minister Mohammad Javad Zarif noted in 2013 that Tehran's rivals were "fanning the flames" and that "fear-mongering has been a prevalent business."[16] The Arab Gulf States assume a similar pose of innocence, typically by calling on Iran to commit to a good neighbors' policy and noninterference in their internal affairs without mentioning their backing of co-sectarians to counter Iran.

Middle Eastern leaders foment sectarianism to attack external adversaries. Equally insidiously, the same tropes are often leveled at internal opposition to delegitimize their demands. Bahraini government leaders attempt to portray oppositionists as advancing a distinctly Shi'a and pro-Iran agenda, and the Hadi-led government in Yemen uses a similar message to discredit its Zaydi rivals, the Houthis. It is not always the recognized power that mobilizes sects, however. In Syria, Sunni groups whip up hatred against the "Nusayris" (a derogatory term for 'Alawis) or "Majus" (a derogatory name for Iranians, alluding to their Zoastrian heritage). On the other side of the ledger, Hizbullah uses the religious symbolism of the Sayda Zeinab shrine to mobilize supporters to fight for their co-sectarians.

Although playing on sectarian fissures was a hallmark of the colonial period, Western leaders typically do not overtly wade into those issues today. That said, leaders across the political spectrum are quick to attribute violence in the Middle East to sectarian hatred and to explain away inaction or failed action by noting the intractability of this problem. A major theme of President Barack Obama's March 2016 interview with Jeffrey Goldberg, for example, was "the reversion to sect, creed, clan, and village . . . [as] the source of much of the Muslim Middle East's problems."[17] The 2015 National Security Strategy's treatment of the Middle East begins with the assessment that "nowhere is the violence more tragic and destabilizing than in the sectarian conflict from Beirut to Baghdad, which has given rise to new terrorist groups such as [the Islamic State of Iraq and the Levant (ISIL)]."[18] More recently, the administration of

---

[14] Al-Arabiya, "In an Interview Today, Mohammed bin Salman to Tackle Saudi, Regional Issues," May 1, 2017.

[15] Takfiri is derived from the word *kafir*, meaning unbeliever. In this context, takfiris are those that excommunicate Shi'a and sometimes Sunni co-sectarians based on different interpretations of religious orthodoxy.

[16] BBC News, "Iran FM: Sectarian Strife Is Worst Threat in World," November 11, 2013.

[17] Jeffrey Goldberg, "The Obama Doctrine," *The Atlantic*, April 2016.

[18] The White House, *National Security Strategy*, Washington, D.C., February 2015. The organization's name transliterates from Arabic as al-Dawlah al-Islamiyah fi al-'Iraq wa al-Sham (abbreviated as Da'ish or DAESH). In the West, it is commonly referred to as the Islamic State of Iraq and the Levant (ISIL), the Islamic State of Iraq and Syria, the Islamic State of Iraq and the Sham (both abbreviated as ISIS), or simply as the Islamic State (IS). Arguments abound as to which is the most accurate translation, and the different case study chapters in this report refer to the group differently. For the purposes of this report, we thus use all three abbreviations.

Donald Trump has focused on building a Sunni, Saudi-led bloc to counter Shi'a Iran, a theme prominently on display during the President's visit to Riyadh in spring 2017. The 2017 National Security Strategy acknowledges "sectarian grievances" as drivers of violence and terrorism in the Middle East.[19]

Knowledge Gaps

Despite all the attention sectarianism receives from scholars and policymakers alike, major gaps exist in our understanding of how to counter it. The premise of this research is that a useful place to start is by building on community resilience that already exists in the region. Although the violent manifestations of sectarianism are easy to identify and the horrific nature of them sticks in our minds, sectarian violence remains an aberration and not the norm in the Middle East.

Even in the darkest periods in Iraq during the height of sectarian conflict in the mid-2000s, Ami Carpenter identified five neighborhoods in Baghdad—spanning majority Sunni and majority Shi'a areas—that resisted the retreat to sectarianism.[20] In Lebanon, Melani Cammett documents welfare-providing groups that cater to both in-groups and out-groups.[21] Regional bridge-builders, such as Oman, a country at the forefront of efforts to de-escalate sectarian tensions, receive less attention than the headline-grabbing rivalry between Saudi Arabia and Iran.[22] And countless examples of survey research show Middle Eastern publics with complicated views on religious identity that transcend simple sectarian prejudice.[23]

Given this backdrop, the natural question is what factors account for some communities' ability to resist the slide into sectarian violence, or, once it is unleashed, recover from it? And, based on those factors, how can the international community best advance local efforts within the Middle East to counter sectarianism by supporting those resiliencies?

This research effort is intended to shift the focus by identifying and analyzing cases of resilience in which leaders or societal groups are actively countering sectarianism or where its attraction has been contained or managed. Resiliencies exist at

---

[19] The White House, *National Security Strategy of the United States of America*, Washington, D.C., December 2017, p. 49.

[20] Ami C. Carpenter, "Havens in a Firestorm: Perspectives from Baghdad on Resilience to Sectarian Violence," *Civil Wars Journal*, Vol. 14, No. 2, 2012.

[21] Cammett, 2014.

[22] Marc Valeri, "Oman's Mediatory Efforts in Regional Crises," Norwegian Peacebuilding Resource Centre, March 2014.

[23] See, for example, Mansoor Moaddel, Jean Kors, and Johan Gärde, *Sectarianism and Counter-Sectarianism in Lebanon*, Ann Arbor, Mich.: University of Michigan Population Studies Center, Report 12-757, 2012.

multiple levels of society and are commonly expressed in the shared bonds and values that cut across in-groups and out-groups. At the level of personal relations, resiliencies include intermarriage and neighborhood ties; at the level of civil society, they include participation in groups with cross-sectarian memberships; and at a national level, resiliencies include political projects and business interests that span sectarian fault lines. These resiliencies are easiest to find in countries at peace, but they also exist, if dormant, in conflict zones.

Examples of resilience or active countering of sectarian pressures demonstrate the potential to mute destructive sectarian conflicts in the Middle East, even though they cannot stop conflict entirely. Drawing attention to resiliencies and active counter-sectarian strategies can provide lessons for how to structure policies more successfully to counter sectarianism and reduce conflict in the future.

Conceptual Issues

Sectarianism is defined in Western scholarship as "the politicization of religious, ethnic, or other ascriptive group identity."[24] Forms of sectarianism include mobilizing support around religious affiliation or, conversely, mobilizing opposition to other religious groups. Similar definitions prevail in Arabic-language scholarship. For example, the Iraqi author Falah 'Abd al-Jabar identifies one defining feature of sectarianism as "the politicization of [religious] identity as the unit for collective action."[25]

What sectarianism is not is devotion to, or identification with, a specific sect. It is only when religious identification is used to break societies into in-groups and out-groups for the purpose of advancing a political project that religious identification becomes sectarian. Thus, a defining feature of sectarianism is that it is associated with exclusion of the "other." This aspect is well developed in religious studies literature, such as Rodney Stark and William Bainbridge's *A Theory of Religion*, which asserts that sectarians claim unique legitimacy to their particular belief systems.[26] A negative—but containable—manifestation of sectarianism is when the sectarian group withdraws from society to avoid diluting its identity. A more destructive manifestation is when sectarianism is used as a rationale to impose a belief system on others. ISIL's brand of sectarianism, in which identification with another belief system is punishable by death or enslavement, is the most virulent.

---

[24] Justin Gengler, "Understanding Sectarianism in the Persian Gulf," in Lawrence Potter, ed., *Sectarianism in the Persian Gulf*, New York: Oxford University Press, 2014.

[25] Falah 'Abd al-Jabar, "al-Mushkila al-Ṭā'ifiya fī al-Waṭan al-'Arabī" (The Sectarianism Problem in the Arab Nation), *Al-Mustaqbal al-'Arabī Journal*, Vol. 408, January/February 2013.

[26] Rodney Stark and William Sims Bainbridge, *A Theory of Religion*, New Brunswick, N.J.: Rutgers University Press, 1996.

Scholars of sectarianism often lament that their research interests can be misinterpreted as primordialist or neo-colonialist;[27] the study of sectarianism does not need to be essentialist. Primordialism—i.e., where identities are treated as fixed—has led to the assertion of cultural stereotypes that ignore variation within a society, the multiplicity of identities, and the evolution of identities over time.[28] In the policy realm, primordialism has led to mono-causal assessments of regional developments, such as a "Shi'a crescent" rising.[29] This research begins from the principle that identities are constructed and that their salience ebbs and flows according to conditions.[30] Societies are not inherently sectarian; identification by sect operates in parallel to competing identities (e.g., national, tribal, class-based, ideological), and the salience of these identities fluctuates over time.

The rejection of primordialism does not mean that we are ignoring or downplaying the very real phenomenon of sectarianism. The Middle East contains individuals and movements that genuinely embrace sectarianism. Sometimes the sectarian agenda is used as a means to an end, but there are many instances in which sectarianism is real and literal. There are Salafi clerics who genuinely believe that practicing Shi'ism is the equivalent of apostasy. There are violent extremists who genuinely believe that those who do not follow their interpretation of Islam are legitimate targets of violence. We are not contesting that. Rather, we are suggesting that the breadth of this behavior and the characteristics of those who adopt it are not presupposed.

Resilience (or *resiliency*) is a term used across academic disciplines; for example, in psychology, the unit of analysis is typically the individual and the focus is often on a person's resilience after trauma.[31] It is also used in the context of humanitarian efforts in which the objective is to improve the resilience of a community in the face of natural and man-made disasters.[32] In peacebuilding, *resilience* refers to "the ability to rebound, maintain, or strengthen functioning during and after a disturbance, or to cope successfully in the face of extreme adversity or risk."[33]

---

[27] John Warner, "Questioning Sectarianism in Bahrain and Beyond: An Interview with Justin Gengler," *Jadaliyya*, April 17, 2013.

[28] Raphael Patai, *The Arab Mind*, rev. ed., New York: Scribner, 2002.

[29] Nasr, 2006.

[30] James D. Fearon and David D. Laitin, "Violence and the Social Construction of Ethnic Identity," *International Organization*, Vol. 54, No. 4, 2000.

[31] George Bonnano, "Loss, Trauma, and Human Resilience: Have We Underestimated the Human Capacity to Thrive After Extremely Aversive Events?" *American Psychologist*, Vol. 59, No. 1, January 2004; George Bonnano and Anthony Mancini, "Beyond Resilience and PTSD: Mapping the Heterogeneity of Responses to Potential Trauma," *Psychological Trauma: Theory, Research, Practice, and Policy*, Vol. 4, No. 1, 2012.

[32] Katie Harris, David Keen, and Tom Mitchell, *When Disasters and Conflict Collide: Improving Links Between Disaster Resilience and Conflict Prevention*, London: Overseas Development Institute, 2013.

[33] Carpenter, 2012.

Resiliency can take different forms.[34] One such form is immunity to the spread of conflict, while another is the ability to rebound from conflict. Thus, a community in Lebanon that resisted the descent into the 1975–1990 civil war would be described as resilient. Likewise, a community that fell into violence but recovered might also be described as resilient. The fact that resilience encompasses both the maintenance of peace in the face of sectarian actors and the ability to rebound from conflict is an important point developed in Ken Menkhaus's work.[35] Resiliencies are best understood as relatives rather than absolutes in the sense that a community might be described as more or less resilient than communities that chronically sit on a knife's edge.

Because the concept of resiliency cuts across disciplines, its definition and form differs, making it difficult to identify common factors that promote or stymie it. Indeed, existing literature on resilience—whether by academics or practitioners—often suffices with identifying those factors that, when absent, override resilience and lead to conflict.[36] This could be because resilience is context-specific and unique to the "complex adaptive system" of a particular conflict environment,[37] making resilience difficult to reduce to generalizable associated factors.

Resiliency also is featured in the U.S. government's approach to diagnosing and treating conflict. The U.S. Agency for International Development's *Conflict Assessment Framework* describes resiliencies as "those institutions, mechanisms, or other factors in society that provide the means to suppress or resolve conflict through non-violent means."[38] The framework provides some concrete examples of how strengthening institutions can make a community more resilient to conflict. For example, judicial actions perceived as fair reinforce the rule of law and build faith in nonviolent resolution of disputes. Similarly, security forces protecting nonviolent demonstrators reinforce peaceful action.

Research Approach and Organization of This Report

This report starts from common understandings of sectarianism and resilience and includes several case studies designed to explore how the impulse of sectarianism and

---

[34] Ken Menkhaus, "Making Sense of Resilience in Peacebuilding Contexts: Approaches, Applications, Implications," Geneva Peacebuilding Platform, Paper No. 6, 2013.

[35] Menkhaus, 2013.

[36] See, for example, Menkhaus, 2013; Jennifer Milliken, "Resilience: From Metaphor to an Action Plan for Use in the Peacebuilding Field," Geneva Peacebuilding Platform, Paper No. 7, 2013; Lauren Van Metre, "Fragility and Resilience," Fragility Study Group, Policy Brief No. 2, September 2016; and United States Institute of Peace, "Resilience as a Peacebuilding Practice: To Realism from Idealism," webpage, undated.

[37] Milliken, 2013.

[38] U.S. Agency for International Development, *Conflict Assessment Framework, Version 2.0*, Washington, D.C., June 2012.

the antibody of resilience interact. This effort is intended to highlight cases that have demonstrated varying levels of sectarianism and resilience in different subregions—namely, the Gulf and the Levant—specifically in Lebanon, Bahrain, Syria, and Iraq. Each case has sectarian fissures of different kinds, but the intensity and duration of sectarianism across the cases vary. As a result, the commonality among the four cases is the degree of sectarian diversity within their borders, and the difference is the level of sectarian conflict.

Our case-selection criteria led us to focus on Lebanon, Bahrain, Syria, and Iraq, which all include the key risk factor (sectarian diversity) but have experienced different scales of sectarian conflict. Yemen and Iran are two other states with significant sectarian diversity and some history of sectarian conflict, making them potentially interesting cases for follow-on research.

Figure 1.1 depicts the levels of sectarian conflict in the Middle East at the time of this writing. Because identifying a conflict as sectarian in nature is ultimately a subjective judgment, the figure simply categorizes countries based on levels of violence and sectarian diversity. The countries shaded in orange have a moderate level of sectarian diversity, while those shaded in red have a high level of sectarian diversity. The states that have experienced more than 1,000 battle deaths—the highest commonly used threshold for a civil war—as of 2016 (the last year for which data are available) are signified by diagonal lines. As seen in the figure, the four case studies this report treats in depth—Lebanon, Bahrain, Syria, and Iraq—are all characterized by moderate or high levels of sectarian diversity.[39] Two of the four cases focus on countries in the midst of civil wars (Syria and Iraq), while the remaining two cases treat a country that experienced previous civil wars (Lebanon) or sectarian tension and some violence but not a full civil war (Bahrain).

The four case studies identify resiliencies already present in the societies, as well as potential resiliencies that could be cultivated to counter and mitigate further sectarian conflict. Each case focuses on a particular episode of resilience or a counter-sectarian strategy and examines the underlying political, economic, and social conditions that supported or undermined it. Factors considered across cases include political and social mechanisms for mediating between sectarian communities, the nature of the physical environment, and the proximity and access of outside forces that might have an interest in instrumentalizing sectarian identity. Such an analysis can inform policies for how to counter sectarianism more effectively and identify the challenges that are likely to remain.

The cases draw on different disciplinary perspectives and include analysis at the subnational level. One of the limitations of much of the current research is that it

---

[39] Figure 1.1 depicts the *largest minority sect* as a percentage of the total population. In the case of Syria, this means that the 'Alawi population is depicted as sitting within the range of 10 percent to 20 percent of the total population. However, if 'Alawis, Christians, and other non-Sunni minorities were summed, they would eclipse the 20-percent threshold and Syria would be colored red to signify high sectarian diversity.

Figure 1.1
Levels of Sectarian Division and Conflict in the Middle East, 2018

Minority sect, % of total population
- <10%
- ≥10%
- ≥20%
- Active civil war with 1,000+ battle deaths as of 2016

SOURCE: For minority sect populations, see Todd M. Johnson and Brian J. Grim, eds., *World Religion Database*, Boston, Mass.: Brill, 2015; for battle deaths, see Uppsala Conflict Data Program, "Armed Conflict Dataset," Uppsala, Sweden: Uppsala University, Department of Peace and Conflict Research, 2016.

begins with the state or society writ large as the unit of analysis, missing the most logical control group: a community that shares many attributes with its neighboring communities but displays a different degree of resilience in resisting sectarian impulses. The subsequent chapters outline measures for judging resilience in a particular case, which include such factors as how a community self-identifies, the religious composition and outlook of state institutions, and the levels and types of societal conflict. Once an empirical basis for describing an example of resilience is established, each case analyzes the factors that account for that resilience.

In her treatment of Beirut Madinati in Chapter Two, Amanda Rizkallah charts the development of civil society as a factor that enabled cross-sectarian cooperation during Beirut's 2016 municipal elections. Because Rizkallah's comparison is temporal—the city of Beirut at different points in time—she is able to analyze how changes in underlying conditions contributed to the emergence of Beirut Madinati. Rizkallah argues that Beirut Madinati's impressive performance in the 2016 municipal elections owed partly to the window of opportunity created by Lebanon's 2015–2016 trash crisis, which eroded the legitimacy of traditional elites and provided the movement with a cross-sectarian issue around which to mobilize voters. The second explanation advanced by Rizkallah focuses on the time and space necessary for a group of activists and professionals to develop the wherewithal to launch a political challenge to established elites. She argues that Beirut Madinati was the beneficiary of propitious political conditions but also was able to leverage the efforts and learn from the successes and failures of forerunner movements.

In Chapter Three, and in contrast to Rizkallah, Justin Gengler analyzes Bahrain via a cross-sectional approach, comparing outcomes in two different locations: 'Isa Town and Hamad Town. Although geographic segregation has long been cited as a tool of states to promote sectarian agendas, bolster sectarian identification, and reduce pressure for conflict resolution, Gengler tackles how urban planning can engender or inhibit resilience to sectarianism. In comparing the spatial layout of mixed 'Isa Town with the more sectarian and homogenous Hamad Town, Gengler argues that physical infrastructure and spatial layout contribute to 'Isa Town's resilience to Bahrain's sectarian conflict. Specifically, 'Isa Town's greater walkability leads to intercommunal mixing, whereas Hamad Town's more-austere roundabouts, with few public spaces for interaction, inhibit such mixing. Gengler asserts that the impact of physical infrastructure is strengthened by its effect on the provision of government public services, with mixed areas more immune to the state's strategy of cultivating sectarian loyalty by targeting subsidies to the regime's preferred recipients (Sunnis), because residents are embedded in a mixed Sunni-Shi'a community.

Kathleen Reedy's analysis of Syria's civil war in Chapter Four identifies foreign involvement as a key factor feeding sectarian mobilization. In her comparison of sectarian violence in the northern governorate of Idlib and the southern governorate of Dara'a, Reedy notes how external actors with sectarian agendas exacerbated conflict in Idlib by providing support (sanctuary, funding, armaments) to sectarian-oriented militias, whereas Dara'a remained resilient, in part, because Syrian rebels were seeking support from external patrons committed to "moderate" factions. Reedy is one of two case-study authors who focus on border management as a critical factor in explaining resilience.

Finally, in Chapter Five, Ami Carpenter highlights the role of border monitoring in limiting sectarian actors from infiltrating Iraqi areas that avoided internal conflict during the 2003–2011 war and again during the 2014 ISIL takeover of portions of western and northern Iraq. In her analysis of stable areas in Baghdad and Dohuk, Carpenter identifies preexisting social networks in both areas as important ingredients in explaining community resilience.

Collectively, these cases point to several factors that can enhance a community's resilience. No one factor is likely to be sufficient on its own, but the cases suggest that formal and informal mechanisms for mediating the early onset of conflict, preexisting levels of trust between community leaders, activists with experience in building movements, strong border monitoring, and physical infrastructure that encourages mixing all help. Of course, readers should be cautious in generalizing these findings. For example, Syria—a republic of more than 20 million people dominated by an 'Alawite minority that engaged in a state-building project based on Ba'thist ideology—is certainly distinct from the Arab Gulf monarchies or even from Lebanon. The lack of comparability across societies misses the important fact that, at a subnational level, there are communities that share many key traits. For example, Beirut shares many characteristics with Damascus, including that each is a multiconfessional capital city of 1–2 million people. Within societies, comparing the experience of one neighborhood in Manama with another provides useful insight into what factors accelerate or slow sectarianism.

In Chapter Six, the report concludes by applying lessons from the case studies and exploring policy implications for countering sectarianism and promoting community resiliency in the Middle East. The premise is not that Western governments need to save the Middle East from its sectarian prejudice but rather that external powers—including the U.S. government—should be cognizant of indigenous factors that act as antibodies against sectarianism, and that Western involvement in regional affairs should be calibrated to strengthen—or, at a minimum, not to undermine—these resiliencies. Such awareness will certainly not eliminate conflict in the Middle East, but it can reduce that conflict.

CHAPTER TWO

Transcending Sectarian Politics: The Case of Beirut Madinati

Amanda Rizkallah
Assistant Professor of International Studies
Pepperdine University

On May 8, 2016, Lebanon held the first of four rounds of municipal elections. These elections were the first since 2010 and represented the first opportunity for citizens to exercise their political voices since the beginning of the Syrian civil war, the ensuing influx of refugees, Parliament's unconstitutional extension of its term in office, and popular protests against a paralyzing trash crisis that had rattled Lebanon's political elite. In the wake of widespread protests and public frustration targeting the ruling elite in its entirety, Beirut's citizens decided to take matters into their own hands. For the first time in the city's recent history, an independent nonsectarian volunteer-based campaign, called Beirut Madinati (Beirut, My City), presented the city's voters with an alternative to sectarian political parties and their candidates. The group mounted a grassroots campaign, raising funds through individual donations and reaching voters through town hall meetings. It presented a program that prioritizes "the primacy of the public good, social justice, transparency, and stewardship of our city for future generations."[1] Although Beirut Madinati lost the election, it still managed to get 32 percent of the vote (or 40 percent when blank and invalid ballots are excluded). It offered voters a glimpse of a path forward and a new way of doing politics in a country and region where *politics* has long been a dirty word.[2]

This chapter examines the rise of Beirut Madinati. In a moment when regional politics have polarized the Middle East along sectarian lines, and in a place where sect is the institutionalized currency of the political system, how did a movement of cross-sectarian unity and resistance to the status quo emerge? To answer this question, this chapter traces the development of the Beirut Madinati campaign. It compares the 2016 municipal election with the previous round in 2010 to gain insight into how changes in key structural and organizational variables opened a window of opportunity for Beirut Madinati. A temporal comparison is preferable to a cross-sectional one in this

---

[1] Beirut Madinati, *Municipal Program 2016–2022*, Beirut, Lebanon, archival copy, 2016.

[2] Kim Ghattas, "Beirut's Lovable Losers," *Foreign Policy*, May 2016; Amanda Rizkallah, "Beirut's Election Was Surprisingly Competitive. Could It Shake Up Lebanese Politics?" *Washington Post*, May 11, 2016.

case. Beirut is a rather unique city in Lebanon: It is unusually diverse, cosmopolitan, and home to a critical mass of activists and intellectuals. Comparing its elections to contemporaneous ones in another city would overwhelm the study with confounding variables. Data are drawn primarily from structured in-depth interviews with key players in the movement, including founding members, candidates, volunteer coordinators, and legal advisers.[3]

The findings suggest that Beirut Madinati emerged for two reasons. The first is a structural window of opportunity that had opened in the political environment. Unusually weak elites and heightened public awareness and discontent as a result of the trash crisis provided a conducive environment for challengers. The second reason for the emergence of Beirut Madinati is the increasingly rapid accumulation of experience and dense network formation within civil society that supplied the campaign with personnel, expertise, and organizational know-how.

This chapter is organized into six main sections. First, this chapter provides some background about Lebanon's electoral institutions. It then examines the formation of Beirut Madinati and the importance of historical antecedents in civil society. The next two sections delve into the details of the campaign, including its successes, failures, and transformation into a more permanent political movement. The analysis then turns to an investigation of why the window of opportunity opened for Beirut Madinati in 2016 and examines the sustainability of the movement. The final section concludes with a discussion of policy implications.

Lebanese Political Institutions and Elections

Since its independence in 1943, Lebanon has had a political system that rests on a sectarian power-sharing agreement. Both before and after the civil war (1975–1990), preserving a sectarian balance has been the chosen mechanism for managing conflict among Lebanon's various religious communities. The largest among these are Shi'a Muslims, Sunni Muslims, Orthodox and Maronite Christians, and Druze. In parliamentary elections, this consociational arrangement means a strict sectarian quota, in which particular seats are allocated to religious communities. In contrast, no sectarian quotas exist in municipal elections.[4] However, similar norms have evolved in which municipal candidate lists often are put together with sectarian considerations in mind. Such an institutionalization of religious identity reifies these differences and produces a politics more centered on identity than on substantive policy debate. In municipal elections, each voter has as many votes as there are seats. Although the system allows

---

[3] Interviews took place between August 2017 and January 2018. To maintain the anonymity of the interviewees, individuals are not identified by name, but rather by number.

[4] Ziad Abu-Rish, "Municipal Politics in Lebanon," *Middle East Report*, Vol. 46, 2016, p. 280.

voters to cast ballots for candidates from different electoral lists, in practice, many cast their ballots for a single list. Candidates with the highest numbers of votes are elected. The system enables a winner-takes-all outcome. In heterogeneous municipalities, this system encourages cross-sectarian alliances in order to capture the votes of constituencies outside one's own.[5]

Sectarian patronage machines dominate Lebanese politics, and municipal elections are no exception. One study of the 2009 parliamentary elections concluded that political parties bought an estimated 60 percent of the votes cast. Standardized ballots did not exist until reforms came into effect in 2018. Parties and coalitions prepared their own ballots with candidate lists on them and distributed them to their voters. By changing small details, such as honorific titles, name order, and paper color, parties were able to trace ballots back to particular extended families and supporters. This compromised the secrecy of the ballots and made the targeted provision of goods and services in exchange for votes much easier.[6] The systemic barriers in the face of new political forces seeking to crowdfund a campaign and win votes on a nonsectarian basis were formidable. This was exactly what Beirut Madinati sought to do during the 2016 municipal elections in Beirut.

Although municipalities were important sites of executive power in the prewar period, municipal councils lost much of their influence during the civil war.[7] Even though the war ended in 1991, new elections were not held until 1998. Since then, municipal elections have proceeded at regular six-year intervals. A sizable portion of municipal revenue comes directly from the national-level Independent Municipal Fund, but local taxes also are an important source of revenue. Officially, funds are disbursed according to population size, but a lack of transparency plagues the distribution process. A 1977 law codified relatively far-reaching municipal powers, stating that any "work having a public character or utility" is within the jurisdiction of the local municipality.[8]

Despite these formal powers, municipalities often are heavily constrained in their ability to implement local policies and projects. This is mostly because of their small size. The country is divided into 985 municipalities. Many municipalities contain fewer than 4,000 residents. Under current laws, in which municipalities receive most of their revenue from local taxation, the size of most municipalities makes them too small to undertake needed public works projects and local development.[9] With a little less than

---

[5] Abu-Rish, 2016.

[6] Daniel Corstange, "Vote Trafficking in Lebanon," *International Journal of Middle East Studies*, Vol. 44, No. 3, 2012.

[7] Abu-Rish, 2016.

[8] Sami Atallah and Diana Kallas, "The Role of Regional Administrations in the Context of Decentralization," Lebanese Center for Policy Studies, Roundtable Report Series, August 2012.

[9] Atallah and Kallas, 2012.

2 million residents, the capital city of Beirut is exceptional in this regard. Governing a population orders of magnitude larger than that of most municipalities, the municipal council of Beirut is among the most consequential bodies of local government in the country, affecting the lives of nearly half the Lebanese population.[10]

In recent years, gridlock and inaction at the national level have turned municipalities into the de facto front line in managing both the flow of Syrian refugees and the trash crisis that began in 2015.[11] In response, international donors have directed aid flows for Syrian refugees in Lebanon through municipalities instead of the central government.[12] In this political context, municipal elections have taken on additional symbolic and practical importance.

Formation: What Is Beirut Madinati?

The original vision and aim of Beirut Madinati was well defined and limited in scope—to organize a nonsectarian campaign and contest the May 2016 municipal elections in Beirut, providing voters with a clear alternative to the candidates of traditional establishment parties. Most interview participants strongly emphasized that, at its founding, Beirut Madinati was fundamentally an electoral campaign and not the broader political movement that it has become since the end of the elections. Yet despite its initial short-term goals, Beirut Madinati's formation cannot be understood apart from long-standing efforts at political, legal, and urban reform in Beirut. It represents a coming together of disparate preexisting networks of activists, urban planners, and political aspirants with a common interest in improving the quality of life for those living in the city.

There are multiple overlapping—yet different—historical movements that preceded Beirut Madinati and supplied it with critical personnel, experience, and expertise. In one sense, Beirut Madinati is an outcome of the historical evolution of postwar civil society in Lebanon. After the end of the civil war in 1990, civil society began advocating for various legal reforms, lobbying elites in power, and, in particular, calling for the holding of municipal elections. Civil society was successful in this regard, and the first postwar municipal elections were held in 1998.[13] Since then, civil society has been careful to remain nonpartisan and has organized only narrow, issue-based campaigns. These include campaigns to remove sectarian identity from identification cards and legalize civil marriage. Others were active in the cultural sphere, working to

---

[10] Rizkallah, 2016.

[11] Rizkallah, 2016.

[12] Abu-Rish, 2016.

[13] Interview 1.

preserve and strengthen Arabic literature or to restore historic buildings.[14] However, recent defeats led some in civil society to consider seeking political power in order to make significant change.[15]

A second current is an urban renewal movement led by two generations of urban planning scholars and practitioners who know the city intimately. They have advocated for the importance of planning in urban life, and, more specifically, planning that prioritizes public spaces and the common good.[16] From this perspective, Beirut Madinati is the result of decades of work by urbanists that began in the aftermath of the civil war. In the immediate postwar years, Rafik Hariri spearheaded a parliamentary decision to give unprecedented power to Solidere, a real estate company that set about erasing "most of [Beirut's] urban fabric and [altering] the scale of its squares and neighborhoods" to transform the capital city into a global destination. This neoliberal approach to urban planning marginalized the city's own residents, reducing mobility and access to public spaces and affordable housing.[17] The first postwar generation of urban scholars mobilized and protested against Solidere's activities. Although they ultimately failed in achieving their goals, their struggle led to two important developments: first, the consolidation of urban planning and urban studies curricula at Lebanese universities and, second, the formation of a new generation of activists, many of whom were students of the first generation who were inspired by their work. A critical urban discourse emerged and a robust network of activists pursued successful projects throughout the city. Mona Harb, one of these urban scholars and a member of Beirut Madinati, chronicles three successful examples in her recent scholarship: the nongovernmental organization (NGO) Nahnoo's campaign to reopen Beirut's largest park, Horch Beirut; the Dalieh Civil Coalition's delay of plans to develop a large historic area of coastal Beirut; and the efforts of the coalition to stop the building of a highway that would have cut through the Achrafieh neighborhood of Beirut and build a park instead.[18] This network of urbanists joined forces with activists working in other domains of civil society to launch the protest movement against the garbage crisis. These same networks were mobilized for the creation of Beirut Madinati after their failure to achieve concrete gains through protest.

A third current, which overlaps with the first two in many ways, emanates primarily from the American University of Beirut (AUB). A first generation of student activists often is associated with the campus movement Bala Hdoud, or No Frontiers, which was actively working on such issues as gender equality in personal status law and civil

---

[14] Interviews 3 and 7.

[15] Interview 1.

[16] Interview 1.

[17] Mona Harb, *Cities and Political Change: How Young Activists in Beirut Bred an Urban Social Movement*, Rome, Power 2 Youth, Istituto Affari Internazionali, Working Paper No. 20, September 2016.

[18] Harb, 2016.

marriage in the early 2000s. Many of these students continue their activism as part of the civil society and urban renewal movements described earlier.[19] More recently, activist students at AUB have organized through the Secular Club, which runs in student body elections as an independent group, unaffiliated with traditional sectarian parties. As recently as 2011, the Secular Club was considered a fringe group on campus, but it now has one of the largest followings of any campus organization, demonstrating the appeal (perhaps surprisingly to outside observers) that such ideas have to youth living in the current political climate.[20] University networks were critical, both by providing Beirut Madinati's core members and during the campaign itself by getting previously apolitical students and faculty involved as volunteers or supporters.[21]

Another current that contributed to Beirut Madinati's formation is a group of activists that consistently aspired to run for office or participate in formal politics. Many of these members were involved in other political parties and joined Beirut Madinati out of frustration borne from not being able to accomplish their goals through other avenues.[22] Many of these activists turned to local politics after the cancellation of the 2013 parliamentary elections.[23]

Deep roots in these preexisting networks produced a Beirut Madinati membership that was united and like-minded in several ways. All members supported a vision that puts the individual at the center of city policy.[24] Furthermore, Beirut Madinati's members are nonsectarian, independent, and unaffiliated with other political parties. The few who had memberships in other political parties were required to dissolve those ties as a condition of entrance into the organization.[25] Although the members are not all personally secular, they share a secularism with regard to politics.[26] Members are moderately left-leaning on social issues and are generally supportive of civil marriage and of gay and transgender rights.[27] Beirut Madinati's core members and candidates had little to no experience in formal politics or elected office and had a reputation for "clean hands"—i.e., they were free of the corruption endemic in Lebanese politics.[28]

---

[19] Interview 1.

[20] Interview 7.

[21] Interview 9.

[22] Interview 1.

[23] Interview 2.

[24] Interview 2.

[25] Interview 8.

[26] Interviews 1 and 4.

[27] Interview 9.

[28] Interview 8.

Many of the members are professionals who are well known in the fields of architecture, urban planning, engineering, medicine, law, and art.[29]

These similarities might falsely suggest that the members of the organization knew each other beforehand or that the organization is lacking in diversity. The reality is quite the opposite. Many members became involved with Beirut Madinati because a single person they knew from a previous experience of activism or through their workplace invited them to a meeting. In this sense, Beirut Madinati is much more than a cobbling together of two or three activist networks. It represents the building, formalizing, and growing of a new, larger network of people who were only loosely connected beforehand. Whether through Beirut Madinati or outside of it, members desiring to launch a campaign, protest a policy, or undertake a local initiative now have access to each other in an unprecedented way.

Anatomy of a Campaign

In September 2015, Beirut Madinati began through a series of small, informal meetings. These meetings gradually became larger and more formalized.[30] Public input through town hall meetings was taken into consideration, the program was developed and disseminated, and volunteers were recruited through universities and social networks. The candidate list was the last piece to fall into place, with names announced only three weeks before election day. Announcing the program before the candidates was an intentional strategy used to avoid the personalization of the campaign and to maintain a focus on substantive policy issues.

The centerpiece of the Beirut Madinati campaign was the Municipal Program, which prioritized the livability of the city. The program addressed the need for greater mobility, public spaces, waste disposal, security, and the preservation of cultural and natural heritage.[31] This was novel in Lebanon. Most interviewees cited the program as one of the most successful components of the campaign's credibility, inspiring confidence in residents and forcing traditional elites to plagiarize the program in order to bolster their legitimacy among voters. However, one interviewee expressed the opinion that the program, although a huge step in the right direction, was not progressive enough. It avoided the issues of migrants, refugees, and noncitizens in general. Although this was a pragmatic electoral calculation, the respondent suggested that silence on these human-rights issues might have been a wasted opportunity to use a public platform to raise awareness.[32]

---

[29] Interview 8.

[30] Interview 2.

[31] Beirut Madinati, 2016.

[32] Interview 7.

From September 2015 to May 2016, Beirut Madinati was structured as a campaign, with no written document except the program. There were no bylaws and no post-election plan had been articulated.[33] The campaign had a flexible and fluid structure. It was divided into three wings, one for operations, which contained all efforts to coordinate volunteers, as well as communications, legal, and fundraising teams. Another wing was in charge of developing the program for the city, and the third wing was a candidate-selection and -vetting committee. Together, the leaders of each wing formed a steering committee.[34] Members acknowledged the virtues of such a fluid and flexible structure while running a campaign for the first time, even as an unclear chain of command led to numerous bottlenecks.[35]

When asked to identify the successes of the campaign, interviewees tended to give similar answers. They pointed to the remarkable feat of trying to build an electoral machine from scratch in the space of a few months. A software application coupled with old-fashioned university networks helped to solve collective-action problems among young supporters. Faculty and student activists successfully tapped their networks on campus to generate a base of volunteers. Television appearances were effective in reaching an older demographic and brought national name recognition to the campaign.[36] Beirut Madinati succeeded in creating a powerful and appealing brand that could be deployed in future mobilization efforts.[37]

Another success was the fundraising effort. Once the program, website, and candidates were announced, the money poured in at a rate that surprised those working on the campaign. Beirut Madinati raised $440,000 in donation amounts ranging from $7 to $50,000, which was a self-imposed ceiling for any one individual contribution. The announcement of a slate of unknown candidates was critical to this fundraising effort. A lack of name recognition was paradoxically reassuring to those seeking a new alternative.

When asked to identify the internal weaknesses or challenges to the campaign, interviewee responses converged on particular elements. Timing and election day logistics were consistently noted as weak spots.

Candidates were not announced until three weeks before the elections. The interviewed members all had a sense that the timing was too late. For instance, when the donations started to come in after the announcement of the candidates, the campaign struggled to spend the money quickly enough as the elections approached, whereas

---

[33] Interview 6.

[34] Interviews 7 and 8.

[35] Interview 9.

[36] Interviews 4 and 9.

[37] Interview 7.

they were short of funds earlier in the campaign. One interviewee asserted that the number of people who heard about Beirut Madinati peaked only after the election.[38]

Beirut Madinati's electoral machinery was woefully insufficient to mobilize the city's voters.[39] The most basic difficulty was because of Lebanon's electoral law, which requires citizens to vote in their town or village of origin. Because of this provision, only a fraction of Beirut's residents are eligible to vote in Beirut. Identifying these voters requires a significant amount of intelligence on neighborhoods and their populations. Establishment parties have huge databases that monitor voter turnout and keep track of particular families' needs. They use this information in combination with pre-prepared ballots to monitor their voters, provide transportation to polling stations, and strategically target their vote-buying efforts. One interviewee explained that Beirut Madinati had accumulated a list of 4,000 phone numbers of eligible voters. In comparison, the Beirutis establishment list had about 100,000 phone numbers. The respondent recounted that every Sunni he or she knew was called by Hariri's Beirutis list.[40] Beirut Madinati also was limited by the fact that its members were, by their own accounts, unwilling to buy votes and were attempting to mobilize voters around a programmatic platform rather than through patron-client relationships.[41]

Despite these organizational challenges, the most serious internal threat to the campaign's existence came from a profound disagreement over strategy, namely whether to field 18 or 24 candidates. A list of 18 candidates would leave the door open to alliances with other parties or groups. Some were adamant that Beirut Madinati would be crossing a red line if it allied with almost any other group, although others saw this approach as shortsighted or counterproductive. The decision ultimately was made to field 24 candidates and make no alliances. An interviewee admitted that, at one point, the internal friction over this decision was so great that it threatened to tear apart the movement.[42] Some indirect evidence suggests that this decision might have cost Beirut Madinati the election. In Tripoli, a list of relative outsiders incorporated some neighborhood leaders in order to draw on their local networks and won against the establishment. Beirut Madinati made the strategic choice to forgo this route. It also made a similar choice when it failed to back any candidates for mukhtar (local headman), despite the fact that these candidates often can bring entire neighborhoods to the polls.[43] Finding a way to broker such alliances without losing independence will be key to tapping into larger networks of voters in future elections.

---

[38] Interview 9.

[39] Interview 7.

[40] Interview 6.

[41] Interviews 1 and 8.

[42] Interview 1.

[43] Abu-Rish, 2016.

All respondents reported that intimidation from establishment parties was minimal for most of the campaign. The most tangible way in which establishment parties limited Beirut Madinati's activities was by making it difficult to organize in certain places. For example, Beirut Madinati was prevented from campaigning and meeting in some lower-income neighborhoods where sectarian sentiments and loyalties were high. Most respondents cited an incident in which they had to cancel a public meeting they were planning in the lower-middle class Sunni neighborhood of Tariq El Jedideh, a well-known stronghold of Saad Hariri's Future Movement.[44] Once Beirut Madinati became a perceived threat, the establishment parties took steps to heighten sectarian fears. Rumors were spread accusing the campaign of being supported by Hizbullah, which was a deliberate tactic designed to tap into Sunni fears and push them to vote for familiar faces.[45] One respondent said that the costs of participation in Beirut Madinati became more apparent after the election, when some members who worked with government contracts stopped getting new contracts.[46] Toward the end of the campaign, as Beirut Madinati's success became a possibility, traditional parties also attempted a strategy of cooptation rather than repression. The establishment parties submitted a proposal to include five of the Beirut Madinati candidates on the establishment list if they would pull out of the race. Beirut Madinati refused.[47] On election day, according to the Lebanese Association for Democratic Elections, 647 violations were observed, which is double the number for the 2010 elections, signaling that establishment parties might have felt seriously threatened.

There were some indications that voters felt pressure to conform. One interviewee described how a man from a Sunni area traditionally affiliated with the Future Movement came to Beirut Madinati a few days before the election to pick up Beirut Madinati ballots. He explained that he and his neighbors could not be seen publicly supporting the movement but that he represented 200 people who wanted to defect. In order to do so, they needed to take their Beirut Madinati ballots discreetly.[48] Disgruntled members of the Free Patriotic Movement (a Christian party) who broke ranks to advocate for Beirut Madinati were disciplined or expelled from the party.[49]

Election Results

On May 8, 2017, Beirut Madinati lost the municipal elections and won no seats on the municipal council. Voter turnout stood at 21 percent, exactly the same as in 2010.

---

[44] Interviews 3 and 6.

[45] Interview 1.

[46] Interview 3.

[47] Interview 3.

[48] Interview 9.

[49] Abu-Rish, 2016.

Several factors explain the low turnout. It is estimated that 25 to 30 percent of voters do not actually live in Lebanon. A further 5 to 10 percent represent deceased voters. It is unclear why voter lists are not adequately updated, but these discrepancies might be linked to fraud tactics.[50] This translates to 40 to 50 percent of voters in Beirut staying home on election day. One of Beirut Madinati's glaring challenges was its lack of an electoral machine and its inability to mobilize apathetic and skeptical voters.

There were some notable differences between 2016 and earlier elections. Not since the first postwar elections in 1998 had there been any significant competition in Beirut's municipal elections. Since 1998, most of Lebanon's elites have put their differences aside and run on the same electoral list in the capital, with the Future Movement routinely nominating the head of the list. This strategy discouraged challengers until the emergence of Beirut Madinati. Table 2.1 shows the share of the votes won by the winning list and the runner-up in each election.

In an unofficial post-election assessment, several members of Beirut Madinati examined more–fine-grained election data to understand how different sectarian communities voted.[51] It is important to note that municipal Beirut does not extend beyond the traditional boundaries of the city. The Hizbullah strongholds in the southern suburbs are not part of the municipality. This results in a diverse but overwhelmingly Sunni and Christian electorate. Shi'a voters form a substantial minority, but, according to tradition, only two of 24 seats in Beirut are Shi'a seats. In other words, municipal Beirut is a district in which Hizbullah is not a central player and in which Hariri's Future Movement historically dominates. This context helps to explain some of the results.

The aforementioned unofficial report found that Sunni voters were the least likely to vote for Beirut Madinati, largely choosing the establishment list or staying home. Hizbullah did not participate in the establishment list and did not give Shi'a voters specific directives. The result was a Shi'a electorate that evenly distributed its votes between Beirut Madinati's list and the establishment list. Armenian voters followed

Table 2.1
Beirut Municipal Election Results

	1998	2004	2010	2016
Share of votes: winning list	40%	41%	69%	48%
Share of votes: runner-up list	25%	12%	13%	32%

SOURCE: Chaaban et al., 2016.

---

[50] Jad Chaaban, Diala Haidar, Rayan Ismail, Rana Khoury, and Mirna Shidrawi, "Beirut's Municipal Elections: Did Beirut Madinati Permanently Change Lebanon's Electoral Scene?" Arab Center for Research and Policy Studies, September 2016.

[51] Chaaban et al., 2016.

their parties' directives and voted for the establishment list. Christian voters (non-Armenian) defected from traditional parties and gave most of their votes to Beirut Madinati.[52] These results have mixed implications for Beirut Madinati as a movement. The only religious group that deviated from politics as usual was Christians. It is difficult to know if this is because of Beirut Madinati's appeal or particular weaknesses within Christian parties. Still, despite defeat at the polls, it is important to note that Beirut Madinati forced the establishment list to adopt a similar substantive program in the final days of the campaign. The movement raised citizen expectations of their government.

From Campaign to Political Movement

Beirut Madinati found itself in a difficult and ambiguous position after election day. Although the campaign ultimately failed to produce an electoral victory, candidates affiliated with the group received a share of the vote that exceeded popular expectations. International news outlets covered Beirut Madinati as more than an alternative slate in a municipal election: It was billed as a turning point in Lebanese politics.[53] Interviewees described public expectations as impossibly high, given that the group had no seats and no means to execute its plan. Ordinary people would come to Beirut Madinati's offices with complaints about problems, expecting immediate change.[54] This was both a blessing and a curse from the perspective of those inside the organization. Although the members were motivated to continue working for the city, the campaign was not structured as a permanent political party and was thus unprepared to meet public expectations.[55]

To remain relevant and meet the challenges of the post-election period, the organization turned inward and began to totally restructure into a sustainable political movement. The size of the group's general assembly doubled, from about 70 to 150, and procedures for inclusion in the body were institutionalized. The general assembly elected a steering committee in October 2016 to restructure the movement and write bylaws that would formally govern operations.[56] The new structure includes a collegiate body of seven elected members. Three of the body's members lead three committees whose collective work embodies Beirut Madinati's agenda for sustained political action. The first committee is an alternative municipality, which acts as a watchdog for the municipality in power. Members monitor the municipality's activities and pressure

---

[52] Chaaban et al., 2016.

[53] Interview 3.

[54] Interview 3.

[55] Interview 7.

[56] Interview 3.

officials to release the budget, which they are required to do by law but never do in practice. Members also propose items to be placed on the municipality's agenda.[57] The second committee consists of neighborhood groups, which seek to extend Beirut Madinati's grassroots presence. They act as local pressure groups, aggregating demands of ordinary citizens and lobbying the municipality to address those concerns. The third is an elections committee, which is preparing for future municipal elections and addressing electoral laws and their flaws from a research perspective. Other internal groups include committees to manage membership and grievances.[58]

Why Now?

The 2010 municipal elections were the least competitive in Lebanon's postwar history, with the results a foregone conclusion. This section discusses key changes that took place between 2010 and 2016 that laid the groundwork for the establishment of a non-sectarian political movement and a competitive municipal election contest.

General Political Environment

In 2010, the international and regional political environment stood in marked contrast to 2016 in ways that indirectly influenced the coalescing of Beirut Madinati. The Arab Uprisings had not yet occurred. Although the direct effect of the uprisings on Lebanon was marginal, protests across the Arab world expanded the realm of what kind of change was possible through activism. Although it did not gain much momentum, this was the beginning of a protest movement demanding the downfall of the sectarian system in explicit terms.[59]

Domestically, the country was still politically polarized along the lines of the March 8 and March 14 Coalitions. These movements had not been discredited in the public eye, and even secular activists tended to have sympathies. For those looking to present an alternative to the sectarian establishment, there was no political opening to do so. Multiple respondents cited the absence of an alternative as an important factor differentiating the political climate preceding the 2010 and 2016 municipal elections. One interviewee explained that, in 2010, some people were still hopeful that reform could be achieved from within March 14, the coalition of traditional parties that had adopted and then co-opted the 2005 Independence Intifada protests, demanding the withdrawal of Syrian troops from Lebanon.[60]

---

[57] Interview 5.

[58] Interviews 1, 2, 4, 6, and 9.

[59] Interview 7.

[60] Interviews 1 and 6.

In 2010, traditional elites were also stronger. By 2016, escalating tensions among regional patrons had led to gridlock at the national level. A restive public was outraged by the resulting trash crisis. This difficult climate, in combination with decreased funding from outside patrons, had put elites on the defensive. This was especially true of Saad Hariri's Future Movement, the most powerful political party in municipal Beirut. Saudi Arabia had withdrawn its patronage of the Hariri family after decades of support. In fact, Saad Hariri was nearly bankrupt and was facing multiple challenges to his leadership from within the Sunni community.[61] One way in which the elites responded to this moment of weakness was to join forces to overcome such popular movements as Beirut Madinati. In districts all over the country, the March 8 and March 14 Coalitions chose to band together to put forward one list.[62] One interviewee explained how this weakness served as an important window of opportunity for a grassroots and crowdfunded effort like Beirut Madinati. Activists knew that they would be fighting an uphill battle. They explained that "it would not have been possible unless it was during a moment of weakness for them, during a weak spot. They were not ready or able to spend in the same way that they had in the past, so we took advantage of this."[63] This is direct evidence that the relative financial weakness of elites in 2016 was part of the calculus of those who organized the Beirut Madinati campaign.

Finally, in 2010, members of Parliament had not yet unconstitutionally extended their terms. Parliamentary elections were still following their regular schedule and would have been held in 2013. Parliament canceled the 2013 elections after citing security concerns and fearing that elections would invite further spillover from the civil war in neighboring Syria. This spawned yet another cycle of protest.[64] The municipal elections in 2016 were held at a time when Lebanese voters had lost the only other formal mechanism for holding their leaders accountable. One respondent traced the interest of those with political ambitions in a group like Beirut Madinati to the 2013 election cancellation, explaining that "[in] 2010, there was still the hope of parliamentary elections coming. Many of those who had been traditionally interested in running were planning for that election. And then it got canceled. So they turned their focus very deliberately to the local [elections]."[65] This is evidence that the cancellation of parliamentary elections made the municipal elections the only remaining focal point for those organizing against the establishment.

---

[61] Thanassis Cambanis, "People Power and Its Limits: Lessons from Lebanon's Anti-Sectarian Reform Movement," in Thanassis Cambanis and Michael Wahid Hanna, eds., *Arab Politics Beyond the Uprisings: Experiments in an Era of Resurgent Authoritarianism*, Washington, D.C.: Century Foundation Press, March 2017.

[62] Abu-Rish, 2016.

[63] Interview 2.

[64] Interviews 6 and 7.

[65] Interview 2.

The "You Stink" Movement

One of the most important differences between the municipal elections of 2010 and those of 2016 is that one occurred before and the other after the trash crisis of 2015. It is difficult to understand the emergence of Beirut Madinati without the trash crisis, popular outrage concerning it, the "You Stink" protest movement that developed in response to it, and the ultimate failure of that movement to effect political change.

In July 2015, the contract providing the Sukleen Company with a monopoly on waste disposal in Beirut came to an end after two decades. Why the contract came to an end is unclear, but it seems to have been related to the breakdown of a long-standing agreement between Saad Hariri and Walid Jumblatt, the leader of the Druze community. Garbage started to pile up in Beirut and Mount Lebanon, creating a major health crisis.[66] In contrast to the gradual deterioration of infrastructure and services, one of the unique features of the trash crisis lay in the undeniable clarity of blame for its occurrence. The fact that politicians failed to secure a waste management contract, one of the most basic parts of their job description, provided a focal point for public anger and outrage.

Another important feature of the trash crisis is that it halted the provision of a public service for which no readily available private or party-based solution existed.[67] Postwar Lebanon has chronically suffered from an underprovision of water and electricity by government agencies. In response to these shortages, Lebanon's population has resorted to buying electricity and water privately. This unregulated private sector is closely connected to sectarian parties who benefit from the monopoly they have over water and electricity.[68] Despite the fact that residents overpay for a suboptimal provision of these essential services, their discontent is dampened by the fact that a private solution exists. Furthermore, once it is arranged, the problem recedes from view. The public does not directly witness the environmental damage caused by these makeshift solutions.[69]

Trash collection proved to be different. Once the contract with Sukleen expired, there was no ready makeshift alternative. People were faced with an ugly and unsanitary reminder of how the political class had failed them. Although politicians had arranged for a solution to water and electricity that placated the public and strengthened their own leverage, they were unable to do so with trash. The power of sectarian elites rests not only on playing identity-based politics and stoking communal fears but also on dense patronage networks through which votes are exchanged for practical,

---

[66] Harb, 2016.

[67] Interview 1.

[68] Éric Verdeil, "Les Services Urbains à Beyrouth: Entre Crise Infrastructurelle et Réformes Contestées," *Géosphères*, 2013; Harb, 2016.

[69] Interview 1.

material benefits and services.[70] Politicians' inability to even selectively deliver a basic service to their supporters in the city undermined one of the key pillars of the sectarian contract between voters and politicians.

By the time trash had inundated the streets of Beirut in 2015, civil-society and activist networks in Lebanon were robust and well established, as discussed earlier. However, they remained organized around narrow issues that touched the daily lives of only a small percentage of voters. Even the 2013 extension of Parliament's mandate did not appreciably affect the life of the ordinary Lebanese citizen. The trash crisis was a critical moment in which the long-standing work of activists suddenly collided with the lived experiences of ordinary people. For the first time in decades, nonsectarian activists had a window of opportunity. Public discontent touched all segments of society and was high enough to make mass mobilization around the issue of trash management possible. One interviewee, a long-time activist, explained that analysts might easily take popular discontent for granted and assume that it had always existed. By this respondent's account, it had not; the trash crisis was instrumental in bringing it to the forefront. Public outrage about the trash crisis was a positive surprise to seasoned activists who had tried to mobilize the public since the end of the civil war.[71]

The acuteness of the trash crisis led directly to the growth and development of the You Stink movement and its offshoots. The movement brought existing networks of activists and civil-society groups together to protest the corruption and inaction of an entire political class. At its height, there were between 60,000 and 70,000 protesters in the streets, which was significant in a small country like Lebanon.[72] For those who participated, it was a powerful experience. For some, it was the first time they were involved in politics. The government's harsh response against protesters, coupled with the regime's dismissive rhetoric downplaying the protesters' grievances, convinced some newcomers that change was necessary.[73] You Stink brought unity to civil society in a way that opened a political space for the formation of Beirut Madinati. Although support for the March 8 and March 14 Coalitions was already in decline, the universality of the You Stink movement's critique broke the polarization between the two coalitions' supporters and created consensus around the idea that the entire political class was to blame.[74] The mood within civil society changed. Activists became bolder in their critiques of the establishment, even in written work.[75] The thawing of this political divide was important in making a diverse effort like Beirut Madinati possible.

---

[70] Cammett, 2014.

[71] Interview 7.

[72] Interview 1.

[73] Interview 9.

[74] Interview 9.

[75] Interview 1.

Paradoxically, the most important legacy of the You Stink movement was its failure to achieve political change. The movement solved collective-action problems among activists, brought newcomers into political advocacy, and generated momentum for continued action. However, it simultaneously discouraged people.[76] Students, frustrated by the failure to achieve tangible gains through You Stink, needed to find a way to shift from protest politics to official politics. Activists learned important lessons from You Stink's lack of focus. The protesters had demanded a solution to the trash crisis, an end of the sectarian system, and everything in between. Bickering, disorganization, and a loss of direction weakened the movement.[77] Many became convinced that nothing would ever change if they continued protesting and lobbying instead of running for election.[78] One respondent described a sense of incompleteness after the movement fizzled out. It seemed that the demand for an alternative was present among the public and that activists had to move to supply that alternative.[79] Another respondent described it as a turning point in the thinking of those who desired change.[80]

There were other lessons learned from You Stink's mistakes. Besides choosing an electoral rather than a protest strategy, another lesson was to avoid negative language and sweeping demands to overthrow the system. When Beirut Madinati emerged, its strategists were explicit in trying to focus on a concrete and positive message. The campaign's rhetoric was diplomatic toward elites and zeroed in on the goal of making Beirut more livable.[81] The rationale was that the negatives were common knowledge, particularly after the trash crisis. Beirut Madinati avoided pointing fingers. In fact, the campaign rarely commented on what others did.[82] Furthermore, the steering committee chose to prioritize transparent communication, pursue local influencers and celebrities, and invite people to use their particular skill set in creative ways—to make art, design the logo, give legal advice, and develop a program grounded in the expertise of engineers, architects, and urban planners.[83] These decisions were attempts to build on the momentum generated by You Stink while explicitly pursuing a nearly opposite organizational strategy.

---

[76] Interview 8.

[77] Interview 1.

[78] Interviews 4 and 7.

[79] Interview 8.

[80] Interview 6.

[81] Interview 2.

[82] Interview 3.

[83] Interviews 1, 2, and 3.

Sustainability and Continuity

The future of a nonsectarian political movement like Beirut Madinati is far from certain. Both internally and externally, there are factors that point to the movement's sustainability, adaptability, and flexibility to changing circumstances. However, there are also reasons to doubt Beirut Madinati's ability to survive internal divisions, win elections within a system designed to benefit sectarian parties, and replicate their movement in municipalities outside the capital.

Signs of Sustainability

One of the most important signs of the movement's sustainability is its ability to adapt, restructure, and continue working after the May 2016 elections. As discussed, the movement weathered disagreements in order to write bylaws that provided a permanent structure and procedures for internal governance.[84] This was a critical moment in which Beirut Madinati could have disbanded after the failure of its electoral bid. Turning this corner intact and reorganized made it possible for Beirut Madinati to continue its work, even when not in office. The alternative municipality and neighborhood committees also have survived since the elections and continue their work.[85]

One of the most important accomplishments of the election was to establish Beirut Madinati as a recognizable and trustworthy brand.[86] The greatest evidence of this has been the victory of Jad Tabet, an independent endorsed by Beirut Madinati, in the April 2017 elections to head Lebanon's Order of Engineers. To place this victory in context, the Order of Engineers is among the largest and most important syndicates in Lebanon, with a membership of 64,000 and competitive elections for leadership. Jad Tabet won despite running against a candidate supported by nearly every establishment party, including both Hizbullah and the Future Movement.[87] Tabet ran on a list calling itself Naqabati (My Syndicate), deliberately identifying with the values of Beirut Madinati's nonsectarian independent brand. Although the rest of the Naqabati list did not win their seats, Tabet won against his opponent by several hundred votes. One interviewee described this as a watershed moment: Beirut Madinati demonstrated that it could actually win an election. The organization was still active and producing results one year after the municipal elections. The election outcome and Tabet's leadership have generated new activism and energy among the Order's members for using their profession to improve urban life in Beirut and in Lebanon more generally.[88]

---

[84] Interview 1.

[85] Interview 2.

[86] Interviews 1 and 3.

[87] *Daily Star*, "Jad Tabet Wins Beirut Order of Engineers Polls," April 8, 2017.

[88] Interview 1.

The new electoral law, which came into effect during Lebanon's 2018 parliamentary elections, is another encouraging sign for the longevity of Beirut Madinati and other small nonsectarian political groups. For the first time in Lebanon's postwar history, elections were held under a system of proportional representation. According to one simulation, if the Beirut municipal elections had been run under the new law, Beirut Madinati candidates would have taken eight seats on the council. The law includes several other reforms that also could benefit small parties and newcomers in the long term. These include pre-printed ballots, which make it more difficult for sectarian parties to monitor voters. Another is a double-counting system. In addition to traditional manual counting, an automated counting system was introduced, which places an additional logistical barrier in the way of those seeking to commit fraud. Finally, Lebanese living abroad were allowed to vote for the first time.[89] Although only 82,970 expatriates registered to vote in the 2018 election,[90] which is a low number, given the estimated millions in the Lebanese diaspora, this provision could have serious political consequences if nonsectarian groups can find ways to mobilize this sizeable voter bloc—a bloc that might be less beholden to sectarian patronage networks.

Admittedly, the new electoral law divides Lebanon into small homogenous districts that benefit the political elite. This advantage was on full display in May 2018 with the resounding victory of traditional parties. On the other hand, the new law also led to the first instance of a civil-society candidate winning a parliamentary seat.[91] If maintained, this new law could create unprecedented opportunities for nonsectarian and independent groups to win seats in future elections. Furthermore, if these nonsectarian voices can coordinate their actions once in Parliament, they will have the potential to influence policy. Despite its serious flaws, the electoral law is a net positive for new political actors. All interview respondents were positive in their assessments of the law's impact on groups like Beirut Madinati.[92]

A final sign of sustainability for Beirut Madinati is the appeal that it (and nonsectarian movements like it) have among youth. One respondent assessed that time is simply not on the side of the establishment elites. Lebanon's high voting age of 21 is kept in place to protect sectarian elites precisely because the younger generation is more educated, less sectarian, and less embedded in the networks of traditional sectarian

---

[89] Interview 3.

[90] Ghinwa Obeid, "Doing the Numbers: Ministers Break Down Expat Vote," *Daily Star*, April 19, 2018.

[91] Asma Ajroudi, "Unpicking the Results of Lebanon's Elections," *Al-Jazeera*, May 10, 2018.

[92] The reasons establishment elites would have agreed on such a law are complex and outside the scope of this case study. Broadly speaking, the reform is a product of two factors. It is the result of intra-elite bargaining and compromise in a moment when an elite consensus was absent. It is also the product of decades-long efforts by civil society to propose and keep a proportional representation alternative on the negotiating table. If elites have opened a window for independents, it is accidental from their perspective (Interview 1).

strongmen.⁹³ As this generation gradually comes of voting age, elites will have to adapt or could be voted out of office.

Challenges to Continuity and Replication

The earlier analysis risks painting too rosy a picture of Beirut Madinati's prospects. Serious challenges remain. The most obvious challenge is that grassroots movements like Beirut Madinati cannot control international developments that can impact Lebanon's domestic politics. The most recent example of this was Prime Minister Saad Hariri's detainment and forced resignation while on a trip to Saudi Arabia in November 2017. This was part of a larger campaign by the Saudi crown prince to pursue a more aggressive foreign policy of containing Iran's influence in the region, which included pressuring Hariri to take a harder line against the growth of Hizbullah's political power. Contrary to the Saudi crown prince's expectations, however, Lebanon's elites and population did not accept the resignation and almost immediately suspected that it was coerced. Domestically, both Hariri's allies and opponents stood with him against such a brazen display of foreign interference.⁹⁴ At the popular level, this has generated unity and sympathy for politicians trying to prevent gridlock and maintain stability in Lebanon while placating their foreign patrons.⁹⁵ Paradoxically, Hariri has returned to Lebanon stronger and more popular.⁹⁶ If this sentiment persists, it will make elections more difficult for groups challenging the ruling elite. There is also a perennial concern within the movement that instability and uncertainty will cause voters to retreat into familiar sectarian enclaves and vote for the status quo.⁹⁷ The region's volatility highlights the little control that small nonsectarian grassroots organizations have over the larger opportunity structures that can determine their success or failure.

At the domestic level, important gaps in Beirut Madinati's ability to mobilize certain segments of voters in 2016 point to similar challenges in future electoral contests. One respondent noted that Beirut Madinati failed to mobilize the majority of the middle-aged population, the generation that came of age during the civil war. This is despite the fact that the older generation of activists spearheading the campaign comes from this demographic. Young voters were enthusiastic about the campaign and so were some of their grandparents. However, many middle-aged voters, skeptical of all religious or political organization, refused to participate in elections in any way.

---

⁹³ Interview 6.

⁹⁴ Anne Barnard and Maria Abi-Habib, "Why Saad Hariri Had That Strange Sojourn in Saudi Arabia," *New York Times*, December 24, 2017.

⁹⁵ Interview 9.

⁹⁶ Ben Hubbard and Hwaida Saad, "Lebanon's Vanishing Prime Minister Is Back at Work. Now What?" *New York Times*, November 25, 2017.

⁹⁷ Interview 7.

Although some of these voters could change their attitudes after seeing more of Beirut Madinati's advocacy work, the organization has yet to successfully turn them out in an election.[98]

Beirut Madinati also struggled to reach lower-income voters, the less educated, and those more embedded in sectarian patronage networks. One respondent explained that the campaign was more visible in cosmopolitan neighborhoods like Hamra, Mar Mikhael, and Achrafieh. The campaign's presence at private colleges like AUB or the Lebanese American University was much more robust than at the public Lebanese University.[99] Respondents were aware of this problem but acknowledged that it is natural for a movement to mobilize those within its personal networks first, because they are the easiest to reach. Moving beyond this demographic will be critical to success in future elections. Some interviewees expressed concerns about the movement's elitist label. Although the members of Beirut Madinati are not wealthy, their educational pedigrees signal a middle- and upper middle–class background. One respondent argued that "Education shouldn't be a bad word. Education can help you serve your country better. It makes you more politically aware, more conscious."[100] This interviewee hoped that education would be an advantage, not a liability. However, another respondent expressed other concerns, explaining that the risk of appearing condescending remains; speaking in a certain way can put people on the defensive. Expanding the movement's reach into lower-income areas will be important in future elections.[101]

Beirut Madinati also failed to attract the majority of Sunnis in a stronghold of the major Sunni political party. Most voter defections from sectarian networks came from Christian voters whose parties are weaker junior players within the boundaries of municipal Beirut. If Beirut Madinati cannot inspire sufficient defections from voters of the identity group corresponding to a region's dominant party, parliamentary elections will present a formidable challenge; districts are designed to be homogenous and comfortably within the strongholds of particular sectarian leaders. National success hinges on bleeding establishment parties of a critical mass of their co-sectarians. The question remains whether Beirut Madinati or any explicitly nonsectarian actor could attract Sunni voters in Tripoli, Shi'a voters in Tyre, or Christian voters in Metn.

A related challenge is the ability to replicate a movement like Beirut Madinati in other regions and localities in Lebanon, particularly in less-urban locales with less educated voters and where a secular discourse is less acceptable or simply less familiar.[102]

---

[98] Interview 9.

[99] Interview 9.

[100] Interview 2.

[101] Interview 9.

[102] Despite these challenges, it is important to note that other nonsectarian movements emerged in other regions. The most important example is Baalbek Madinati (Baalbek, My City). The group emerged in a Hizbullah-controlled district and explicitly borrowed Beirut Madinati's brand.

Conditions in Beirut are specific and relatively unique within Lebanon. For example, a base of secular voters exists. In other areas where this base may not exist, campaigns might need to do more work to persuade voters. One respondent also pointed out that Beirut, despite the importance of Hariri's party, is no sectarian group's home turf. Beirut is diverse and symbolically important as the capital city. Sectarian parties usually find compromises behind closed doors and run together in elections. This allows challengers like Beirut Madinati to confront the elite while avoiding the divisive national issues embodied in the March 8 and March 14 Coalitions.[103] If Beirut Madinati transports its model to a stronghold of one of these coalitions, keeping the campaign focused on local matters will be difficult and the movement will be more vulnerable to exploitation.

Also, challenging parties that have armed militias in their strongholds could invite a harsher response than that which Beirut Madinati encountered in 2016. In fact, intimidation and voter fraud are likely to be more serious across the board in future electoral contests. Now that Beirut Madinati is a recognizable brand capable of threatening the status quo, members are unlikely to be permitted to campaign so freely in the future.[104]

The 2018 Parliamentary Elections

Of all the challenges to Beirut Madinati's sustainability and continuity, there may be none more formidable than its own pluralism and political diversity. During the campaign for municipal elections, national issues were avoided and left unaddressed in the interest of building a diverse coalition. Members come from every part of the left-right ideological spectrum. Members do not necessarily have the same views on Hizbullah. Some see it as a constitutionally problematic force, while others believe that the problem is a more systematic one created by a sectarian system that produces and allows movements like Hezbollah to exist and thrive.[105] There also are debates about the extent to which Beirut Madinati should identify as a secular organization. Some fear that such a stance will alienate the public and risk misunderstandings. Beirut Madinati does not want to put restrictions on religious life; rather, it wants to keep religion and politics separate spheres.[106] However, this nuance might be difficult to communicate. One interviewee explained that something must change within the movement for it to become relevant at the national level. It is currently staying out of divisive but important debates like refugees and relationships with neighboring countries. By doing so, it leaves sectarian parties to shape both discourse and policy in this realm. This respondent reported believing that this is a mistake but was also at a loss for how

---

[103] Interview 2.

[104] Interview 7.

[105] Interview 9.

[106] Interview 9.

to authentically enter the world of high politics while still seeking consensus within the movement and appealing to voter desires for stability.[107] This could prove to be the thorniest challenge to Beirut Madinati's viability at the national level.

This pluralism was connected to internal divisions over whether to run for parliamentary elections in 2018. Those who were against running in the elections explained that Beirut Madinati's members simply do not occupy the same political space on the spectrum of national politics.[108] A national campaign would force decisions on secularism and Hizbullah's weapons that the movement might not survive.[109] Others emphasized the supremacy of local issues and argued that concrete successes at the local level are the most efficient and effective way to build credibility and undermine the sectarian system. There is a fear of getting lost in traditional Lebanese politics and losing sight of the everyday concerns of the individual.

Another argument is that Beirut Madinati does not currently have the capital and human resources to divide itself between the two levels of government. People in this camp advocated allowing members to participate in elections under other labels but argued that Beirut Madinati should focus on organizing the battle in Beirut around its agenda, building local institutions and a grassroots presence, and preparing for the municipal elections of 2022. They contended that Beirut Madinati simply did not have a clear alternative to present at the national level.[110] There were also short-term strategic reasons to oppose running. Some thought that they might be able to do better outside of Beirut Madinati. Others were concerned that, because the movement's supporters tend to be more sympathetic to the March 14 Coalition, running would weaken March 14 and indirectly enhance the relative power of Hizbullah's March 8 Coalition.[111]

Another faction within Beirut Madinati believed that real change would not come without entering national politics. Members of this group argued that local and national politics in Lebanon are interrelated and that the organization should be working within each layer in order to bring about policy change. Decisions to decentralize government and empower and fund municipalities are made at the national level. Transforming the city could not happen without engagement in national politics.[112] This group also highlighted the issue of momentum. Members of this group believed that the elite agreement on an electoral law and holding national elections for the first time in nine years presented a window of opportunity that should not be wasted. They argued that Beirut Madinati had a moral responsibility and obligation to run. If Beirut

---

[107] Interview 7.

[108] Interview 2.

[109] Interview 9.

[110] Interview 7.

[111] Interview 3.

[112] Interviews 1 and 8.

Madinati was absent from electoral politics for six years, it might have squandered the political capital and goodwill it built during the municipal contest.[113] Although members of this group acknowledged the reasonableness of the strategic concerns of the other camp, they rejected the notion that running would indirectly strengthen Hizbullah and argued that Beirut Madinati's success would weaken all sectarian actors.[114] One respondent also voiced concerns that establishment lists had been trying to lure members with tempting offers. Such suspected attempts at co-optation could harm Beirut Madinati by breeding mistrust within the organization.[115]

Ultimately, Beirut Madinati voted not to participate in parliamentary elections. Such strategic decisions have to pass with a two-thirds vote in the general assembly. The pro-running faction received more than 50 percent of the vote but less than the necessary two-thirds. A second vote was conducted with a similar outcome.[116] Despite this organization-level decision, several respondents mentioned that groups within Beirut Madinati chose to run their own campaigns for parliamentary elections. For example, the LiBaladi (For My Country) civil-society group that ran as part of the Kollouna Watani (All Are My Nation) civil-society coalition has overlapping membership and supporters with Beirut Madinati.[117] The continuity with Beirut Madinati is also evident in LiBaladi's branding and grassroots mobilization approach. This is just one example of Beirut Madinati members running as part of other coalitions.

Beirut Madinati will continue to wrestle with the thorny implications of its members running as part of other organizations in national elections. It is possible that some Beirut Madinati members might end up on opposing lists in certain districts. The organization is keen to avoid this and sees it as a serious threat to its cohesion. At the time that the interviews were conducted, efforts were ongoing to rewrite bylaws to address conflicts of interest and prevent such a situation.[118]

As these details make clear, the coordination of a strategy for parliamentary elections presented Beirut Madinati with a formidable test. It remains to be seen whether Beirut Madinati can build cohesion despite significant internal disagreements on overall strategy. If the organization maintains its momentum long enough to be a relevant player in the 2022 municipal elections, it is likely to survive external challenges from the sectarian establishment.

---

[113] Interviews 3 and 8.

[114] Interview 3.

[115] Interview 3.

[116] Interview 9.

[117] Interview 8.

[118] Interviews 1 and 3.

Implications and Conclusions

Beirut Madinati emerged because of a confluence of factors emanating from both the external political environment and internal developments within civil-society networks. Embattled elites, cut off from their foreign patrons and short on cash, were a critical factor. A public confronted daily with a tangible and disruptive reminder of the failures of the political elite was another. A protest movement uniting activists and disparate strands of a well-established civil society, but failing for lack of organization and direction, was the final piece. It is difficult to imagine the emergence of Beirut Madinati without all three of these conditions present. Once the campaign began, it took full advantage of Lebanon's imperfect but noteworthy freedoms of assembly and press.

This analysis of Beirut Madinati's emergence reveals that instances of cross-sectarian cooperation and resilience to sectarian pressures are multilayered processes, likely because of multiple variables coming together in a particular moment. Yet this study does suggest some implications and ways forward for international policymakers seeking to promote such resilience in the region.

Encouraging movements like Beirut Madinati requires a two-pronged approach. The first is a concerted effort to promote substantive rather than procedural liberalization in the region. Instead of trying to sponsor particular organizations (which may end up delegitimizing those movements), U.S. and international actors should use their leverage to pressure allies to open the political space in general. This includes broadening the focus beyond holding elections to encouraging greater freedom of the press and freedom of assembly. This carries some risks, but it is the only way to create an opportunity for the development of truly independent nonsectarian grassroots political action.

Although it is easier said than done, the second approach requires taking steps to limit the foreign funding of sectarian parties and actors throughout the region. Weaker sectarian leaders, with less funding and foreign support, have a more difficult time providing the goods and services that are the backbone of sectarian patronage networks. This creates public discontent and an opportunity for those seeking to provide a nonsectarian alternative. Outside of comprehensive political solutions to larger regional conflicts between Iran and Saudi Arabia, this case study suggests that making it more difficult for regional powers to funnel resources to sectarian actors is an indirect but effective way to de-escalate sectarian tensions in the region. For new nonsectarian alternatives to emerge, their sectarian competitors must be weak, embattled, and unable to deliver on material promises to their voters.

CHAPTER THREE

Segregation and Sectarianism: Geography, Economic Distribution, and Sectarian Resilience in Bahrain

Justin Gengler
Research Assistant Professor
Social and Economic Survey Research Institute
Qatar University

For most of the modern history of Bahrain, and especially since the 1979 Iranian Revolution, episodes of political tension have naturally overlapped with strained relations between the island kingdom's Sunni and Shi'i citizens. Shi'a Muslims constitute approximately 55 to 60 percent of the population but are politically and economically disenfranchised, making Bahrain the only remaining Arab state—after the 2003 fall of the Ba'thist regime in Iraq—still dominated by a Sunni minority elite. Given this demographic makeup, popular efforts to limit the largely unconstrained authority of the ruling Al Khalifa family are synonymous with Shi'a empowerment for many Bahrainis, and even grievances shared by citizens of both confessional communities—grievances such as corruption and financial mismanagement, appropriation of public lands, and the importation of foreigners, among others—have not given rise to sustained cross-sectarian political mobilization. Bahraini Sunnis hesitate lest their cooperation with the Shi'a-led opposition end in a radical change to the political status quo that finds the fortunes of the two groups reversed.[1] Moreover, Sunnis who dare to join forces with Shi'i actors are generally the first to be targeted for state reprisal, both as a punitive measure against alleged defectors and because a vigorous cross-societal reform movement represents the only real domestic threat to the Al Khalifa monarchy.[2]

Bahrain's most recent and violent episode of sectarian-based political conflict—the popular uprising of February 2011—saw these dynamics exaggerated to their extreme, in line with the severity of the challenge to the prevailing order. Mass protests involved the better portion of the adult Shi'a population, while pro-government counter-demonstrations claimed to turn out an equal number of mainly Sunni loy-

---

[1] Daniel Brumberg, "Transforming the Arab World's Protection-Racket Politics," *Journal of Democracy*, Vol. 24, No. 3, 2013.

[2] Justin Gengler, "Royal Factionalism, the Khawalid, and the Securitization of 'the Shi'a Problem' in Bahrain," *Journal of Arabian Studies*, Vol. 3, No. 1, 2013.

alists.³ On several occasions, members of the two sides engaged in direct armed confrontation. The breakdown of law and order spanned a month and was put down only with the intervention of the Bahraini military at the encouragement of ground forces dispatched by neighboring Saudi Arabia and other Gulf Cooperation Council states. An extended period of martial law followed, during which the leaders of, participants in, and even sympathizers with the protest movement were systematically sought out for punishments ranging from incarceration to dismissal from work to revocation of academic scholarships. Ordinary citizens were invited to take part in this task of rooting out those whom the government and its supporters termed "terrorists" by helping to identify demonstrators from photographs shared via state television and social media. Meanwhile, a labyrinthine network of official and makeshift security barriers effectively cut off much of the Shi'a population, concentrated in outlying villages, from the rest of the island. The political and physical gulf long separating Bahrain's sectarian communities was widened incalculably.

And yet, amid this turmoil and division, Sunni-Shi'i relations in some locations and arenas, even if strained, fared better than elsewhere. Although some mixed districts were sites of regular clashes between protesters and loyalists, other districts saw few clashes. In some sectors of the economy, Shi'a employees were summarily fired for absenteeism during the early days of the protest, whereas striking workers in other industries were granted relative reprieve by management and colleagues. Such variation in the intensity of sectarianism during the initial period of the 2011 uprising suggests sources of resilience that can help counteract pressures toward conflict, even in such an acutely polarized environment as Bahrain's. This chapter seeks to draw out these mechanisms, aided by insights from interviews with Bahrainis who lived through communal relations in 2011 and empirical evidence from a nationally representative public opinion survey of citizens completed in early 2017.

Results of the analysis point to residential integration as the key factor associated with sectarian resilience. First, mixed neighborhoods provide shared physical space that encourages positive intergroup contact, militating against negative feelings that can lead to escalation and violence in times of social tension.⁴ Second, and perhaps more important in the context of an authoritarian distributive state such as Bahrain, integrated settings complicate elite efforts to target resources to coethnics as presumed political supporters while excluding non-coethnics from these benefits, because many of the goods demanded by supporters—hospitals, schools, municipal offices—are nonexcludable. This inability to segregate political constituencies efficiently reduces local inequality among communities and thus feelings of resentment stemming from unfair economic distribution. A final factor underlying the association between residential

---

³ Jane Kinninmont, *Bahrain: Beyond the Impasse*, London: Chatham House/Royal Institute of International Affairs, 2012.

⁴ Thomas F. Pettigrew, "Intergroup Contact Theory," *Annual Review of Psychology*, Vol. 49, No. 1, 1998.

integration and sectarian resilience in Bahrain is geographic self-selection. It is reasonable to expect, and historical accounts seem to substantiate, that citizens who already hold more-positive sectarian orientations have been disproportionately likely to choose or accept living alongside members of the other community in mixed neighborhoods. The link between local intergroup mixing and resistance to sectarianism is, in this way, partly endogenous.

The remainder of this chapter unravels these mechanisms of resilience through an examination of Bahrain's sectarian geography and of the public-policy choices that have helped shape patterns of citizen settlement since the country's first large-scale state housing efforts in the 1960s. The analysis begins with a qualitative comparison of the country's two largest planned settlements, 'Isa Town and Hamad Town, with attention to the divergent physical attributes of these confessionally mixed urban spaces, how they encourage or discourage positive intergroup contact, and how they relate to the dissimilar government priorities motivating their respective creations. A second section widens the scope of the inquiry to evaluate the systemic impact of local intersect mixing on sectarian resilience via state goods distribution in Bahrain. It leverages subnational demographic variation captured in the survey data to assess the extent to which individual-level economic outcomes vary according to the degree of local confessional segregation. The aim is to understand how the expected economic payoffs of Sunni and Shi'i citizens in Bahrain differ depending on the confessional makeup of their neighborhoods, and how these patterns should be expected to stimulate or dampen local sectarian tensions. In a final section, this chapter returns to the cases of 'Isa Town and Hamad Town to trace the impact of these pathways to resilience on local sectarian relations during the 2011 uprising.

A Tale of Two Bahraini Cities: 'Isa Town and Hamad Town

Patterns of settlement in Bahrain have been closely connected to the country's economic and political development. Bahrain was the first Arab Gulf State to exploit oil in large quantities, and in the decades after oil's discovery in 1932, the capital, Manama, was transformed under British tutelage to become "the central place of oil modernity in the Gulf."[5] Yet, by the time of Bahrain's first large-scale government housing projects outside of the capital, begun in the 1960s, oil was already beginning to run out: Production from the main onshore field would peak in 1970.[6] The largest undertaking, the new city of 'Isa Town, located south of the capital near Bahrain's oil facilities,

---

[5] United Nations Educational, Scientific and Cultural Organization, World Heritage Centre, "Manama, City of Trade, Multiculturalism and Religious Coexistence," webpage, July 20, 2018; and Nelida Fuccaro, *Histories of City and State in the Persian Gulf: Manama Since 1800*, Cambridge, U.K.: Cambridge University Press, 2009.

[6] Gengler, 2015.

was built expressly for workers at the state petroleum company, many of whom were Bahraini Shi'a from remote agricultural villages or migrant laborers in need of housing. However, as Nelida Fuccaro states, for the former group of Shi'i "peasants turned oil and service workers," employment in the modern economy did not need imply "physical dislocation from their homes."[7] Those who felt strong connections to their villages chose to remain, while new "suburban Shi'i dormitory communities" proliferated around Manama and around the oil refinery in Sitra.[8]

Thus, the early phase of post-oil public housing in Bahrain represented by 'Isa Town did not coincide with mass urbanization, even among the relatively narrow category of workers in the new oil economy for whom it was primarily intended. The option of modern, state-provided housing occasioned instead a selection effect whereby Shi'i villagers with weaker familial or emotional attachments to their agrarian communities were more likely to relocate to what would become a far more diverse environment, while others with stronger attachments tended to remain in rural or suburban sectarian enclaves. Although the communities were not necessarily tied to religious orientations, Bahraini interviewees with family links to modern-day 'Isa Town suggested that religion might have played a role in determining internal migration decisions, with more-secular and left-leaning families tending to exit village life for the wider social and economic opportunities of the mixed urban setting.[9]

If Bahrain's first efforts at mass government housing were spurred by the needs of the new oil economy, then its ongoing second phase, embodied in the sprawling, fingerlike Hamad Town, reflects the contemporary rise of a very different sector: security. Aptly named for current ruler King Hamad bin 'Isa Al Khalifa during his three-decade tenure as defense minister and architect of the Bahrain Defense Force, Hamad Town was established in 1984, ostensibly to accommodate the growing number of Bahraini families priced out of a booming local property market.[10] Unlike in 'Isa Town, housing in Hamad Town took the form of explicit government welfare—a gift, or what Abdulhadi Khalaf terms a royal *makrama*[11]—rather than compensation provided by an employer in return for labor. The list of applicants thus came to include much of the citizenry, and the state needed to prioritize cases.

In practice, since the time of its founding, Hamad Town has been noted among both Sunni and Shi'i Bahrainis for its conspicuously high concentration of households, especially those of foreign nationals and newly naturalized citizens, whose members

---

[7] Fuccaro, 2009, p. 207.

[8] Fuccaro, 2009, p. 225; and Fuad I. Khuri, *Tribe and State in Bahrain: The Transformation of Social and Political Authority in an Arab State*, Chicago: University of Chicago Press, 1981, pp. 234–235.

[9] Interviews with the author via Skype, May 2017.

[10] Gengler, 2013, pp. 53–79.

[11] Abdulhadi Khalaf, "The New Amir of Bahrain: Marching Sideways," *Civil Society*, Vol. 9, No. 100, 2000.

are employed in the police, military, and various other security services.[12] Three years prior to the founding of the town, Bahrain witnessed a failed coup attempt by the Iranian Revolution–inspired Islamic Front for the Liberation of Bahrain, and one might speculate that the settlement was conceived at least in part for the purpose of housing newly imported soldiers viewed as essential to safeguarding the regime.[13] Whatever the case, extended periods of Shi'a unrest in the 1990s, in the 2000s, and following the uprising of February 2011 coincided with a massive security buildup that saw Bahrain's annual military spending increase by 118 percent between 2001 and 2010 alone (leading the Middle East).[14] With this spending came an influx of Sunnis from Syria, Yemen, Jordan, Pakistan, and elsewhere recruited for police and military service. These groups often clashed with Bahrainis and with each other. During the author's stay in Bahrain from 2008 to 2009, it was not uncommon to see signs in Hamad Town shop windows warning, for example, "No Syrians allowed." At the same time, the author listened to several Shi'i villagers complain of public housing applications pending since the 1980s.[15]

Beyond conceptual differences related to the impetus behind their creation and the nature of the housing they provide, Hamad Town and 'Isa Town also are distinguished by their physical layouts. 'Isa Town proper possesses all the attributes of a typical urban setting: a city of approximately 40,000 citizen residents extending more or less evenly from a center core, with roads named after Arab capitals and dwellings of various types alongside such points of public congregation as mosques, malls, university campuses, government offices, restaurants, the national stadium, and a noted traditional market. As described by one Bahraini interviewee, its layout is such that a person driving or walking to retrieve takeaway food from a restaurant will very likely have to cross through various districts and interact with citizens and noncitizens of different backgrounds. To the east, the city merges almost imperceptibly into the mainly Arab and Persian Shi'i settlements of Jidd 'Ali, Tubli, and Jurdab. With the exception of some more-rural portions, these villages form an effective extension of the urban space. An aerial view of the typical urban landscape of 'Isa Town is given in Figure 3.1.

Hamad Town, by comparison, is something of a misnomer, being not so much a town as a collection of deliberately organized roundabouts and walled villa compounds separated by empty desert landscape. Hamad Town is purely residential, home to about 85,000 citizens, and broken only intermittently by an isolated public school or convenience store. Points of common gathering, such as markets and shopping malls, are located beyond the boundaries of the town proper, and pedestrian activity is mini-

---

[12] Interviews with the author via Skype, May 2017.

[13] Hasan T. Alhasan, "The Role of Iran in the Failed Coup of 1981: The IFLB in Bahrain," *Middle East Journal*, Vol. 65, No. 4. 2011.

[14] Gengler, 2013, pp. 72–73.

[15] Gengler, 2015.

Figure 3.1
'Isa Town

SOURCE: Google Maps, August 7, 2017.

mal. The streets and 22 roundabouts of Hamad Town are laid out with industrial sterility in a geometric north-south pattern and are known only by their numbers. Thus, a resident will refer to himself as hailing from, say, "Hamad Town Roundabout 14." Crucially, many of these sectors are dominated by members of a single sectarian and/or national community. So, although Hamad Town is often referred to as a rare "mixed" region of Bahrain,[16] it is mixed mostly in the aggregate and tends to be balkanized at the local level both between Sunni and Shi'i Bahrainis and between citizens and noncitizens. Moreover, unlike the seamless integration of 'Isa Town with its eastern periphery, Hamad Town is flanked to the west by several of Bahrain's most restive Shi'i villages, including Karzakan, Dumistan, and al-Malikiyya, with clear boundaries separating them from the edges of town. A view of a typical stretch of Hamad Town is shown in Figure 3.2.

---

[16] See, for example, U.S. Department of State, "Bahrain," from Bureau of Democracy, Human Rights, and Labor, *July–December 2010 International Religious Freedom Report*, September 13, 2011.

In short, Hamad Town is a commuter city, providing housing and little else. Its residents generally work, do their shopping, and seek entertainment in other urban centers and need never interact with any but a localized and often homogenous group of neighbors. Indeed, the layout of the settlement suggests that this lack of communal fabric was perhaps by design. Yet, despite these social shortcomings and Hamad Town's reputation for sectarian tensions, Bahrain's housing shortage remains urgent enough that most citizens are happy to take advantage if they are fortunate enough to be offered a home there. 'Isa Town represents the opposite dynamic: Founded around the peak of Bahrain's resource wealth, it is a city born of abundance rather than poverty. Bahrainis chose to relocate to 'Isa Town in search of employment in the burgeoning oil and service sectors, and migration was more likely among families with higher

Figure 3.2
Hamad Town

SOURCE: Google Maps, August 7, 2017.

levels of education and greater openness to mixed cultural environments. In this way, 'Isa Town attracted a group of settlers that was relatively diverse demographically but similar ideologically. This history has continued to differentiate 'Isa Town from other parts of Bahrain throughout the modern period: It is one of the last strongholds of secular and leftist political movements and candidates since the reopening of Parliament in 2002.

As noted earlier, the divergent characters of Bahrain's two largest planned urban spaces are not mere accidents of history but have been influenced by deliberate design decisions reflecting very different periods and corresponding to elite approaches to housing policy. The impetus behind 'Isa Town was economic efficiency at a time of regime security, when the position of the Al Khalifa was still guaranteed by the British crown. Hamad Town, on the other hand, was meant to bolster political stability amid economic decline and in the wake of a failed revolution.

Bahrain and other distributive authoritarian regimes preserve power by maintaining a coalition of supporters who are materially invested in the political status quo and who enjoy a preponderance of military wherewithal with which to enforce it. In the Arab Gulf region, significant variation exists in the manner by which and among whom this political support is cultivated. Such variation in ruling strategy is underlied by substantial cross-national differences in resource wealth and demography, among other factors. In richer, more-homogenous states, such as Qatar and the United Arab Emirates, rulers can afford to distribute oil and gas revenue liberally among citizens, yielding a broad popular consensus around the legitimacy of the regime. In poorer, more ethnically fractionalized states like Bahrain and Saudi Arabia, however, leaders lack both the resources to patronize all citizens and confidence in the loyalty of all groups in society, creating more-difficult allocation choices with clearer winners and losers. For these leaders, the provision of welfare benefits to communities seen as inclined toward opposition represents a poor political investment, because the same limited resources could be used to reinforce support among loyalists.

In the context of Bahrain, then, a set of problems arises around distribution. The first is a coordination problem: The state aims to reward supporters without allocating scarce resources to nonsupporters, but it cannot know with certainty whether a citizen is of one or the other type. That is, the Al Khalifa monarchy faces a challenge in targeting beneficiaries-cum-supporters effectively. A compounding issue is that many goods demanded by supporters—e.g., quality roads, schools, and clinics—are public in nature, such that the state might be unable to target loyalists with resources without benefiting opponents. This problem of nonexcludability means that leaders, even if capable of identifying constituents and targeting them effectively, still might find it difficult to do so efficiently within acceptable limits of spillover to nonsupporters. Thus, the political return on the state's economic investment decreases as a function of geographic heterogeneity: Provision of public goods in a district populated only by supporters involves no dissipation of resources on nonsupporters, but deploying resources in a neighborhood evenly mixed between supporters and nonsupporters entails a high level of misallocation. Meanwhile, areas known to be dominated by nonsupporters can be disproportionately underresourced.

One tool that can help ease these problems is geography. In the post-oil Arab Gulf States, land and housing distribution generally has involved the creation of new settlements to accommodate ever-expanding numbers of citizens and foreign workers. In the process, skillful elites have seized the opportunity to shape a nation's political geography in a way that hampers coordination between societal factions while also earning the gratitude of citizens who benefit from financially consequential public housing and land allotments.[17] At the same time, citizens who wish to increase their likelihood of capturing government resources can relocate to areas perceived to be populated by regime supporters or, at a minimum, migrate away from regions perceived to be opposition strongholds. These dynamics encourage the political-cum-ethnic segregation and self-segregation of communities.

In Bahrain, geographic segregation of social groupings as political constituencies is both more extensive and more deeply engrained than in neighboring states. Although Bahrain's population is confined to a tiny island and compacted by the world's second-highest population density, Sunni and Shi'a citizens are separated into sectarian enclaves; maintain competing histories; speak distinct Arabic dialects; are employed in different sectors of the economy; tend to have wildly divergent political orientations toward the monarchy; and are readily distinguishable to fellow nationals by given and family names, dress, and any number of other outward cues. More fundamentally, the foundation of modern Bahrain is rooted in a military conquest widely perceived, and indeed celebrated officially, as possessing a clear sectarian dimension: the 1783 capture of the archipelago, then a Persian protectorate, by an alliance of Sunni tribes based in modern-day Qatar. In the decades after their victory, the allies would divide the territory into independent feudal estates on which native Shi'a agricultural workers served tribal landlords. Such a system persisted until legal reforms were imposed by British colonial administrators in the 1920s over the strong objections of the ruling family.[18] This historical legacy underlies the two communities' continued

---

[17] Farah Al-Nakib, for example, traces how state housing policies that were implemented from the 1950s through the 1980s in Kuwait "divided the population into discrete social residential zones" and stratified the urban and tribal classes. In Qatar, land allocation is an opaque process, leading to complaints over plot size and location, particularly with regard to plots far from the urban center that are seemingly reserved for specific descent-based groups. See Farah Al-Nakib, "Revisiting Ḥaḍar and Badū in Kuwait: Citizenship, Housing, and the Construction of a Dichotomy," *International Journal of Middle East Studies*, Vol. 46, No. 1, 2014; and Jocelyn Sage Mitchell, "Beyond Allocation: The Politics of Legitimacy in Qatar," Ph.D. thesis, Georgetown University, Washington, D.C., 2013.

[18] Khuri, 1981.

geographical separation, which the linguist Clive Holes has described as an "almost apartheid-like system of voluntary segregation."[19]

Segregation and Distribution in Bahrain

Measuring Sectarian Segregation

This section discusses the impact of spatial segregation on local sectarian relations in Bahrain as a way of understanding the causes of disproportionate resilience to conflict in some confessionally mixed areas relative to others. In particular, this section empirically tests the notion that geographic segregation of social groupings facilitates unequal distribution of resources in Bahrain and in other allocative states, and that these economic inequities drive local sectarian competition and resentment. Conversely, where communities are interspersed residentially, the state cannot efficiently target benefits toward a specific group as presumed political supporters, resulting in reduced sectarian-based economic inequality and, thus, in reduced animosity and tension at the local level. The quantitative analysis relies on the results of a nationally representative survey of 500 Bahraini households carried out by the author in late 2016 and early 2017.

The survey provides previously unavailable, nuanced data on local sectarian composition in Bahrain.[20] A total of 89 of Bahrain's administrative districts were sampled for the survey, with an average of 5.5 respondents interviewed from each. By sampling numerous subjects in each neighborhood, this approach offers a quite straightforward and reliable estimate of district-level sectarian composition.[21] The author created a variable capturing the sectarian composition of a respondent's district. This variable ranges theoretically from zero to one, with zero meaning that no members of a respondent's sectarian community reside in his or her district and one meaning that the district is populated entirely by members of the respondent's community, again as estimated by sampled respondents. The lower bound of zero is logically impossible, because each respondent represents an observed member of his or her community in a district, so the smallest observed value of segregation is one in six, or 0.167. That is, for instance, one of the six respondents interviewed in that district was Sunni, while the remaining

---

[19] Clive Holes, "Dialect and National Identity: The Cultural Politics of Self-Representation in Bahraini Musalsalāt," in Paul Dresch and James Piscatori, eds., *Monarchies and Nations: Globalization and Identity in the Arab States of the Gulf*, London: I. B. Tauris, 2005, p. 60.

[20] The survey was conducted face to face with 500 adult citizens at respondents' homes using traditional paper-and-pencil methods. It was commissioned by the Social and Economic Survey Research Institute at Qatar University and funded by a grant (NPRP 6-636-5-064) from the Qatar National Research Fund, a member of The Qatar Foundation. The statements herein are solely the responsibility of the author.

[21] For present purposes, this method is an upgrade of the sampling employed in a 2009 household survey also carried out by the author. That study surveyed a larger number of districts, but the average number of respondents in each surveyed district was much lower. Gengler, 2015, p. 103.

five were Shi'i, or vice versa. The group-specific distributions of the resulting measure of local segregation, expressed as a percentage of the total number of Sunni and Shi'i observations, respectively, is visualized in Figure 3.3.

As shown in Figure 3.3, the data confirm Holes's and others' qualitative impressions of extreme sectarian segregation. According to the survey, around one-third (31 percent) of Bahraini Sunnis and one-half (54 percent) of Shi'is live in districts that are populated almost exclusively by citizens of their own confessional community.[22] An estimated 60 percent of Shi'a and 45 percent of Sunnis live in neighborhoods where their community represents at least 80 percent of the local citizen population. By contrast, the data reveal that very few Bahrainis of either sect live in neighborhoods where they represent a minority: A startlingly low 14 percent of Sunnis and 12 percent of Shi'a live in areas where their community constitutes less than half of the local citizens. Segregation is also apparent at the governorate level. In the Capital (Manama) Governorate, Shi'is represent approximately 75 percent of the population and no less than 33 percent of any single district. Shi'a likewise represent an estimated 71 percent of the population of the Northern Governorate. In the Southern Governorate, by contrast, Sunnis constitute around 69 percent of the population, and no district within the governorate is estimated at less than 40 percent Sunni. Muharraq Governorate, at

Figure 3.3
Sectarian Segregation in Bahrain

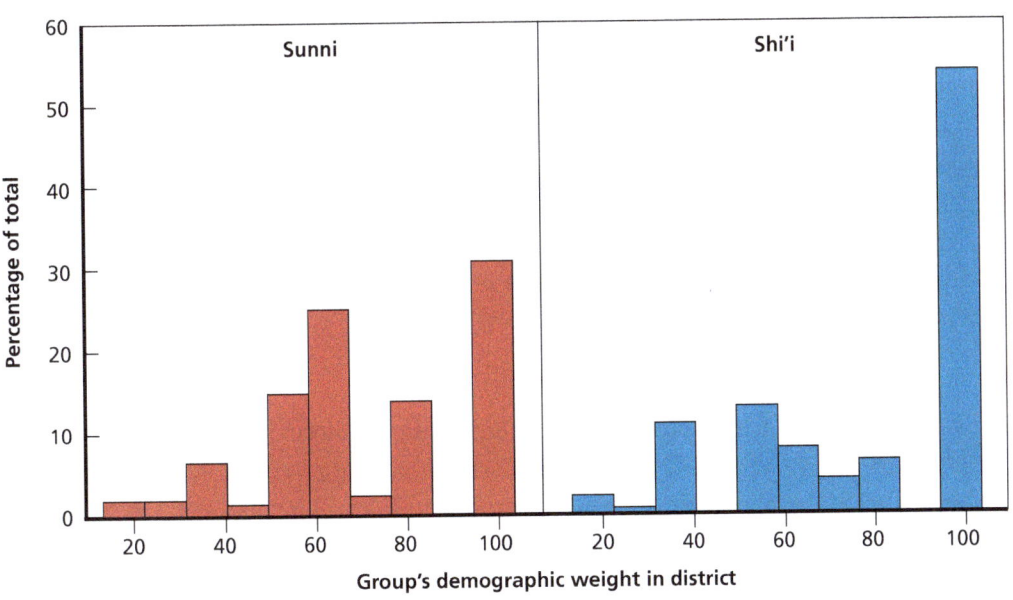

---

[22] Because noncitizens were not included in the survey, here, as elsewhere, population estimates and other survey results correspond only to Bahrain's citizen population.

around 65 percent Sunni versus 35 percent Shi'i, is the closest to approaching sectarian balance.

Finally, and notably, the 2017 survey corroborates previous survey-based estimates of Bahrain's overall sectarian balance. A 2009 household survey also conducted by the author found that Shi'a Bahrainis constitute an estimated 58.2 percent of the citizen population, or somewhere between 54.1 percent and 62.3 percent within the standard level of statistical confidence.[23] In the 2017 survey, Shi'a citizens are estimated to be 56.6 percent of the population, with a corresponding 95-percent confidence interval of 52.1 percent to 61.2 percent. It is worth noting that the decline in estimated means over this eight-year period from around 58.2 percent to 56.6 percent is within the margin of error and thus is not indicative of a change in the country's overall confessional demography. Instead, the data give further evidence that Shi'a Muslims most likely account for between 55 and 60 percent of Bahrain's citizenry, rather than the much higher ratios of 65 percent or even 75 percent often cited by journalists and scholars alike.

Beyond the physical separation of Bahraini Sunnis and Shi'is, survey results from 2009 also revealed stark socioeconomic disparities distinguishing the two groups. Compared with Sunni respondents, Shi'i citizens reported greater difficulty in accessing basic public services, including procuring official documents, enrolling children in school, accessing nearby medical care, receiving police assistance, and accessing the justice system. Shi'a also reported much lower levels of neighborhood safety, with three times as many Shi'is as Sunnis describing their area as "less safe" than it was three years ago.[24] Finally, findings from the 2009 survey gave substance to long-standing accusations of sectarian-based discrimination in hiring in the government sector. Conditional on employment and controlling for other determinants such as age, gender, and education level, a Bahraini Shi'i was an estimated 42 percent less likely to be employed in the public sector, compared with a 65-percent probability for a Sunni of identical employment-related attributes. This relative premium of 56 percent enjoyed by Sunnis was significant with a high degree of statistical confidence.[25] Furthermore, among Bahrainis who were working in the public sector, Shi'a were associated with an occupational level that was significantly lower compared with equally qualified Sunni employees.[26]

The Impacts of Sectarian Segregation on Economic Outcomes

The updated data from the 2017 survey both corroborate and extend these findings. Although it did not include questions about local government services, the survey did

---

[23] Gengler, 2015, p. 96.

[24] Gengler, 2015, pp. 106–107.

[25] Gengler, 2015, p. 108.

[26] Gengler, 2015, pp. 115–117.

capture household economic and demographic data that allow one to evaluate the factors that increase or decrease a Bahraini citizen's likelihood of receiving various types of state benefits. These new data show, first, that the overall percentage of citizens working in the public sector would appear to have declined somewhat since 2009. Whereas 51 percent of working Sunnis and 38 percent of working Shi'a reported working in the government or semi-government sectors in 2009, the corresponding percentages in 2017 were only 47 percent and 33 percent, respectively. This downward trend likely reflects Bahrain's lower capacity for government spending following the 2014 crash in oil prices, and it possibly also reflects the impacts of mass public-sector firings in the wake of the 2011 uprising.

More importantly, however, the new data on local sectarian demography contained in the 2017 survey permit direct quantitative assessment of not only overall Sunni-Shi'i disparities in economic outcomes in Bahrain but also how these outcomes are influenced by the geographical segregation (or integration) of the two communities at the local level. Leveraging local variation in sectarian demography, one can readily evaluate the effects of residential sectarian composition on the quality and magnitude of economic benefits that accrue to individuals. The analysis in this section considers three economic outcome variables in particular: the likelihood of employment in the public sector, total household income, and subjective overall economic satisfaction as assessed by survey respondents.[27] The author's hypothesis, again, is that higher levels of residential integration are associated with reduced between-group disparities in economic well-being because of the state's practical inability to target benefits disproportionately toward local Sunnis as presumed political supporters. It is this relative equality in distribution among neighbors that helps foster local resilience against sectarian conflict.

The results of this analysis in the case of public-sector employment are depicted in Figure 3.4, which shows the likelihood of being employed by the government (conditional on being employed and according to local sectarian composition).[28] These probabilities are estimated separately for Sunni and Shi'i respondents. The results are striking and intuitive. Among Bahraini Sunnis, the probability of working in the public sector increases directly as a function of the local concentration of Sunnis, whereas conversely among Shi'a citizens the chances of working for the government decline, if not as markedly, with the local population of Shi'a. As denoted by the 95-percent confidence intervals surrounding the individual point estimates, this between-group

---

[27] I model economic outcomes as a function of the variable capturing sectarian segregation, as well as a multiplicative interaction with a respondent's sectarian identity. This specification tests the effect of local segregation on outcomes separately for Sunnis and Shi'is, respectively. All models also include standard demographic control variables, namely gender, age, education level, and others as noted.

[28] Apart from the additional variables capturing geographic segregation and its interaction with sectarian group membership, this statistical model is identical to the two-step Heckman estimation described in Gengler, 2015, p. 108.

Figure 3.4
Public-Sector Employment and Local Sectarian Segregation

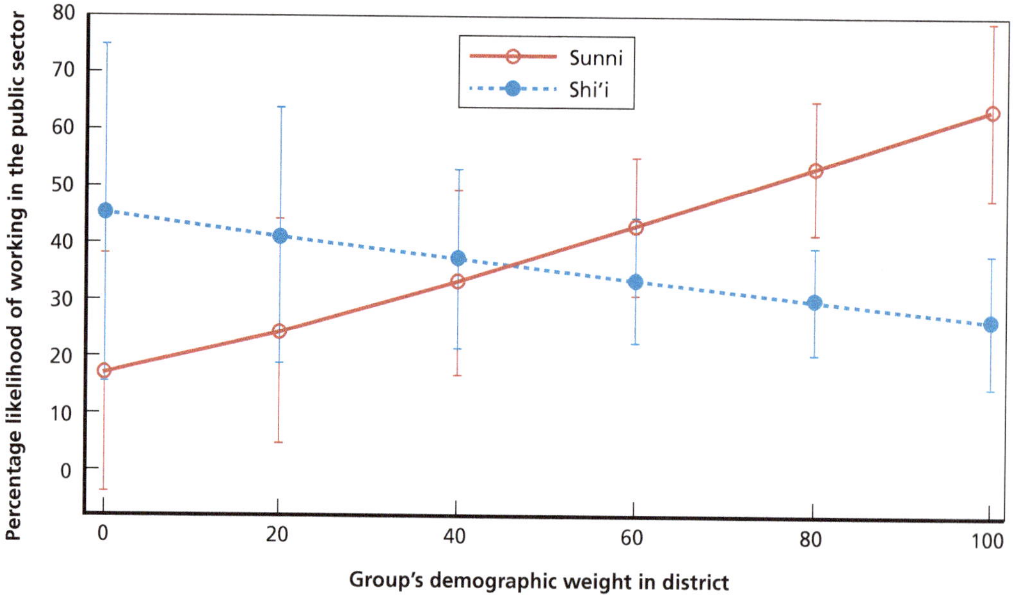

gap is statistically significant at levels at or above 75-percent local segregation. At the extreme, a Sunni in a Sunni-exclusive district has an estimated 64-percent likelihood of working for the government, compared with just 27 percent for a Shi'i of identical age, gender, and education level who resides in a Shi'i-exclusive district. By contrast, the results show that no such discrepancy exists among respondents in more-mixed districts, where there is no statistically significant difference in the probability of public-sector employment between Sunni and Shi'a. Yet, as shown earlier in Figure 3.3, about two-thirds of Shi'a and half of Sunnis live in neighborhoods where their communities represent at least 80 percent of the local citizen population. In reality, then, the disproportionate access to public-sector employment among Sunnis residing in Sunni-dominated areas and the disproportionate exclusion of Shi'a residing in Shi'a enclaves has an enormous practical impact on Bahraini households.

The real-world impact of this unequal distribution of welfare benefits is even more apparent when one considers the effect of local segregation on overall economic outcomes as measured by reported household income. This result is depicted in Figure 3.5. As in the case of state employment, the survey data show that the income of citizens is closely tied to the demographic character of their local communities, with Bahrainis residing in neighborhoods dominated by one sect witnessing exaggerated positive or negative outcomes. After accounting for the effects of a respondent's gender, age, education level, marital status, and employment status, the predicted household income of a Sunni living in a 100-percent Sunni neighborhood is more than 2,000

Figure 3.5
Household Income and Local Sectarian Segregation

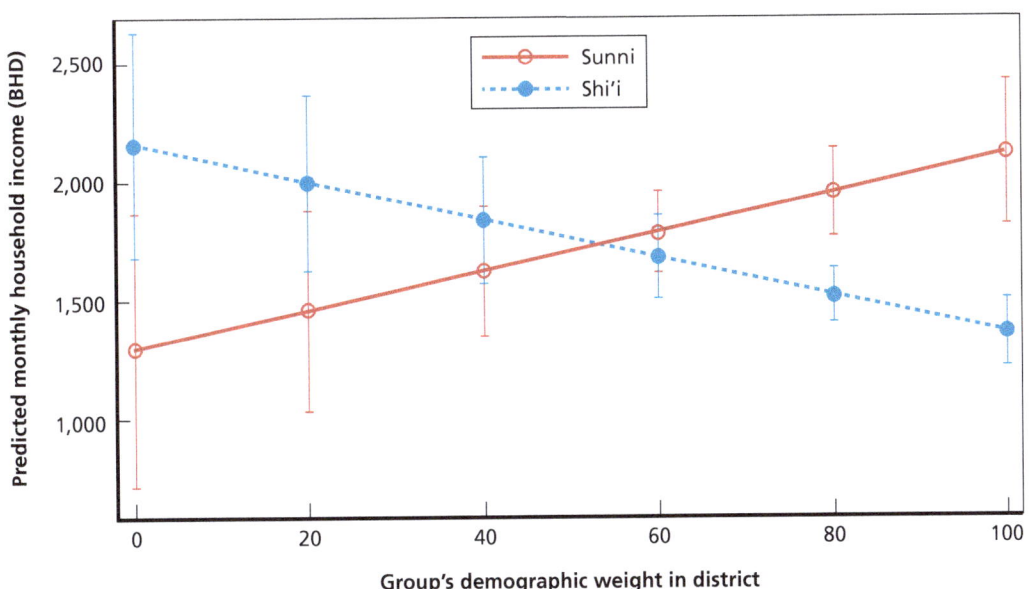

Bahraini dinars (BHD; about $5,300 U.S. dollars [USD]) per month. Conversely, the predicted monthly household income of a Shi'i in a 100-percent Shi'i district is about 1,300 BHD (about USD $3,500). Once again, group-based discrepancies disappear as neighborhoods become more mixed: At segregation levels of between 35 and 75 percent, there is no statistically significant income disparity based on sect.

Notably, however, at the low end of segregation, the gap in income between Sunni and Shi'a is once again statistically significant—but in the opposite substantive direction. Here, Shi'a residing in Sunni-dominated districts fair far better than Sunnis residing in Shi'a-exclusive areas, despite the small numbers of residents in these situations. (A similar pattern, although not statistically significant because of the small number of Bahrainis who reside in areas where they constitute a confessional minority, is visible in Figure 3.4.) This is strong evidence in favor of the notion that the state deploys resources at the group level, with geography used as an imperfect proxy, rather than at the individual level. Although some individuals might receive a smaller or greater allocation of state largesse than intended, the process is an efficient and cost-effective way of benefiting presumed supporters while not dissipating scarce resources on those thought to be opponents.

The final outcome variable examined is a subjective rather than objective measure of economic well-being. Survey respondents were asked to rate their overall satisfaction with their household's financial situation on an ascending scale from 0 to 10. Overall, Sunnis reported a higher mean satisfaction level of 6.0, compared with an average of

5.4 among Shi'a ($p = 0.001$). But, like in the cases of the two other economic outcomes, the aggregate discrepancy widens significantly when local sectarian composition is taken into account. Figure 3.6 illustrates this familiar pattern: Self-rated economic satisfaction among Sunnis increases with their local demographic concentration, while among Shi'a it declines with Shi'a dominance, in this case quite dramatically. Indeed, a Shi'i residing in a Shi'i-exclusive neighborhood is estimated to have a subjective satisfaction level of less than 5 on the 0–10 scale, compared with a predicted level of 7.5 for a Shi'i living in a Sunni-exclusive neighborhood. In relative terms, this corresponds to a 50-percent premium in expected economic satisfaction for Shi'a living in Sunni rather than Shi'a enclaves.

The data collected in the 2017 survey show a common substantive result: Whether measured in objective or subjective terms, the economic fortunes of Sunni and Shi'i citizens in Bahrain are tied inextricably to their places of residence. Students of Bahraini history might observe that such has always been the case, but the foregoing analysis paints a precise picture of the magnitude and consequences of the country's residential segregation. Members of the Sunni community benefit from geographical homogeneity as the state can be confident that resources deployed in these regions will be well spent. Concentrated Shi'a populations, on the other hand, also facilitate easy state decisionmaking surrounding distribution, but to their detriment. Ironically,

Figure 3.6
Self-Assessed Economic Satisfaction and Local Sectarian Segregation

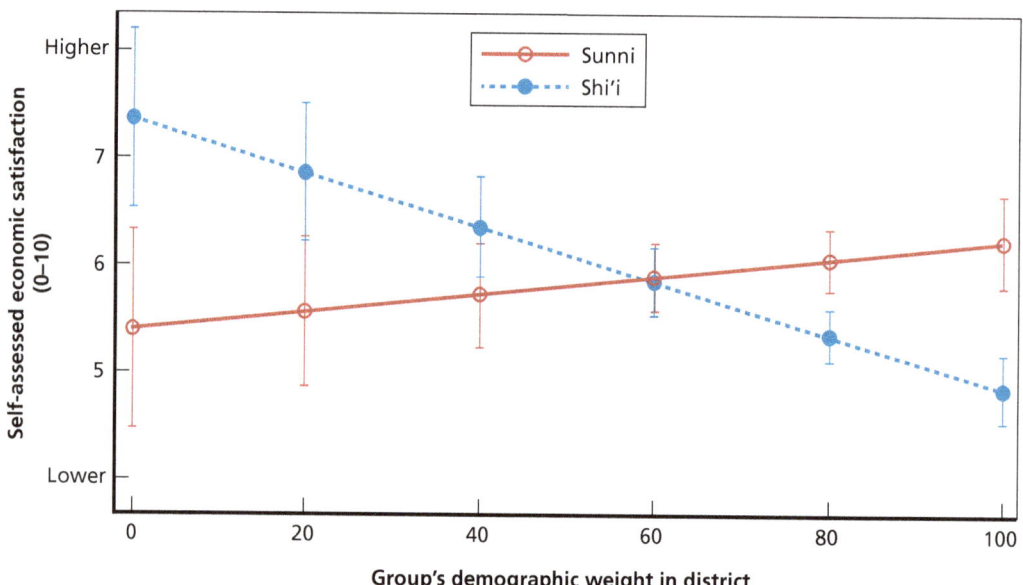

NOTE: *Higher* denotes that members of the group are more satisfied with their economic well-being (e.g., rated higher than 7). *Lower* indicates that members of the group are less satisfied with their economic well-being (e.g., rated lower than 5).

the same outward markers of Shi'a identity intended as symbols of defiance of the Al Khalifa monarchy—black flags flying above houses, anti-regime graffiti, and street banners invoking the martyrdom of the Imam Hussain—serve as veritable beacons, informing the state that such an area is safe to neglect, for its residents are already lost politically. What remains to be done in the final section is to trace how distributive discrimination according to local demographic makeup served as a driver of sectarian resilience, or alternatively of conflict, during the 2011 uprising. For this we return to the illustrative cases of 'Isa Town and Hamad Town.

Local Integration and Sectarian Relations During the 2011 Uprising

As demonstrated earlier, very few Bahrainis live in areas where they represent a sectarian minority, with one-third of Sunnis and more than half of Shi'a citizens residing in neighborhoods exclusive to their communities. The extended period of unrest that followed the February 2011 uprising offered few opportunities for direct confrontation between ordinary Sunni and Shi'a citizens, especially when combined with official and unofficial roadblocks barring travel between residential zones. Indeed, James Fearon and David Laitin cited the island's "metrocommunity scale" to explain why Bahrain has escaped full-scale civil war so far, which they say would be predicted by most empirical models of intrastate conflict.[29] For present purposes, the spatial separation of Bahrain's confessional groups is important because it means that latent sectarian conflict is only rarely observable, given substance primarily in anecdotes recounting destroyed friendships and marriages, vague communal "tensions," and so on.

In addition, rare observed instances of physical confrontation between Sunni and Shi'i citizens during the uprising owed as much to simple opportunity as to the character of local group relations. For instance, the two largest and most violent sectarian clashes, witnessed at the height of the breakdown in law and order in March 2011, occurred outside residential settings altogether. On March 13, violence erupted between opposition and state supporters at the main public University of Bahrain, an isolated campus located on the southern inhabited edge of the country. According to the authoritative account of the Bahrain Independent Commission of Inquiry (BICI), "knives, swords, wooden planks, rocks, and other objects were used"; fire was set to a building in which protesters allegedly had taken refuge from pro-government assailants; and "a number of private vehicles were destroyed."[30] Riot police were dispatched to disperse the opposition demonstrators, and classes were suspended for more than two months.

---

[29] James Fearon and David Laitin, "Bahrain," unpublished manuscript, June 15, 2005, p. 8.

[30] BICI, *Report of the Bahrain Independent Commission of Inquiry*, final revision, December 10, 2011, pp. 128–129.

The second notable case of direct Sunni-Shi'i confrontation took place two days earlier, when hard-line opposition groups organized a march to the Royal Palace compound in al-Riffa', the traditional seat of the ruling family and allied Sunni tribes. Around 3,000 protesters from neighboring Shi'i villages joined the march, while "large numbers of predominantly Sunni residents of Riffa . . . gathered behind [a] police barricade" erected to stop demonstrators from entering the district.[31] In total, an estimated 8,000 individuals armed with makeshift weapons squared off on opposite sides of the barrier, leading to hundreds of reported injuries. Among the participants was local member of Parliament and Salafi imam Sh. Jassim al-Sa'idi, who was caught on video exhorting the crowd and insulting Shi'a while brandishing a sword.[32] Sometime afterward, police used tear gas to clear the marchers and pro-government crowds "gathered in the vicinity of the Prime Minister's residence to voice their support of the [government]."[33]

Both incidents involve a confusing mixture of politics and social relations: Were combatants fighting against the rival sect or against the rival political faction whose membership overlapped with sectarian identity? Although both sides were able to motivate followers through the use of politicized stereotypes of the opposing group—with Sunnis referring to Shi'a protesters as *rawāfyd*, or "rejecters" of rightful religious and political authority, and Shi'a dismissing Sunni loyalists as *baltajiya*, or mercenary "thugs" of the regime—the competition on each side was tied essentially to the state. Shi'a protesters sought to exert pressure on the government by demonstrating popular opposition both domestically and to international audiences, while Sunnis aimed to confront Shi'a, not as followers of a deviant school of Islam but as challengers to a preferable, if not perfect, political system (at least for them).[34] In defending the state, Sunnis aimed to defend their interests enshrined in the status quo: superiority in social and political status over their Shi'a co-nationals and preferential access to state resources. Physical separation perpetuates group-based inequalities, fueling rivalry between regime beneficiaries and outcasts.

This conclusion helps explain the long-standing differences in sectarian relations between residents of the two mixed settlements examined at length earlier. Although

---

[31] BICI, 2011, pp. 121–122.

[32] e14feb, "زعيم البلطجية السعيدي يجيش المليشيات المسلحة" [*Baltajiya* Headman al-Sa'idi Enlists Armed Militias]," YouTube, March 13, 2011.

[33] BICI, 2011, p. 122.

[34] One arguable exception is the December 2011 melee in al-Muharraq involving a procession of Shi'a mourners celebrating the holy festival of 'Ashura' and Sunni residents led by a former state security officer. Organizers apparently ignored Ministry of Interior orders to reroute the procession to avoid Sunni areas, sparking a backlash among residents of one neighborhood. However, given the overtly political nature of 'Ashura' processions in Bahrain (Khuri, 1981; Laurence Louër, *Transnational Shia Politics*, New York: Columbia University Press, 2008; and Gengler, 2015), it is difficult to view the episode purely as a case of religious intolerance. See Mohammed al-A'ali, "Clashes Spark Plea for Calm," *Gulf Daily News*, December 4, 2011.

hostility might have existed during the uprising in both Hamad Town and 'Isa Town—"individual relationships ended in both places," said one Bahraini[35]—only the former saw sustained physical confrontations between ordinary members of the two communities. In fact, Hamad Town even witnessed the rise of self-styled Sunni "militias" that documented their anti-Shi'a exploits on YouTube.[36] By January 2012, conflict was regular enough to prompt a letter to King Hamad from the leader of the main opposition society al-Wifaq, Sh. 'Ali Salman, complaining that "the residents of Dar Kulaib [a Shi'i village adjoining south Hamad Town] . . . are being exposed to attacks by groups of armed civilians under the protection of the security forces, suggesting coordination and collusion between security forces and militias." He continues that the "nightly" attacks and the "failure of the security forces in their role of deterring the militias" left residents with no other choice but to appeal for protection from international organizations.[37]

Part of the explanation for the relatively greater resilience to sectarianism observed in 'Isa Town—both during the uprising and over the previous decades—lies in the physical layout of the city. Compared with Hamad Town, 'Isa Town features far greater demographic integration at the local level and more public spaces where residents have the opportunity to meet and interact. Of the five districts of 'Isa Town included in the 2017 survey, for instance, four reflect a sectarian mix of 60 percent Shi'i to 40 percent Sunni, while the most extreme neighborhood-level imbalance was 67 percent Sunni versus 33 percent Shi'i. By contrast, of the ten Hamad Town neighborhoods surveyed in 2017, three had populations that were 80 percent or more Sunni, two others were 83 percent and 75 percent Shi'i, respectively, and another was 67 percent Shi'i. Thus, half of the surveyed areas of Hamad Town skewed more or less heavily toward majority Sunni or Shi'i citizen residents. (Although not captured in the survey data, nonnational residents will further augment the local Sunni population in areas in which they are numerous.) Although it is a mixed urban space in the aggregate, Hamad Town is largely segregated along sectarian lines at the neighborhood level.

Yet, 'Isa Town too shows signs of communal separation. When the author visited in 2009, its main shopping mall, for example, possessed separate Sunni and Shi'i mosques located at opposite ends of the arcade. So, beyond physical integration per se, what else about 'Isa Town helps explain its residents' noted resistance to sectarian conflict during times of political crisis? A key difference would seem to lie in the larger public versus private nature of Hamad Town relative to 'Isa Town. Residents of the former, both citizen and noncitizen, literally owe their homes—and, for many work-

---

[35] Interview with the author via Skype, May 2017.

[36] One example is the Faruq Militia. See Alfarooqmli, "ميليشيا الفاروق تقتحم كرزكان و تمسح الإساءات" [The Faruq Militia Storms Karzakan and Wipes Out Graffiti]," YouTube, August 10, 2011.

[37] Justin Gengler, "How About That Police Reform," Religion and Politics in Bahrain, blog post, January 8, 2012.

ing in the security sector, their jobs—to the largesse of the state. Moreover, internal segregation of Hamad Town between Sunni and Shi'i enclaves enables the state to target resources to specific constituencies within the city. For Sunnis, vigorous defense against perceived attacks on the regime helps arrest the possibility of a personally injurious shift in the allocation of economic resources resulting from radical political change and sends a strong signal of support that could earn one additional benefits.

By contrast, public housing (*iskān*) constitutes a smaller percentage of residences in 'Isa Town, which is dominated by private homes inherited, purchased, or rented by middle-class Bahrainis. The notably even distribution of Sunni and Shi'i citizen residents at the neighborhood level also means that the state is unable to efficiently target resources to supporters without simultaneously benefiting nonsupporters. Unlike in Hamad Town and most other locations in Bahrain, in 'Isa Town, either everyone benefits or no one benefits from public goods, reducing sectarian inequalities and grievances based on perceptions of unfairness in government service provision. At the individual level, too, residence in 'Isa Town offers a degree of social anonymity not often found in Bahrain. Whether in an employment application or in everyday interaction with fellow citizens, the appellation 'Isa Town itself conveys no sectarian information, whereas a citizen living in Sanabis will immediately be assumed a Shi'i, one from Al-Riffa' a Sunni, and so on. Finally, with personal economic fortune being de-linked from sectarian identity in 'Isa Town, opinions of the government are less likely to reflect standard group-based patron-client dynamics. There, citizen views and behavior toward the state are shaped by individual circumstances, dampening incentives to attack or defend the regime as a member of either a privileged or disadvantaged group.

Further evidence in favor of this interpretation can be found by comparing sectarian relations during the uprising in another domain divided between public and private: the economy. Infamously, soon after the outbreak of protests in February 2011, the Bahraini government took wide-ranging punitive action against public-sector workers accused of taking part in or otherwise assisting protests, including those who joined labor strikes, doctors and nurses who treated demonstrators at Bahrain's public Salmaniya Hospital, and even individuals identified as government employees who expressed critical opinions on the internet. In total, several thousand workers were fired, prompting a labor rights complaint from the U.S.-based American Federation of Labor and Congress of Industrial Organizations on the grounds that the dismissals violated Bahrain's free trade agreement with the United States.[38] BICI received 1,624 statements from individuals fired or suspended in February and March 2011. In total, 84 percent of these cases took place in state or semi-state entities, compared

---

[38] American Federation of Labor and Congress of Industrial Organizations, "Public Submission to the Office of Trade and Labor Affairs Under Chapter 15 of the U.S.-Bahrain Free Trade Agreement: Concerning the Failure of the Government of Bahrain to Comply with Its Commitments Under Article 15.1 of the U.S.-Bahrain Free Trade Agreement," April 21, 2011.

with 259 complaints from employees in "other," private-sector companies.[39] The different criteria used to dismiss workers can explain this public-private disparity. BICI reports that, whereas termination in the private sector was justified by "absence from work" and "involvement in union activity related to the demonstration," in the public sector, another reason was used to fire workers: "public display of opinions incompatible with the internal regulations of the ministries involved."[40] In agencies and corporations linked to the state, workers were expected to be supportive or at least keep quiet as an effective condition of their employment. In other words, whatever the government's political failings, its employees should be grateful to the hand that feeds.

Accounts of Bahrainis working during the crisis tell a similar story. According to one interviewee, Shi'a medical workers at Salmaniya Hospital who either were dismissed or felt unwelcome after the uprising generally found ready employment in private facilities.[41] Another contact employed in the financial sector described isolated tensions that were defused by management efforts to limit rather than exacerbate conflict between Sunni and Shi'i workers. For example, nothing came of an internal memo that purported to list names of bank employees involved in demonstrations. Similarly, workers whose absence coincided with a two-week strike called by opposition groups were excused for safety reasons, on the grounds that their commutes to the office might have put them in danger.[42] Thus, absenteeism, the basis for dismissal in one organization, is tolerated and ostensibly encouraged by another out of concern for workers' welfare. The divergence here again lies in the nature of the relationship between the individual and the corporation: Whereas a bank needs its specialized employees in order to carry on operating efficiently, a ministry views its workers as needing it more than it needs them. When the end itself is welfare distribution through employment, the individual deemed unworthy of the state's benefaction ought naturally to be replaced with another who is worthy. From the perspective of Bahrain's ruling elite, anything else is a misallocation of scarce resources.

Conclusion

This chapter has explained variation in sectarian resilience observed in Bahrain during and after the 2011 popular uprising. The results of a qualitative comparison between the country's two largest mixed settlements, 'Isa Town and Hamad Town, and empirical insights from a nationally representative survey of Bahraini citizens identify resi-

---

[39] The "other" category also likely includes some smaller, quasigovernmental organizations, making this a conservative estimate of the public-private ratio in employee dismissals.

[40] BICI, 2011, p. 331.

[41] Interview with the author via Skype, May 2017.

[42] Interview with the author via Skype, May 2017.

dential integration as the key determinant of such resilience. The chapter argues that the positive effects of communal mixing flow via two separate pathways. The first and most direct mechanism relates to the physical properties of genuinely mixed urban settings, which encourage quotidian interaction between residents and contact between members of different social and political groups. This observation is in line with substantial literature in psychology and other fields suggesting that positive intergroup contact can mitigate feelings of enmity toward and reduce conflict with members of social out-groups.

A second, indirect mechanism elaborated here is the effect of communal mixing on local distributive parity in the context of a rentier economy such as that of Bahrain. Analysis of individual-level survey data collected in 2016 and 2017 offered compelling support for the proposition that economic outcomes in Bahrain depend critically on the demographic character of a citizen's area of residence, with residents of Sunni-dominated districts—of both sects—faring far better than individuals living in Shi'i-populated districts. Such a finding, which is consistent across both objective and subjective measures of economic well-being, indicates a clear geographic-based strategy of resource distribution. Lacking the capacity to allocate benefits on an individual basis, Bahrain and other Arab Gulf States to varying degrees seek to segment political constituencies geographically, targeting known in-group strongholds and neglecting out-group enclaves, even if it means that some individuals will receive more or less than their intended share of benefits. This physical segregation perpetuates group-based economic and political inequalities, fueling rivalry and resentment between members of overserved and underserved communities.

Mixed residential districts counteract this pressure toward conflict by helping to equalize economic distribution at the local level. Bahraini neighborhoods in which Sunnis and Shi'a live side-by-side preclude straightforward targeting of resources toward members of a single sectarian-cum-political constituency. In mixed areas, such public goods as infrastructure, educational and medical facilities, and security will tend to benefit residents either together or not at all. Moreover, residence in a mixed community such as 'Isa Town reveals nothing about likely sectarian affiliation or political orientation, whereas residence in a sectarian enclave can be used to infer such information to a citizen's benefit or detriment. In short, integrated geographic settings offer the state no sectarian proxy to inform allocation decisions, forcing upon it a difficult choice: either neglect an entire area and risk alienating many supporters or deploy resources even if it means that some opponents will likely benefit.

It should be apparent that such a dynamic provides strong incentives for members of both communities to relocate to areas where they can expect to capture a greater share of state resources. For Shi'i citizens, this likely means leaving an underserved village or suburban enclave for a more mixed urban setting, because relocation to a Sunni-dominated area entails considerable formal and informal barriers. For Bahrain's Sunnis, on the other hand, the tremendous economic premium enjoyed by those residing in Sunni-exclusive settings means that there is a universal incentive to be located in a sectarian stronghold. To be sure, Sunni migration to Sunni-dominated parts of Al-Muharraq, and especially to Al-Riffaʻ, has been reported by Bahrainis in the years since the uprising. Absent a perceptible shift in the basis on which economic resources are distributed, self-segregation of Bahrain's confessional communities is likely only to accelerate under intensified competition over dwindling state oil revenues.

Unfortunately for Bahrain, these incentives for relocation fuel a vicious political-economic cycle that works to undermine resilience to sectarianism. As geographic regions become more homogeneous, they permit more-efficient government targeting or withholding of resources, exaggerating local positive or negative economic outcomes. More-efficient geographic discrimination in allocation further widens the gap between served and underserved regions, creating ever-greater perceptions of unfairness and incentives for resettlement. Yet, as observed in earlier periods of internal migration in Bahrain, certain populations are less likely than others to take advantage of the economic opportunities afforded by relocation, especially those with a strong attachment to the land itself or a normative preference for being surrounded by members of their own community. Bahrain's poorest citizens might simply lack the means to move elsewhere. The result is that individuals with a greater cultural openness and pragmatism will be more likely to seek to exit sectarian enclaves, leaving behind those who are more ideologically driven to self-segregation. In this way, regional confessional homogeneity comes to overlap with a certain political orientation, a self-fulfilling prophesy that reinforces the logic behind geographic-based deployment of state benefits in the minds of decisionmakers.

CHAPTER FOUR

Resilience and Sectarianism in Syria: The Role of Foreign Support

Kathleen Reedy
Senior Social Scientist
Johns Hopkins University Applied Physics Lab

The drawn-out civil war in Syria, with its massive numbers of casualties, refugees, and internally displaced persons (IDPs), has sparked an intense debate about whether the nature of the conflict is inherently sectarian.[1] The alignment of various minority groups with the government, the role of international actors with political agendas couched in sectarian politics (i.e., Iran and the Gulf countries), and the purported violence directed specifically against confessional targets—by both certain opposition groups and the regime—all lend a cast of sectarianism to the conflict. Although sectarian-based violence is difficult to verify because of limitations on access to the country,[2] there are enough incidences to suggest that certain populations have been targets of killings and sexual violence based on their religious leanings. This is particularly true of groups like the Islamic State (IS) and, to a lesser extent, Hay'at Tahrir al-Sham (HTS, formerly the al-Qaeda–affiliated Nusra Front), which have claimed responsibility for such attacks.[3] Although the regime has largely denied such attempts, the various Syrian and Iranian militias have been accused of similar abuses.[4]

However, despite these instances of violence, sectarian divisiveness does not seem to have taken hold at a popular level to as great a degree as one might expect based on news reports; but sectarian divisiveness has taken hold more than might have been expected in pre-war Syria. In a 2015 study of 2,500 individuals, 26 percent of respondents said they considered themselves "not sectarian at all," 36 percent said "slightly sectarian," and 24 percent said "somewhat sectarian," while 80 percent of respondents disagreed with the concept that sectarianism in Syria is an "old problem and cannot

---

[1] For an overview of this debate, see Brandon Friedman and Uzi Rabi, "Sectarianism and War in Iraq and Syria," Foreign Policy Research Institute, January 5, 2017.

[2] Phillips, 2015, p. 360.

[3] Lizzie Dearden, "Syria: Bombing Hits Bus Convoy," *The Independent*, April 15, 2017; and Mahmoud Eskaf, "Syria: Tahrir al-Sham Adopts Damascus Twin Bombings," *Middle East Observer*, March 13, 2017.

[4] The Carter Center, "Syria: Pro-Government Paramilitary Forces," November 5, 2013.

be solved." The study acknowledged that views of sectarianism likely are somewhat underrepresented, given that openly admitting to such views historically has been taboo, but this suggests that high levels of sectarianism are not yet prevalent in Syria. More than 65 percent of the respondents suggested that a secular system based on citizenship would be the best option for a postwar government, while only 13.5 percent said Islamic rule would be the best option and 7.4 percent suggested a quota system based on sect.[5]

There has been much work exploring the history of internal violence tied to religion in Syria, including violence between Druze and Christians;[6] Druze and Sunnis;[7] 'Alawis and Sunnis;[8] and, specifically, the sectarian and religious overtones in the Muslim Brotherhood uprising in the 1970s and 1980s.[9] This chapter therefore focuses on the complexities surrounding sectarian violence and policies in Syria between 2011 and 2017 through a comparison of the evolving situations in Idlib and Dara'a in order to identify potential points that have made these areas more or less resilient (or prone) to sectarian-style divides. The lack of reliable information on events and populations within Syria makes such an approach challenging, but this chapter will focus on identifying several of the key variables that make regions of Syria appear to be more or less vulnerable to sectarian ideology. Although the activities of IS in the east of the country might seem an obvious place to start, the heavy influence of foreign fighters who have flocked to this group makes it unclear how much of the sectarian violence undertaken by IS is Syrian in nature, rather than merely taking place in Syria.[10] By contrast, although the violent Sunni Salafist groups in Idlib (primarily HTS and Ahrar al-Sham) and the militias in Dara'a (primarily the Southern Front) do receive fighters and/or funding from foreign sources,[11] a much higher percentage of their fighters are Syrian, so their actions might better reflect possible attitudes and opinions of the Syrian population in that region.

---

[5] The Day After, *Sectarianism in Syria: Survey Study*, Istanbul, 2016, pp. 19–83.

[6] Ussama Makdisi, "After 1860: Debating Religion, Reform, and Nationalism in the Ottoman Empire," *International Journal of Middle East Studies*, Vol. 34, No. 4, 2002.

[7] *New York Times* Archives, "The Syrian Outbreak: Details of the Damascus Massacre, Foreign Intervention in Syria," digitized version of an article from August 13, 1860.

[8] Ayse Tekdal Fildis, "Roots of Alawite-Sunni Rivalry in Syria," *Middle East Policy*, Vol. 19, No. 2, 2012.

[9] Hanna Batatu, *Syria's Peasantry, the Descendants of Its Less Rural Notables, and Their Politics*, Princeton, N.J.: Princeton University Press, 1999, pp. 260–278; Joshua Landis, "Islamic Education in Syria: Undoing Secularism," Minority Rights Group International World Directory of Minorities, 2011a; and Joshua Landis, "Syria: Background," Minority Rights Group International World Directory of Minorities, 2011b.

[10] Karen Parrish, "Official: Stopping Foreign Fighter Flow to ISIS Requires Collaboration," U.S. Department of Defense, April 5, 2017.

[11] Foreign fighters in these groups include Uyghur and Uzbek fighters. Jacob Zenn, "Al-Qaeda-Aligned Central Asian Militants in Syria Separate from Islamic State–Aligned IMU in Afghanistan," The Jamestown Foundation, May 29, 2015.

Idlib and Dara'a make a useful point of comparison because they are similar in many ways. Both are somewhat rural and, before the war, were primarily Sunni with few minorities. Both are relatively close geographically to Damascus as compared with far-flung Raqqa or Deir ez-Zour (see Figure 4.1). Both governorates also were early sources of protest against the regime and both experienced violent crackdowns in response. At the time of this writing, both were controlled by rebel groups.[12] And, most importantly for this research, each abuts one of Syria's neighbors to the north and the south, Turkey and Jordan, which allows us to explore the role of foreign support in

Figure 4.1
Political Map of Syria

SOURCE: Perry-Castañeda Library Map Collection, "Syria Maps: Syria (Political) 1976," University of Texas, 2017.

---

[12] This is no longer the case: Government forces retook Dara'a in July 2018. Kareem Shaheen, "UN Calls for Access to Syrians Stranded in Desert After Deraa's Fall," *The Guardian*, July 13, 2018.

fanning or mitigating sectarian ideology. Although other comparisons might be useful in addition to this one (e.g., between rebel- and regime-held areas, or areas with diverse and homogenous populations), this case study attempts to control for both of those variables in order to examine the roles of civil society and foreign actors in suppressing or abetting sectarianism.

Although these two governorates share many of the same characteristics, they differ in their levels of sectarianism, at least as measured by the territorial control of sectarian-oriented rebel groups and acts of sectarian violence. On the metric of territorial control, HTS is currently the strongest armed actor in Idlib and, as an Al-Qaeda affiliate, exhibits a Sunni sectarian hue. Ahrar al-Sham is the second-strongest actor in the governorate, and although analysts intensely debate its true colors, it is Islamist and, its critics allege, Sunni sectarian. In contrast, the Southern Front dominates in rebel-controlled Dara'a and is generally considered by observers to be more moderate and secular in its orientation. The one exception is the Khalid Bin Waleed Army, a Syrian group aligned with IS, which operated in Dara'a along the border of the Golan Heights before being expelled by Syrian regime forces in summer 2018. During regime operations against the group, the Khalid Bin Waleed Army carried out a spate of reprisal attacks in Dara'a and As-Suwaydah (the governorate bordering Dara'a to the east).

Still, Dara'a has seen fewer instances of sectarian attacks and a slightly lower percentage of such acts originating there. Idlib is a much more violent area, and, in absolute terms, it registers many more attacks than Dara'a, including sectarian attacks. However, when sectarian violence is isolated as a percentage of attacks, Idlib is only slightly more prone to this type of violence.

The aim of this chapter, then, is to identify the variables that might make Idlib more welcoming to sectarian actors and Dara'a less so as a means of understanding elements that could make populations more or less resilient in the face of sectarian violence. The following sections will address some of the variables across the two locations, including attitudes toward the conflict and religious diversity, demographics, levels of political and economic engagement, local governance efforts, and likely the most influential variable—key foreign actors engaged in those governorates.[13] The chapter ends with a discussion of the variables most likely to contribute to differences in the types of violence in the two regions and the implications those variables have on resilience to sectarianism.

---

[13] For readers familiar with comparative methods, this approach is one way to execute Mills's method. Specifically, the two cases vary on the dependent variable in that one case (Dara'a) exhibits greater resilience to sectarianism than the other (Idlib). Because the outcome variable is different, the independent variables are compared to see which vary and thus might account for the different outcome. This is the method of difference.

Experiences in the Civil War

Daraʿa was the spark of the Syrian uprising. In February 2011, 15 school children were arrested in the capital of the governorate for spraying anti-regime graffiti. News that the children were being beaten and abused in prison sparked rallies and protests in Damascus and Daraʿa, which led to further detentions and, in March 2011, to four deaths as security forces fired into a crowd at a rally. Similar protests began across the country, and increasingly violent government crackdowns sparked the civil war that continues to rage.[14] In 2013, the Syrian government lost much of Daraʿa governorate to U.S.-backed armed groups, including the Free Syrian Army,[15] and the Nusra Front, al-Qaeda's Syrian affiliate.[16] The Southern Front was formally organized in February 2014 as an umbrella organization of nearly 50 smaller groups of mixed orientations,[17] including those with secular and moderate outlooks,[18] despite coordinating with the Nusra Front as late as 2015. The Southern Front's popularity and strength slowly edged out the Nusra Front's place in the southwestern governorate, although IS-affiliated groups remained active in the region through 2018. The Southern Front took on the IS groups directly, leading to several suicide attacks in retribution, although they targeted the combatants rather than civilians, suggesting that it was a military tactic rather than a sectarian-fueled approach.[19] Although the area has remained relatively quiet since 2015 as the regime focused on other fronts, violence began to increase again in 2017 as the government attempted to gain control of Daraʿa city, which previously had been controlled by the rebels, and open a corridor to Jordan.[20]

Over the past several years, one of the consistent elements of Daraʿa governorate is that it has not been subject to acts of sectarian violence to the degree that other governorates have. According to the Global Terrorism Database, of the 39 terrorist attacks in Daraʿa between 2011 and 2016, only five were likely sectarian in nature (two against likely Shiʿa targets, two against mosques that were likely Sunni, and one in a Christian-centric area). Another attack that targeted civilians and was claimed by IS

---

[14] Joe Sterling, "Daraa: The Spark That Lit the Syrian Flame," CNN, March 1, 2012.

[15] Michael B. Kelley, "Damascus Is 'Totally Exposed from the South' After Rebels Take Key Towns," Business Insider, March 29, 2013.

[16] "Syria: Amid Rebel Buildup, Fear of New War," UPI, March 28, 2013.

[17] It is believed that Western states and Jordan, who were providing assistance to Syrian rebel groups at an Amman-based military operations command center, pushed for the establishment of the Southern Front. Their motivation was to increase intrarebel coordination and identify groups that were moderate enough in their orientation to merit foreign assistance.

[18] Aron Lund, "Does the 'Southern Front' Exist?" Carnegie Middle East Center, March 21, 2014.

[19] Waleed Khaled a-Noufal and Dan Wilkofsky, "On the Defensive in Daraa, Reported Islamic State Affiliates Deploy 'Unheard of' Suicide Bombings," Syria Direct, April 5, 2016.

[20] Suleiman al-Khalidi, "Syrian Army and Allies Step Up Bombing of Rebels in Deraa City," Reuters, June 11, 2017a.

affiliates might have been sectarian in nature (there is not enough information to be certain). The other attacks targeted primarily military and government personnel and infrastructure.[21] These data suggest that just under 13 percent of the terrorist attacks in Dara'a during that time were sectarian in nature.[22]

Idlib, by contrast, has endured a much higher number of terrorist attacks writ large (155 in total between 2011 and 2016), and a somewhat higher rate of these were likely sectarian in nature (27, accounting for about 17.5 percent of all terrorist attacks in the governorate). Of these, 18 were against Shi'a targets, four were against Christians, three were against Sunni religious targets, and one each was against the Druze and the 'Alawi. A further 12 attacks did not have enough data to indicate likely targets, so they might have been sectarian. In-fighting between opposition groups in 2016 could reflect intra-Sunni sectarian tensions as well.[23] This higher rate of sectarian attacks, particularly against non-Sunni targets, suggests that Idlib has been a stronghold for more-extreme Islamist groups, particularly since Idlib city fell to rebels in 2015, because all but four of those sectarian attacks occurred in 2015 and 2016.[24]

Like Dara'a, Idlib was an early location for anti-regime demonstrators, and protests were put down with violence, first by police and then through the use of the Popular Committees—regime militias who were, by and large, made up of Sunni members in Idlib and led and funded by several prominent local Sunnis, despite their characterization across the country as being largely made up of Shi'a individuals. Although the regime retained control of the city of Idlib, there was increasing unrest in the surrounding governorate, especially when rebels secured control of one of the border crossings with Turkey (i.e., Bab al-Hawa), allowing them to access weapons and funding from the Gulf countries (primarily Saudi Arabia and Qatar), as well as more-extreme Islamist organizations, such as the Nusra Front and Ahrar al-Sham.

Once the rebels took the city, there was a purge of President Bashar al-Assad supporters, which might have involved targeting minorities but was political rather than sectarian in its focus.[25] However, several of the 27 incidents of sectarian violence are worth highlighting, including an attack on a Shi'a site of worship,[26] the killing of 20 Druze villagers in the village of Qalb Lawzeh, the forced conversion of hundreds of

---

[21] Exact data on most of the targets are unavailable, meaning that the author of this chapter made assumptions based on coordinates and other supplemental information.

[22] National Consortium for the Study of Terrorism and Responses to Terrorism (START), "Global Terrorism Database," data file, 2017.

[23] START, 2017.

[24] Suleiman al-Khalidi, "Rebels Capture Last Syrian Town in Idlib Province," Reuters, May 28, 2015; and START, 2017.

[25] Aron Lund, "Assad's Broken Base: The Case of Idlib," The Century Foundation, July 14, 2016.

[26] Human Rights Watch, "Syria: Attacks on Religious Sites Raise Tensions," webpage, January 23, 2013.

Druze to hard-line Sunni Islam,[27] and the siege of two small Shi'a villages.[28] In April 2017, a convoy with Shi'a civilians from the besieged villages who were being swapped with a similar set of pro-rebel villagers from the outskirts of Damascus was hit by a suicide attack (which no group openly claimed).[29] The government, with the aid of Russia, tried to make inroads into Idlib, but it remained solidly in the control of armed groups, although there was in-fighting between the Nusra Front (now reorganized into the coalition group HTS) and Ahrar al-Sham that saw the latter pushed out of Idlib city and much of the governorate in July 2017.[30] Although there has been a greater presence of Islamist groups that espouse sectarian violence in Idlib than in Dara'a and a few more attacks or increased pressure on the local population, overall, the incidences of sectarian-based violence in Idlib are still relatively low when compared with territory held by the IS or in parts of Iraq.

In addition to attack data, the informal justice structures established by armed groups in Idlib are evidence of these groups' sectarian orientations. Amnesty International documented that armed groups in Idlib, including the Nusra Front and Ahrar al-Sham, targeted Christians for abductions and property confiscation.[31] The United Nations Commission of Inquiry documented detainees separated by faith at a Nusra Front–run prison, with Shi'a prisoners subjected to torture and other practices in front of their relatives.[32]

Variables in Sectarianism

Although there has not been a vast number of violent incidents motivated by sectarian tensions in either Idlib or Dara'a,[33] the question remains why and how more-extreme Islamist movements that might have promoted such divides are flourishing in Idlib

---

[27] Patrick Cockburn, "Syrian Civil War: Jabhat al-Nusra's Massacre of Druze Villagers Shows They're Just as Nasty as Isis," *The Independent*, June 14, 2015.

[28] Robert Fisk, "Syria Civil War: The Untold Story of the Siege of Two Small Shia Villages—And How the World Turned a Blind Eye," *The Independent*, February 22, 2016.

[29] John Davison, "Death Toll from Aleppo Bus Convoy Bomb Attack at Least 126: Observatory," Reuters, April 15, 2017.

[30] Hilary Clarke, "Blast Kills Fighters After Jihadists Take Control of Syria's Idlib," CNN, July 24, 2017.

[31] Amnesty International, *"Torture Was My Punishment": Abductions, Torture, and Summary Killings Under Armed Group Rule in Aleppo and Idlib, Syria*, London, July 2016.

[32] United Nations Human Rights Council, "'I lost My Dignity': Sexual and Gender-Based Violence in the Syrian Arab Republic," Independent International Commission of Inquiry on the Syrian Arab Republic, A/HRC/37/CRP.3, March 2018.

[33] In comparison with the 13 percent of terrorist attacks in Dara'a and 17.5 percent in Idlib being sectarian in nature, the percentage of attacks that were likely sectarian was more than 38 percent in Latakia governorate (presumably because of the far higher numbers of minority citizens present), more than 40 percent in Raqqa

more than in Dara'a. Understanding where these differences lie could better enable policymakers to ensure that sectarianism does not gain a greater foothold in Syria and could provide models for how to consider engagement during and after conflict in societies susceptible to identity-based violence.

To that end, this section considers several different variables that might impact the resilience of the populations in these two governorates. This list is not exhaustive but instead includes the variables for which there is some degree of reliable data for comparison and that are similar to factors identified in other studies on sectarianism. When comparing variables on attitudes toward sectarianism, demographics, levels of political and economic enfranchisement, and local governance efforts, Idlib and Dara'a overall look fairly similar. There are some differences, particularly with the advent of the war and the vast numbers of IDPs who wound up in Idlib. The most striking difference between the two is the location and, more specifically, the foreign donor support that is able to cross the border into these governorates. The proximity of Dara'a to Jordan and the southern opposition groups' access to support from the U.S.-led coalition have created a very different environment than Idlib's border with Turkey, where weapons and money have been flowing much more freely from pro-Islamist funders in the Gulf and elsewhere. The practicalities of controlling territory around these regions and having access to supply lines seem to play the most significant role of all the variables in shaping whether these governorates are more or less susceptible to sectarianism.

Attitudes Toward the Conflict and Religious Diversity

One measure of how resilient a local population is to sectarian ideology is popular attitudes toward religious diversity and, specifically, the role of religion in the current conflict. The available information allows for two approaches to assess these attitudes: through the use of a survey conducted across Syria about sectarianism in 2015 and through more-indirect measures, such as how extreme Islamist groups have directed attacks and used messaging. The hypothesis here is that sectarian attacks and messaging, such as proudly claiming to have carried out a sectarian attack, would be more pronounced in areas that are more tolerant of sectarian ideologies. Relatively lower numbers of these phenomena might indicate less popular support for these ideas.

The survey on sectarianism had 178 respondents from Dara'a and 536 from Idlib, with the overwhelming majority being Sunni Muslim (92 percent and 98 percent of the samples, respectively).[34] In Dara'a, 83 percent of the respondents identified themselves as of moderate ideology (on a five-point scale between extreme political Islam

---

(although those were often Sunni-on-Sunni attacks), and nearly 48 percent in Homs (where there also are higher numbers of minorities) (START, 2017).

[34] The researchers involved in the survey explicitly noted their limitations in conducting this work in a war zone and in a country that historically has not allowed much popular polling, but they offer the survey up as the only real data of its kind.

and extreme secularism) and 13 percent identified as Islamist. In Idlib, there was a much wider scale, with 9 percent identifying with extreme political Islam, 18 percent as Islamist, 34 percent as moderate, 25 percent as secular, and 14 percent as extreme secularist (see Figure 4.2).[35] Any findings from this survey should be taken with caution, however, particularly given that there is a high number of IDPs currently living in Idlib (see the next section, on demographics), which might have uncertain impacts on the results.

For many measures, respondents in Dara'a and Idlib provided very similar responses, particularly in contrast to the broader population of polled Syrians. More than 80 percent of the respondents in both areas suggested that sectarianism is a political rather than a historical problem, compared with 62 percent of the Syrian population as a whole (see Figure 4.3).[36] In both areas, just more than 50 percent of those polled thought that the "tyranny exercised by the regime and the demonstrators' pursuance of establishing a civilian democratic state" was the primary driver behind the 2011 demonstrations, followed by 37–38 percent who said the reason was "exposure to sectarian discrimination and Alawites' control over the state."[37] Both governorates had more than 80 percent of respondents say that the sect of any future president was

Figure 4.2
Reported Ideology of Respondents According to a Survey on Sectarianism, 2016

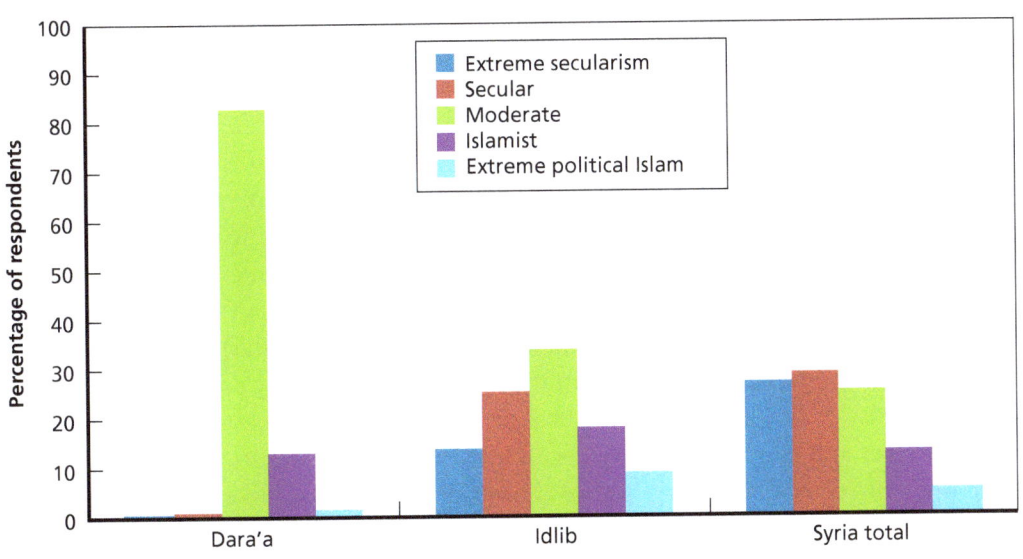

SOURCE: Based on data from The Day After, 2016.

---

[35] The Day After, 2016, pp. 11–12.

[36] The Day After, 2016, p. 20.

[37] The Day After, 2016, p. 30.

Figure 4.3
Perceived Origins of Sectarianism in Syria

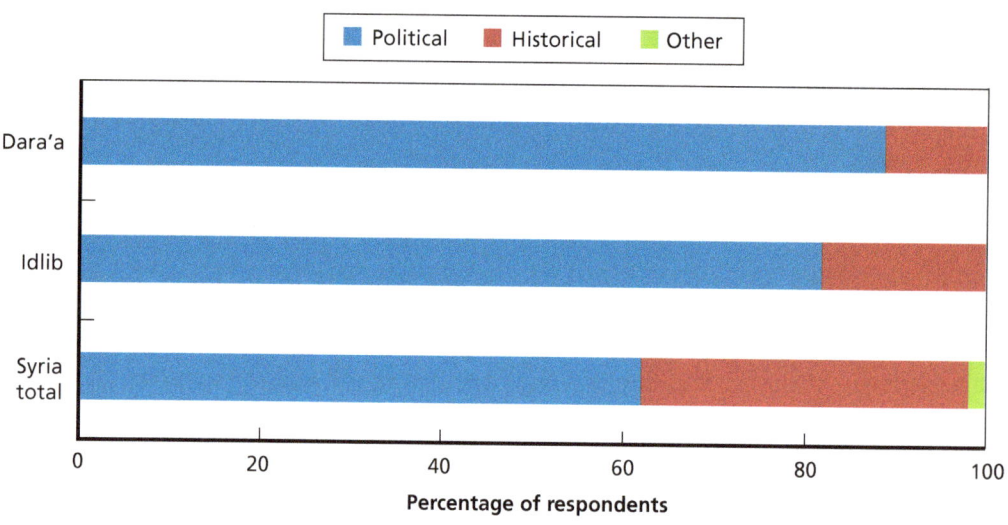

SOURCE: Based on data from The Day After, 2016.

either important or very important.[38] That the responses from the two governorates largely overlap in these areas suggests that there is not much difference in attitudes on some of these key topics around sectarianism and that the popular opinion is that sectarianism is more a political than an inherent and intractable cultural issue, at least as late as 2015.

As noted earlier, attack and messaging data can serve as indirect measures for local attitudes toward sectarian violence because a group might be less likely to act and to advertise those actions in areas that are less supportive of sectarianism. These measures could also reflect territorial control of the area, with greater control leading to greater confidence in making claims regardless of the population's attitudes, but because this chapter focuses on the variables that allow sectarian groups to gain territorial control, the author will focus primarily on the attitudes aspect. In Dara'a, the commitment of rebel groups to remain moderate and to actively combat (at least after 2015) Islamist extremists suggests a broader popular preference to not reify confessional divides and to maintain Syria as a more diverse community (and/or possibly to keep deep extremists like the IS out of the region). Of the five likely sectarian attacks in Dara'a, none was openly claimed by any group, suggesting that messaging that glorifies sectarian violence is not effective or welcome there. Eight of the 28 sectarian attacks in Idlib were claimed, while seven of 16 were claimed in Latakia, four of 17 in Raqqa, and 20 of 87 in Homs (see Figure 4.4). These numbers show that, in all of these governorates, sectarian attacks constituted a minority of overall attacks by opposition

---

[38] The Day After, 2016, pp. 36–38.

Figure 4.4
Attacks in Syria, 2011–2016

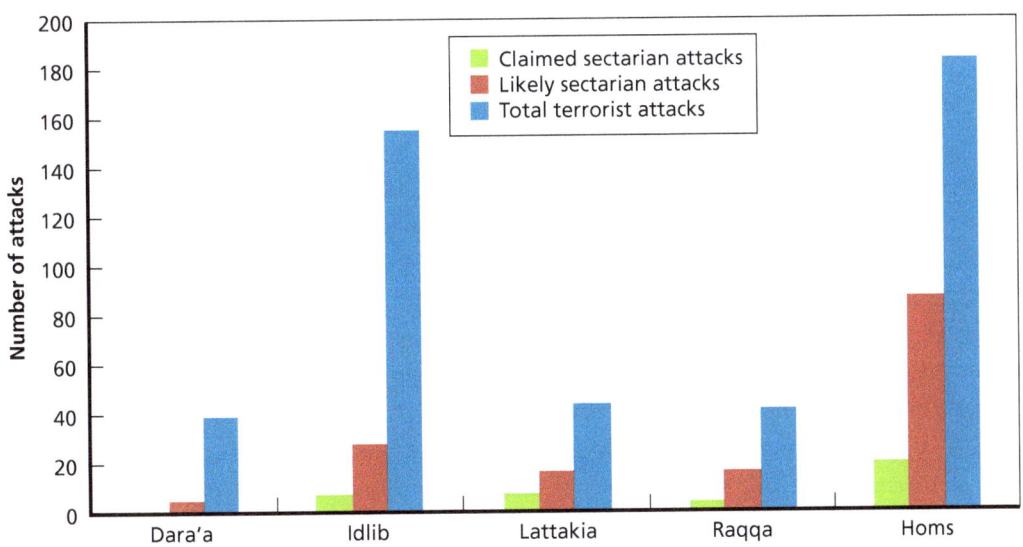

SOURCE: Based on data from START, 2017.

groups, and very few of them were openly claimed, even in Raqqa, where IS was in control. These relatively low numbers of sectarian attacks and minimal positive messaging about them (via claiming them) suggests that popular attitudes across Syria are not highly tolerant of sectarianism.

This pattern held true even in Idlib, where groups with openly sectarian ideologies (such as the al-Qaeda–linked HTS and Ahrar al-Sham) held territorial control. There were more sectarian attacks and more were openly claimed as such, but eight over six years is not a very high occurrence. Of 1,800 terrorist attacks across the country from 2011 to 2016, Idlib also had the only instance of a jihadist (or any) group apologizing for its actions. In the aforementioned 2015 killing of 20 Druze villagers in Idlib by the Nusra Front, the organization released a statement saying that it was an "unjustified error that occurred without the leadership's knowledge, and the village and its people continue to live securely and calmly under our protection."[39] Organization leaders also declared that the perpetrators of the killing would be brought before a Shari'a court. Ahrar al-Sham and other groups in the area also issued a response that praised the village of Qalb Lawza and its "sons of the Druze sect" for their support of the Syrian revolution, condemned the incident, called for arbitration at a Shari'a court, and declared that their only enemies were the regime and IS, not other sects.[40] In no

---

[39] Aymenn Jawad Al-Tamimi, "The Massacre of Druze Villagers in Qalb Lawza, Idlib Province," Syria Comment, June 15, 2015.

[40] Al-Tamimi, 2015.

other instances of sectarian or nonsectarian violence did a group and others in the area release similar statements condemning the violence and making assurances that the perpetrators would be prosecuted.[41] In contrast, in 2016, the Nusra Front and Ahrar al-Sham both claimed credit for attacking an ʿAlawi town in Latakia, and Nusra claimed six sectarian attacks that killed 61 civilians in Homs.

These statements do not suggest that the Nusra Front did not target the Druze in that particular instance and others. It also does not downplay the sectarian elements of the forced conversion of that Druze community. However, it is telling that all of the major militant organizations in the area felt it necessary to employ rhetoric that called it a mistake rather than enthusiastically claiming the event as a victory against members of another sect, as IS might have done and one might expect militant organizations to do to recruit other extremists. Their messaging was targeted at the local population (and, possibly, the international community) and suggests that they felt they needed to be seen as more moderate and tolerant in order to gain legitimacy. This, in turn, points to a possibility that the local population would not find acceptable either extremist, sectarian rhetoric or acts of violence that specifically targeted minorities rather than the regime. Such a view gains further support in light of a 2017 protest in the city of Maʿrat al-Nuʿman in Idlib. When HTS arrived in the anti-regime town, local activists rallied a peaceful protest that was effective enough that it forced the HTS soldiers to retreat that day.[42] Protestors demonstrated that there is popular resistance to the sort of extreme violence that this group exemplifies, including along sectarian lines.

The courts and rule of law that the groups in both locations employ also point to the importance of balancing group ideals with popular sentiments. In Daraʿa, the factions eventually developed a fairly unified court system that, although based on Unified Arab Code, which is itself based on Shariʿa law, was largely run and interpreted by secular legal professionals. In contrast, Idlib's many factions set up a series of Shariʿa courts with judges who were appointed by the armed Islamist groups and were often poorly educated, even in Shariʿa law. These courts often handed down harsh punishments for any infractions of the strict versions of Shariʿa law common to extreme Islamists, especially early on.[43] However, by 2016, some of these restrictions were eased—including strict dress codes—in order to appeal to the broader population

---

[41] At about the same time, Druze populations in the south of Syria were beginning to leave their more moderate pathways and join the regime forces. Some of the placating attitudes in the north might have been to forestall anything similar from happening in Idlib, although the Druze community there had already been known to be pro-government (Patrick J. McDonnell and Nabih Bulos, "Syrian Military and Druze Allies Join Forces to Fend Off 'Terrorists,'" *Los Angeles Times*, June 21, 2015).

[42] Mat Nashed, "Militants Stifle Civil Society in Syria's Idlib," *Al-Monitor*, July 26, 2017.

[43] Mikael Ekman, ed., *ILAC Rule of Law Assessment Report: Syria 2017*, Enskede, Sweden: International Legal Assistance Consortium, 2017, pp. 85–101.

that was not so enamored by the IS lifestyle.[44] Although the Idlibi judicial system and laws were unquestionably more strictly sectarian than those in Daraʻa, they were also less stringent than those of IS, which may indicate a population less comfortable with such a way of life.

Demographics

Prior to the start of the war, Daraʻa and Idlib were fairly similar in terms of demographics. Both are primarily Sunni with a significant rural population focused on agriculture. The people of the Hawran plain that covers part of Daraʻa perhaps had more historical engagement with religious diversity: They are bordered by the Druze-populated Arab Mountain to the east; some of the major tribes in the area were Christian, particularly in neighboring Suwaida; and, prior to the Baʻth era, there was a strong Sufi presence.[45] Idlib's prewar population had a somewhat lesser presence of minorities, although there was a small Christian community in the provincial capital, two Shiʻa villages, and a Druze enclave.[46] Each governorate, then, had a small minority presence, but the Sunnis in both were considered by Hanna Batatu to be more culturally "pacific" than their nomadic and mountainous counterparts in the Euphrates and Druze regions, who were "more independent, more impatient of oppression, and more prone to ignore or defy measures inconsistent with their interests."[47] This similar background suggests that there was nothing preexisting in the religious demographics of the area that would account for differences in resilience apart from slightly more exposure to other religions in Daraʻa than in Idlib.

One historical demographic difference between the two governorates, though, was the presence of tribes as a form of social organization in Daraʻa and not in Idlib. The "People of the Tree" in Idlib were considered "clanless peasants,"[48] while the areas around Daraʻa had several prominent tribes, many of whom had immigrated from the Gulf in the 19th century and continued to have strong ties to Arabian tribes.[49] Although such clans continued to have social resonance through the 20th century, the agrarian land reforms changed many of the local dynamics that empowered shaykhs by breaking up their landholdings. Access to education and work outside the agricultural arena further eroded the power of the shaykhs as the population became less dependent on patronage systems. Many of the tribes in the area did not bother to replace paramount

---

[44] Ammar Shawki and Roy Gutman, "A Letter from Rebel-Controlled Idlib, Syria," *The Nation*, December 1, 2016.

[45] Batatu, 1999, pp. 13, 107–108, 260–278.

[46] Lund, 2014.

[47] Batatu, 1999, pp. 11–12.

[48] Batatu, 1999, p. 23.

[49] Norman N. Lewis, "The Frontier of Settlement in Syria, 1800–1950," *International Affairs*, Vol. 31, No. 1, 1955.

shaykhs when they died in the later part of the century, as tribes and extended families became less important and less clear-cut (because of higher degrees of intermarriage) than immediate families.[50] Researchers have made a strong case that tribalism played a greater role in the Syrian conflict in the east, where Bedouin tribal structures are still relatively influential,[51] but there is not compelling evidence to suggest that similar factors were at play in the uprising in Daraʿa. Indeed, rather than neatly lining up along tribal lines, most of the opposition groups in Daraʿa comprise a wide mix of clans, suggesting that there is no strong unifying tribal force aligning people.[52] Nor is there any indication that tribal allegiances would incline a population to be less supportive of sectarian actors. In fact, IS's domination of the more-tribal eastern portions of Syria might suggest the opposite, if anything, meaning that whatever differences there are in tribal identity between Daraʿa and Idlib are unlikely to have a significant impact on their tolerance of sectarian ideology.

However, although historical demographic patterns might not have contributed to differences between the two governorates, recent changes in population demographics could be enabling the continued existence of extreme Islamist groups in Idlib. Daraʿa has a fair share of refugees and IDPs who are being housed there, given its close proximity to the refugee camps in Jordan,[53] but Idlib has seen a greater demographic shift as a result of population choice, Islamist organization actions, and regime efforts. Many of the 2,000 Christian families in Idlib fled at the beginning of the war, and all but two of the remaining families left when the city fell to rebels in 2015.[54] Idlib also has become host to a large number of IDPs: Of 6.4 million IDPs in Syria, it is estimated that between 700,000 and 2 million are in Idlib, many of whom are fleeing the regime.[55] As noted, Islamist hard-liners besieged the two Shiʿa villages and forced the Druze population to convert to Sunni Islam.

The regime, too, has its hand in changing the local demographics of Idlib. In the swap of villagers mentioned earlier, Iran and Russia helped form an agreement with the regime and the rebels in Idlib to allow the populations of Shiʿa in the two villages in Idlib to move to two largely Sunni, rebel-sympathizing villages under siege in regime-

---

[50] Batatu, 1999, pp. 24–26.

[51] Aaron Lund, "Syria's Bedouin Tribes: An Interview with Dawn Chatty," Carnegie Middle East Center, July 2, 2015; and Haian Dukhan, "Tribes and Tribalism in the Syrian Uprising," conference paper, St. Andrews University, Scotland, 2014.

[52] Nicholas A. Heras, "A Profile of Syria's Strategic Darʿa Province," *CTC Sentinel*, Vol. 7, No. 6, June 2014.

[53] Associated Press, "Aid Groups: Jordan Deports Thousands of Syrian Refugees," Voice of America, May 12, 2017.

[54] Syria Direct, "Airstrike Destroys Church in Idlib, Where Christians Once 'Happily Coexisted,'" August 11, 2016.

[55] United Nations Office for the Coordination of Humanitarian Affairs, *2016 Humanitarian Needs Overview*, Brussels, October 2015; and Omer Karasapan, "The Internally Displaced in the Middle East and North Africa: Harbingers of Future Conflict?" Brookings Institution, July 5, 2017.

controlled territory. This move has been interpreted as an attempt at ethnic cleansing, to replace Sunni rebel supporters with a more regime-friendly population in the south and consolidate restive Sunni rebels in the north.[56] This changing demographic landscape in Idlib could continue to alter popular attitudes toward Islamist extremism and sectarian violence.

Concentrating IDPs who are unhappy with the regime in Idlib could serve to increase antipathy toward the regime, particularly if the government is harsher on this population in the remainder of the conflict and early into the post-conflict period. This could make Idlib a hot spot for recruitment into violent extremist groups. These groups can play on feelings of disenfranchisement by marketing themselves as the only organizations actively continuing the fight. These demographic moves are recent enough that it is hard to say for certain how much of a role such shifts will play, but ensuring that IDPs are returned to their homes and that post-conflict negotiations include these populations will be essential to limiting long-term impacts.

Levels of Political and Economic Enfranchisement

As previously noted, both Daraʻa and Idlib are rural, agricultural areas, with Daraʻa being known as the breadbasket of Damascus, while Idlib has been renowned for its orchards. In the early 1990s, Daraʻa had 4.4 percent of the country's total population but 6.2 percent of the rural population. Similarly, Idlib had 6.7 percent of the country's total population but 10.9 percent of the rural population. In each case, a high percentage of the population was rural.[57] Both governorates benefited from the early land reforms put in place by the Baʻth Party: More than 5,000 families in Daraʻa and nearly 7,000 families in Idlib benefited.[58] As a result of these reforms, the Baʻth Party was relatively popular in both governorates, particularly in the early years of the regime, with active and supporting members of the party being roughly equivalent to the population. Although this might not be a direct measure of local support, other governorates did vary somewhat with regard to regime popularity. For instance, Latakia historically was a stronger supporter of the government and had a higher level of participation than its population size might indicate, while Hasakah was less supportive of the regime and had a correspondingly lower level of participation in the Baʻth Party (see Table 4.1). Daraʻa had a slightly higher percentage of supporters in the 1970s and in the early 1990s, and more officers and politicians in the Baʻthist regime came from Daraʻa, as opposed to relatively few from Idlib.[59] However, in Idlib, the remnants of these supporters likely formed the backbone of the Popular Committees that remained loyal to

---

[56] Martin Chulov, "Iran Repopulates Syria with Shia Muslims to Help Tighten Regime's Control," *The Guardian*, January 13, 2017.

[57] Batatu, 1999, p. 181.

[58] Batatu, 1999, pp. 34–35.

[59] Lund, 2016.

Table 4.1
Active and Supporting Members in the Ba'th Party

	1979			1992		
Governorate	Percentage of Active Members	Percentage of Supporting Members	Percentage of Total Population	Percentage of Active Members	Percentage of Supporting Members	Percentage of Total Population
Dara'a	5.4	3.2	3.7	5.4	4.5	4.4
Idlib	5.6	6.3	6.0	6.4	6.4	6.7
Latakia	8.2	7.9	6.2	8.9	11.1	6.0
Al-Hasakah	5.0	6.1	7.3	4.7	5.8	7.4

SOURCE: Batatu, 1999, pp. 180–181.

Assad, despite their Sunni background, suggesting that politics rather than sect was the true driving factor in deciding allegiance, even after the uprising had begun.

In the 1990s, Idlib began to slide out of focus, receiving less in the way of development than the rest of the country. For instance, as one measure, the doctor-to-inhabitant ratio in Syria overall in 1993 was one to 966, but in Idlib specifically, the proportion was one to 1,760, suggesting that Idlib was becoming more disenfranchised.[60] In the 2000s, Dara'a fared somewhat better than Idlib in terms of service provision. By 2010, the doctor-to-inhabitant ratio (as reported by the Syrian government) was down to one to 661 across Syria, but Dara'a was down only to one to 1,042 and Idlib had the worst ratio in the country at one to 1,186.[61] Both fared better with respect to schools: Dara'a had 4.7 percent of the country's state-run primary schools for only 4.4 percent of the population in 2009, and Idlib had 7.3 percent of the schools for 6.2 percent of the population.[62] However, Dara'a had 5.1 percent of the country's children in schools and Idlib had 8.0 percent, suggesting that there were more students per school and perhaps that the quality of education was poorer than elsewhere in Syria (see Table 4.2, with Assad's home governorate of Latakia included for comparison).[63] Public service provision in Dara'a and Idlib in numerous sectors lagged behind that of places closer to the regime but was not sharply dissimilar from each other in their trends.

Economically, Idlib has been somewhat worse off, with an unemployment rate of 16.8 percent compared with 13.3 percent in Dara'a in 2011. However, given that the

---

[60] Batatu, 1999, p. 68.

[61] Syrian Central Bureau of Statistics, "The Medical Professional, 2005–2010, and Distribution by Governorate, 2010," webpage, 2011d.

[62] Syrian Central Bureau of Statistics, "Basic Education Schools (1st & 2nd Cycle) by Ownership of School and Sex of Pupils 2005–2009, and Distribution of Schools by Governorate for 2009," webpage, 2011a.

[63] Figures for teacher numbers were not available. Syrian Central Bureau of Statistics, 2011a; Syrian Central Bureau of Statistics, "Pupils of Basic Education (1st Cycle) by School Governorate and Sex 2005–2009, and Distribution of Schools by Governorate for 2009," webpage, 2011b.

Table 4.2
Service Provision in Syria, 2009

Governorate	Doctor-to-Inhabitant Ratio	Percentage of the Total Population	Percentage of All State-Run Primary Schools	Percentage of All Students Attending Primary School
Daraʿa	1:1,042	4.4	4.7	5.1
Idlib	1:1,186	6.2	7.3	8.0
Latakia	1:563	5.7	5.2	3.8

SOURCE: Batatu, 1999.

national average was 14.9 percent, with three governorates having rates below 10 percent and four governorates having rates above 20 percent, Daraʿa and Idlib were relatively comparable.[64] Assad's economic reforms to bring in higher levels of foreign direct investment did little for hinterlands like Daraʿa and Idlib and instead further concentrated wealth in the hands of regime cronies.[65] Compounding these economic woes were the global economic depression of the 2000s and a drought that disproportionately impacted the rural, agricultural areas of Syria like Daraʿa and Idlib.[66]

Overall, then, although there were differences between Daraʿa and Idlib in terms of political enfranchisement and economic strength in the 1990s and 2000s, those differences were relatively small in comparison with other parts of the country. The fact that Daraʿa was doing slightly better economically could have played a small role in the intensity of the uprisings, but the gap between them is unlikely to have been significant enough for this to have had a major impact on the rise of sectarian actors.

Local Governance Efforts

Another hypothesis about local conditions that might increase or limit sectarianism in Syria is the role of civil society and local governance initiatives that have sprung up since the war. Activists and local councils have worked to assert control over civilian issues even in places like Idlib and are often more moderate in their ideologies than their militant counterparts. Alternatively, it is possible that the development of such groups is enabled by the fact that a population is already inherently resilient against sectarianism and extremism, but without a great deal of reliable data from the ground, this section will focus on whether there is at least some degree of overlap between the two.

---

[64] These rates might not be entirely reliable, because reported rates for 2011 and 2012 were identical down to the number of precise individuals unemployed, which seems unlikely. Syrian Central Bureau of Statistics, "Rate Unemployment by Governorate and Labor Force," webpage, 2011c.

[65] Bassam Haddad, *Business Networks in Syria: The Political Economy of Authoritarian Resilience*, Stanford, Calif.: Stanford University Press, 2011.

[66] Francesco Femia and Caitlin Werrell, "Syria: Climate Changes, Drought and Social Unrest," Center for Climate and Security, February 29, 2012.

At their height, there were an estimated 76 local councils in Daraʻa formed via various methods, including notable families and elections,[67] with a provincial council that was also selected via nominations from local district councils. The councils were primarily responsible for conducting relief operations, distributing rations, keeping the bakeries running, keeping the school system functioning, providing services, and repairing public buildings. The provincial council got its funding from the Syrian National Council,[68] while others relied on humanitarian aid organizations and, in some cases, residual salaries paid by the government.[69] The councils in Daraʻa made an active attempt to avoid political affiliation and to keep extreme Islamists and designated terrorists, such as the Nusra Front, from being able to participate directly.[70] Although the Daraʻa provincial council provides many of its financial details and workings via its Facebook page,[71] there is little reporting on any active efforts made on the part of these councils to reduce sectarian tensions, apart from the fact that they do not welcome groups like the Nusra Front, suggesting a popular desire to keep the extreme and sectarian ideals of such groups from gaining influence in the governorate. These groups in the south have an advantage over those with similar aims in Idlib in that there is not such a strong presence of extremist groups in Daraʻa in the first place, making a case for correlation between local councils and resilience to sectarianism rather than causation. Conversely, one of the challenges for local councils in Daraʻa is their location—one study found that councils in governorates near Turkey have fared better than their counterparts near Jordan because of Jordan's less approving stance toward local administration.[72]

Activists and councils appeared early on in Idlib, with a group of professionals in the provincial capital forming the National Opposition for Idlib Intellectuals organization as early as August 2011 with the aim of encouraging discourse between the opposition and the government, while other activists began providing humanitarian assistance, traffic control, and city guards in areas outside the government's control. Al-Idlibi House was another such organization that worked hard to pressure armed groups to hand over control of the city to civilians. They worked to push back against

---

[67] Daniel Serwer, "Yes, Mr. Obama, There Is a Syrian Opposition," Middle East Institute, October 23, 2015.

[68] Yaman Yosif and James Bowker, "After 'Marginalizing' the East, Daraʻa's New Electoral System Aims for Equity," Syria Direct, November 10, 2015.

[69] Aymenn Jawad Al-Tamimi, "'Reconciliation' in Syria: The Case of Al-Sanamayn," Middle East Forum, April 27, 2017.

[70] Institute for War & Peace Reporting, *Local Governance Inside Syria: Challenges, Opportunities, and Recommendations*, Washington, D.C., 2014, p. 26.

[71] "Daraʻa Council," Facebook page, undated.

[72] Agnes Favier, "Local Governance Dynamics in Opposition-Controlled Areas in Syria," in Luigi Narbone, Agnes Favier, and Virginie Collombier, eds., *Inside Wars: Local Dynamics of Conflict in Syria and Libya*, San Domenico di Fiesole, Italy: European University Institute, 2016.

the extremists and supported women's activities and rights. They also formed a committee with other civil-rights activists and organized the election of a local council that would negotiate with the armed groups and encourage them to return the court and local security to civilians.[73] Across the governorate, about 150 similar groups have organized to provide local governance and services, including utilities, sanitation, provision of subsidized bread, and coordination of relief aid. These councils are the primary targets for international support and often rely on such support to maintain their legitimacy and efficacy, as they have no alternative revenue streams. Local area councils will often work with police and Shura Councils, which provide the enforcement and judicial aspects of governance. Since 2011, many have greatly expanded their roles but, in general, are not very inclusive of women or minority populations. A Swiss Peace report found that one exception to this is a council in the town of Ma'aret al-Numan in Idlib, where women are included on the council and various advisory boards and where the council actively reaches out to the community for input. In theory, were there a religious minority presence in that town, it would have a voice in these councils, but most other local councils are notable for their lack of inclusion.[74] There is also a broader Provincial Council for Idlib that is meant to support and coordinate the efforts of the local councils, especially in terms of international aid, but many aid organizations prefer to work directly with the local councils, reducing the broader organization's real influence.

The councils are not without their challenges, as many of them risk being co-opted by local powerful families or militant and extremist organizations, as has been noted in the local council of Kafr Takharim in Idlib.[75] Local councils across the governorate also are facing competition for service provision from the civilian wings of HTS and Ahrar al-Sham. These organizations are beginning to use local administrators to bolster their legitimacy,[76] which could eventually create councils that are more extremist and sectarian in their outlook. However, most local councils have managed to maintain their independence to some degree and have improved their standing and legitimacy over time. Reports do not seem to indicate, though, that dealing with social issues like sectarianism is high on their agendas, as most are focused on the day-to-day challenges of governance. Many of the local councils studied in depth are operating in fairly homogenous communities. The leadership is often seen as "a reflection of the

---

[73] Julia Taleb, "Syrians Roll Back Extremism in Idlib Without Military Intervention," *Waging Nonviolence*, May 23, 2017.

[74] Bahjat Hajjar, Corinne von Burg, Leila Hilal, Martina Santschi, Mazen Gharibah, and Mazhar Sharbaji, *Perceptions of Governance: The Experience of Local Administrative Councils in Opposition-Held Syria*, Bern, Switzerland: Swiss Peace, 2017, pp. 11, 17.

[75] Sam Heller, "Keeping the Lights on in Rebel Idlib," The Century Foundation, November 29, 2016; and Hajjar et al., 2017.

[76] Ibrahim al-Assil, "Al-Qaeda Affiliate and Ahrar al-Sham Compete for Control in Idlib," Middle East Institute, June 29, 2017.

local community," so it is possible that in more-diverse communities, these councils could be inclusive and supportive of a natural resiliency in the population.[77] This suggests that local council attitudes toward sectarianism and inclusivity could be a product of local levels of resiliency rather than a driver of it.

It is challenging to determine whether such councils and activists influence the levels of sectarianism in an area or if they are the result of underlying popular resilience to such ideologies. One report suggests that "the less religiously adherent a town's residents are, the more likely they are to embrace a secular local council and be less enthusiastic about sharia courts or other Islamist-controlled bodies," and notes that religious adherence tends to be higher in more-agricultural areas.[78] The great number of councils active in Idlib, then, could suggest a population that is less sectarian and less committed to ideology. One report suggested that the councils across the country do not demonstrate a strong tendency for inclusivity, particularly with respect to gender, but that most are populated with individuals who are relatively secular or at least moderate. When asked about the councils and sectarianism, one individual responded that

> In general, they're non-ideological bodies, particularly at the local level, which, in a way, looks like a way forward. It doesn't matter if one guy is a leftist and the guy next to him is an Islamist. They're there because one of them knows something about how to get the water system working, and another one knows something about education, and they're working [on] practical things for the sake of the community.[79]

In either case, such organizations do seem to be correlated with and actively working toward a more resilient Syria. However, given the role of foreign actors discussed next, actively supporting or developing such institutions in Syria from the outside might ultimately be more detrimental than helpful, as it will allow space for other actors to accuse such groups of being pawns of the United States and Europe. A better option for international actors hoping to encourage resilience would be to wait for such groups to request aid through traditional humanitarian channels and then support them via those means while working to ensure that any aid efforts make it to their intended recipients. However, there should not be expectations that these councils are necessarily viable in the long term, as their legitimacy is tied much more closely to

---

[77] Hajjar et al., 2017.

[78] Centre for Human Dialogue, *Local Administration Structures in Opposition-Held Areas in Syria*, Geneva, April 2014, p. 17.

[79] Daniel Moritz-Rabson, "In Wartime Syria, Local Councils and Civil Institutions Fill a Gap," PBS Newshour, July 31, 2016.

short-term humanitarian aid efforts rather than more-sustainable sources, such as ties to the government and access to steady tax revenue.[80]

Key Foreign Actors

In many ways, then, Daraʻa and Idlib do not seem all that dissimilar in terms of their original, overwhelmingly Sunni demographics; historical exposure to some other religions and sects; economics; historical levels of engagement with and support of the Baʻth regime; attitudes toward sectarianism; and use of local governance structures. Yet the fact remains that Idlib is home to two extremist jihadi groups that espouse sectarian hatred at some level of their ideology while similar groups have largely failed to gain a foothold in Daraʻa. Some of the explanation might reside in deep social, cultural, and historical differences in perspective between the two regions that are nearly impossible to detect without the type of intensive on-the-ground data collection that is currently infeasible. However, the other striking difference between the two governorates, as was briefly discussed in terms of local councils, is their location (in particular, their proximity to a border with Jordan on the one hand and Turkey on the other; see Figure 4.1).

Two of the main supporters of both Ahrar al-Sham and HTS are Qatar and Turkey. One of the reasons that these extremist opposition groups are able to continue to operate so effectively in Idlib might have less to do with local resilience to sectarianism and more to do with the fact that Idlib shares a border with Turkey, allowing these two countries to funnel arms, money, and fighters to the group.[81] The main channel into Idlib and Syria through Turkey is the Bab al-Hawa border crossing. As a major supply line, it has immense strategic value and has been hotly contested since 2011. It was seized first by opposition groups in 2012 and became a "jihadist congregating point" before ultimately falling into the hands of Ahrar al-Sham.[82] In 2017, HTS succeeded in pushing out Ahrar al-Sham and taking control of the crossing to secure its own access to resources.[83] In addition, HTS has made an effort to control numerous towns along the Syrian-Turkish border, as well as key smuggling routes.[84] There are no reliable estimates of the flow of people, funds, and resources across the border or of how much income has been provided to the Islamist groups that controlled Bab al-Hawa and the licit trade across the border, but the crossing has been a regular access

---

[80] However, the success of local councils is tied to the size of the city, the proximity to friendly international borders, and access to natural resources. See Centre for Human Dialogue, 2014, pp. 15–16.

[81] Charles Lister, *Profiling Jabhat al-Nusra*, Washington, D.C.: Brookings Institution, Project on U.S. Relations with the Islamic World, Analysis Paper No. 24, 2016, pp. 29–32.

[82] Rod Nordland, "Al Qaeda Taking Deadly New Role in Syria's Conflict," *New York Times*, July 24, 2012; and Aron Lund, "Showdown at Bab al-Hawa," Carnegie Middle East Center, December 12, 2013.

[83] Suleiman al-Khalidi, "Syrian Rebels Re-Open Main Border Crossing with Turkey," Reuters, July 27, 2017b.

[84] Al-Assil, 2017.

point, particularly for thousands of foreign fighters entering the country.[85] It is estimated that 30 percent of HTS's fighters are foreigners, so such access has considerable impacts on its ability to fight.[86] With Kurdish and IS control of other border areas during much of the conflict, the Bab al-Hawa crossing remained the major option for supply lines for Ahrar al-Sham and HTS. Controlling this territory was therefore both the motivation to maintain a strong presence in Idlib and the source of resources that allowed them to do so.

By contrast, Daraʻa shares a border with Jordan, which has been the source of considerable support from the United States and other Western-aligned countries that have a made an active effort to support moderate groups rather than extreme Islamist ones. Much of the Central Intelligence Agency's investment in training and support programs was based in Jordan and targeted at the moderate Southern Front,[87] which is the dominant opposition group in Daraʻa and is widely considered to be supported actively by a military operations command center based in Amman.[88] Jordan itself sees the matter of extremism on its borders as one of national security; thus, it has actively supported the Southern Front with training and supplies across the Nasib border crossing into Daraʻa.[89] Reportedly, in 2015, Jordan also considered establishing a buffer zone on the Jordanian side of the border, supplemented by safe havens in Daraʻa and using Syrian fighters vetted and supported by Jordanian officials.[90] Jordan border policing has limited the amount of support available to extremist groups in Daraʻa, as well as the numbers of foreign fighters crossing into the governorate, compared with the more open borders in the north.[91] In 2016 and 2017, though, support to moderate opposition groups in Daraʻa and the south has been somewhat reduced.[92] Concurrently, there has been an increase in the presence of extremist opposition groups in this area, which often have much more-sectarian ideologies.[93]

---

[85] Hannah Lucinda Smith, "Jihadists' Tour Guide Shuttles Foreign Fighters into Syria," *Vice News*, February 3, 2014.

[86] Mapping Militant Organizations, "Hay'at Tahrir al-Sham (Formerly Jabhat al-Nusra)," Stanford University, August 14, 2017b.

[87] Greg Miller and Karen DeYoung, "Secret CIA Effort in Syria Faces Large Funding Cut," *Washington Post*, June 12, 2015.

[88] Hugh Naylor, "Moderate Rebels Take Key Southern Base in Syria, Dealing Blow to Assad," *Washington Post*, June 9, 2015.

[89] Kim Ghattas, "Syria War: Southern Rebels See US as Key to Success," BBC News, December 9, 2014.

[90] *The Economist*, "Drawing in the Neighbours," July 2, 2015.

[91] Barbara Opall-Rome, "Jordan Proves Heavyweight in Fight Against ISIS," *Defense News*, May 9, 2016.

[92] Mona Alami, "What's Keeping Syria's Rebel Forces from Consolidating Their Power?" *Al-Monitor*, September 26, 2016.

[93] Mohammad Ersan, "Extremist Expansion in Southern Syria Puts Jordan on Guard," *Al-Monitor*, March 13, 2017.

The provision of funding, weapons, and fighters is essential to maintaining any sort of conflict. Even early on in the fighting in Syria, more-moderate oppositions groups lost fighters to better-funded extremist groups for the simple reason that organizations like IS and Jabhat al-Nusra had the ability to pay them.[94] Securing access to resources and backers has been a main driver in the strategic decisions of many rebel groups. In the south, the major supply lines into Daraʻa come through Jordan, which more strongly regulates the flow of people, weapons, and resources and (along with its pro-secular American and Gulf allies) targets moderate and secular organizations. In contrast, Idlib's border with Turkey is much more open, with opportunities for extremist financing and fighters to cross more readily into Syria.[95] This suggests that international support for sectarian groups and the sheer access those organizations have to funding and resources could be the most significant variables that allow the groups to flourish. If external funding and support are indeed the primary sources driving sectarian violence in Syria today, access to resources might be what drives the presence of sectarian ideology, and a denial of that access—or, better yet, active support for moderate organizations—might help support a seemingly relatively broad Syrian desire to be resilient to such violence.[96]

Discussion

During the Syrian civil war, Daraʻa and Idlib remained two centers of rebel holdouts against the regime forces. Both were home to early protests against Assad and the government, and both saw violent crackdowns that led to continued fighting for control. Both are and have been primarily Sunni Arab by demographics, with a smattering of other minority religious groups. Each is a rural, agricultural area, impacted by the drought in the late 2000s, but each is also a recipient of Baʻth Party land reforms and had active Baʻth Party members in rough proportion to the size of its population, although the citizens of Daraʻa had greater participation in higher levels of the regime. To the extent we can measure, the populations of Idlib and Daraʻa espouse similar ideas about sectarianism and religious difference. Both areas have seen the development of local councils to run service efforts in the absence of the regime's ability to effect governance. And finally, both share a border with another country, and rebels

---

[94] Loveday Morris, "Battling on Two Fronts, Moderate Syrian Rebels Struggle for Funding, Lost Fighters," *Washington Post*, October 18, 2013.

[95] See Tom Keatinge, "The Importance of Financing in Enabling and Sustaining the Conflict in Syria (and Beyond)," *Perspectives on Terrorism*, Vol. 8, No. 4, August 2014.

[96] As of mid-2018, this trend of foreign support does not seem to be diminishing, with Turkey's continued support of armed groups in Idlib challenging its relations with Russia (Fehim Tastekin, "Syria's Idlib Emerges as Achilles Heel in Russia-Turkey Partnership," *Al-Monitor*, July 30, 2018).

are able to receive funds and support across these transit lines more readily than governorates in the interior of the country.

And yet, despite these similarities, Idlib became home to two of the major extreme Islamist organizations that have perpetrated some degree of religious cleansing, while the rebels in Daraʻa actively opposed such groups, suggesting a popular resilience against sectarian ideology.[97] That said, there are certainly elements within Idlib governorate that are willing to confront the Islamist militias, and civilian organizations compete with militants to control efforts at governance. Additionally, HTS's hedging when it comes to messaging about their own sectarian actions suggests that its views are not yet widely held. Nevertheless, HTS remains dominant in Idlib, enabling sectarianism to grow there, a situation that is only likely to get worse with the demographic shifts of other rebels into the area who might feel cornered and liable to turn to terrorism as Assad's forces continue to make advances.

Indeed, this demographic shift seems to be one of the major points of difference between the two governorates that might account for the continued existence of these groups in Idlib. The other—and likely more influential—variable that is clearly divided between the two regions is which border they are close to and, more precisely, which external actors are using these borders to provide resources to rebel groups. In Daraʻa, the Southern Front receives assistance from the United States and European allies via Jordan. In Idlib, where extremist groups control the border crossings with Turkey, it is Qatar and other wealthy Gulf and Islamist benefactors who provide support. Given the lack of reliable data on social dynamics, the strongest conclusion this author can draw is that the practical variable of international support for rebels with particular ideologies is what enables these groups to operate, more than any social or civil-society efforts.[98]

Fortunately, unlike developing civil society or influencing culture, the movement of people and resources, especially from outside the country, is something that policymakers outside Syria can more significantly affect. The first step would be to make a genuine effort to cut off the resources, supplies, and fighters coming from foreign sources. This might involve putting greater pressure on places like Qatar or, perhaps more effectively, cooperating with Turkey to close the border to traffic of this kind. HTS and Ahrar al-Sham almost entirely rely on trade and resources coming from outside Syria, so cutting them off would limit their ability to operate effectively and drive them out of Idlib.[99] As for the changing demographics, to the extent that outside

---

[97] Andrew Parasiliti, Kathleen Reedy, and Becca Wasser, *Preventing State Collapse in Syria*, Santa Monica, Calif.: RAND Corporation, PE-219-OSD, 2017, pp. 7–10.

[98] This is not to say that such elements do not play a role, only that, with the current limits on information and data from Syria, it is impossible to assess the strength of these variables at this time.

[99] Mapping Militant Organizations, 2017b; Mapping Militant Organizations, "Ahrar al-Sham," Stanford University, August 5, 2017a.

powers have any influence in a postwar Syria, they should make it clear that they will not accept the attempts at ethnic cleansing that have left the population more-strictly divided along religious lines. The Balkans has proven that allowing this demarcation to endure can have long-term consequences in terms of solidifying differences based on identity rather than encouraging reconciliation and acceptance of diversity.[100] Reconciliation and reconstruction efforts, then, should emphasize the importance of returning IDPs and refugees to their homes rather than pressuring them to settle in religious enclaves.

What little polling there has been suggests that Syrians in Idlib and Daraʻa, as well as in other parts of the country, largely feel that sectarian divides are not old, unsolvable problems but are political in nature, pointing to a more popular resilience to sectarianism and tolerance for religious diversity. However, with every act of violence committed by an extremist militia or the regime and its allies that is or appears to be based on religious grounds, sectarian divides will be reified in a cycle of action begetting retribution. This makes solutions like cutting off the flow of foreign resourcing and pushing for the importance of inclusivity and diversity essential to preventing long-term cycles of violence and retribution. Resilience is present in Syria, but it could fade if world powers do not make an effort to allow it to flourish.

---

[100] Tom Evans, "Bosnian Leader: 'Ethnic Cleansing' Continues 15 Years After the War," CNN, March 1, 2010.

CHAPTER FIVE
Resilience to Sectarianism in Baghdad and Dohuk

Ami Carpenter
Associate Professor
Joan B. Kroc School of Peace Studies
University of San Diego

This chapter analyzes resilience to sectarian violence in Baghdad neighborhoods in 2010 and in the Kurdistan region of Iraq (KRI) in 2017. The Baghdad section builds off of earlier work that explains why some neighborhoods were better able to resist the descent into sectarian violence during the insurgency of the late 2000s.[1] This chapter introduces a second case study focused on Dohuk governorate in the KRI to test whether similar factors might be at play in explaining that area's resilience to violent conflict, despite its proximity to ISIS-controlled territory and an influx of IDPs.

At the outset, it is important to note that Baghdad and Dohuk differ in size, demography, history, and institutional stability. The premise of this case study is not that these two areas are the same. The primary comparison in this chapter—as in the earlier research—is among different neighborhoods in Baghdad. The intra-Baghdad comparison has the methodological advantage of controlling for many variables, including location, proximity to sectarian diversity, and embeddedness in national politics, an advantage that Dohuk lacks.

The reason for including Dohuk in this treatment of resilience is practical. First, the Kurdistan region was one of the few places in Iraq where fieldwork could be safely carried out by a Westerner in 2017. Although the Kurdish region does not possess significant sectarian diversity, it does contain substantial ethnic diversity. Dohuk has served as a receiving area of many Sunni-Arab IDPs, as well as smaller populations of Christians and Yezidis who fled ISIS control in nearby areas, including Mosul. Given this challenging context (i.e., Dohuk's hosting of non-Kurdish IDPs), which might have been expected to erode Dohuk's stability, and the prior consideration of fieldwork access, this chapter treats Dohuk as a second case to test the portability of the Baghdad findings in a different setting.

---

[1] Carpenter, 2012; Ami C. Carpenter, *Community Resilience to Sectarian Violence in Baghdad*, New York: Springer-Verlag, 2016.

This chapter finds that, despite the different contexts, there is a great deal of overlap in what accounts for Baghdad's and Dohuk's capacity to resist the impulse of violence. Although not an exhaustive classification of resilience factors, social capital (high intergroup trust) has a great deal of explanatory power in both cases. Communities in which people trusted each other and interacted on a regular basis were less likely to become fearful and angry in Baghdad's rapidly shifting and chaotic landscape and were more likely to take strategic action that reinforced and protected their relationships and values.

Resilience, Conflict Escalation, and Social Capital

Multiple studies have found that community resilience depends on the strength of intergroup trust and cooperation among community members.[2] This is particularly true when theorizing about resilience to violent social conflict, because strong intergroup relations provide a buffer against conflict escalation. Violent social conflicts do not emerge suddenly and without warning; they escalate through a series of stages.[3]

Escalation usually is triggered by an event that unsettles relationships between groups. Within a group, higher levels of fear and anger drive changes that separate groups further: Each group coheres, cuts off communication with the "other," and prepares to defend itself. Because "victim" and "aggressor" are contested roles in violent conflict, and because the desire for revenge is an emotion tied to the trauma of violence, readying for defense often leads instead to offensive attacks. Violence then

---

[2] Betty Pfefferbaum, Rose L. Pfefferbaum, and Richard L. Van Horn, "Community Resilience Interventions: Participatory, Assessment-Based, Action-Oriented Processes," *American Behavioral Scientist*, Vol. 59, No. 2, 2015; Daniel P. Aldrich and Michelle A. Meyer, "Social Capital and Community Resilience," *American Behavioral Scientist*, Vol. 59, No. 2, 2015; and Mary B. Anderson and Marshall Wallace, *Opting Out of War: Strategies to Prevent Violent Conflict*, Boulder, Colo.: Lynne Rienner Publishers, 2012.

[3] Thomas E. Boudreau, "When the Killing Begins: An Epistemic Inquiry into Violent Human Conflict, Contested Truths, and Multiplex Methodology," in T. Maytók, J. Senehi, and S. Bryne, eds., *Critical Issues in Peace and Conflict Studies: Theory, Practice, and Pedagogy*, Lanham, Md.: Lexington Books, 2012, pp. 21, 33.

spreads through exposure[4] as victims become perpetrators[5] and the visibility of violence increases.[6] The longevity of violent conflict only exacerbates these dynamics.[7]

High levels of social capital buffer against the negative effects outlined above. People who trust each other and interact on a regular basis are less likely to become fearful and angry at each other and therefore are less likely to demonize the "other." They are less vulnerable to mobilization and recruitment by sectarian actors because of "competing loyalties to other identities, competing shared histories from a broader religious affiliation [and] conflicting loyalties from their memberships in other groups on other cleavages."[8]

Background

After Saddam Hussein was deposed, the conflict in Iraq evolved from an insurgency against the interim U.S.-led government (the Coalition Provisional Authority) into a sectarian civil war. Al-Qaeda in Iraq (AQI) was formed in late 2003 and led by Abu Mus'ab Al-Zarqawi, a Jordanian who adapted the Jihadist organization to which he belonged—Tawhid wal Jihad—to the Iraqi context. His initial goals included armed and ideological opposition to American and foreign involvement in Iraq, the overthrow of the new Iraqi government, and the establishment of an Islamic caliphate. But AQI's strategy shifted quickly from attacking coalition forces to attacking Shi'ite civilians, first in western Al-Anbar province and then in Baghdad's mixed sectarian and Shi'ite-dominant neighborhoods. Al-Zarqawi's explicit aim was to provoke sectarian violence, despite warnings from Osama bin Laden's then-deputy, Ayman Al-Zawhari, that such a strategy undermined the overarching goal of ousting coalition forces and establishing a pan-Islamic state.

---

[4] People exposed to violence are more likely to become perpetrators of violence. Exposure includes observing, witnessing, or being subjected to violence. See Gary Slutkin, "Violence Is a Contagious Disease," in *Contagion of Violence: Workshop Summary*, Washington, D.C.: Forum on Global Violence Prevention, National Academies Press, 2013.

[5] Sarah Kelly, "The Psychological Consequences to Adolescents of Exposure to Gang Violence in the Community: An Integrated Review of the Literature," *Journal of Child and Adolescent Psychiatric Nursing*, Vol. 23, No. 2, May 2010.

[6] L. Rowell Huesmann and Lucnya Kirwil, "Why Observing Violence Increases the Risk of Violent Behavior in the Observer," in D. J. Flannery, A. T. Vazsonyi, and I. D. Waldman, eds., *The Cambridge Handbook of Violent Behavior and Aggression*, Cambridge, U.K.: Cambridge University Press, 2007.

[7] Simha F. Landau and Danny Pfeffermann, "A Time-Series Analysis of Violent Crime and Its Relation to Prolonged States of Warfare—The Israeli Case," *Criminology*, Vol. 26, No. 3, August 1988.

[8] Joshua R. Gubler and Joel Sawat Selway, "Horizontal Inequality, Crosscutting Cleavages, and Civil War," *Journal of Conflict Resolution*, Vol. 56, No. 2, 2012.

Among the Shi'a community, Muqtada Al-Sadr formed the Mahdi Army in 2003. Sadr is the son of the late Grand Ayatollah Muhummad Al-Sadr, who was a figurehead of Shi'a resistance under Saddam Hussein's regime. The organization began as a religious and social movement, based in Baghdad's marginalized Shi'ite-dominant areas (particularly in Al-Thawra, since renamed Sadr City) and provided social services and spiritual support. Like Al-Zarqawi, Al-Sadr opposed the presence of U.S. and coalition forces in Iraq. Unlike Al-Zarqawi, Al-Sadr publicly rejected sectarian violence against Sunni Muslims. However, as internal violence increased, the Mahdi Army played a larger public-security function in Baghdad neighborhoods, with the goal of protecting both Baghdad's Shi'a population and religious shrines. The organization expanded rapidly between 2004 and 2005 and decentralized into different (and often rival) factions, many of which adopted sectarian tactics despite Al-Sadr's policy.

In 2005, Al-Zarqawi called for a comprehensive war against Shi'ite Iraqis. The bombing of the Shi'a Al-'Askari shrine in Samarra in February 2006 became a symbol of the scope of sectarian violence in the country. It occurred at a time when Baghdad was becoming increasingly divided into Sunni and Shi'ite enclaves as 80 percent of Baghdad's households fled their formerly multiethnic neighborhoods. Sectarian violence continued largely unchecked until 2008, when Sunni tribes realigned themselves against AQI and drove them out of Al-Anbar and other Sunni areas. Afterward, Al-Sadr entered into a ceasefire agreement with Prime Minister Nouri Al-Maliki's government.

By 2012, AQI had reconstituted as the Islamic State (IS). Its seizure of territory in northern Syria caused an exodus of refugees east across the Syria-Iraq border into Dohuk governorate in the KRI.[9] In June 2014, 48 miles southwest of Dohuk City, IS captured Mosul and the governorate received hundreds of thousands of IDPs fleeing the violence. Two months later, IS attacked the KRI directly, capturing Sinjar, the Mosul Dam, and eight other towns. This "Northern Iraq offensive" displaced 40,000 Yezidi and other minorities and generated the third wave of IDPs into Dohuk. As of this writing, refugees and IDPs constitute 50 percent of the population in Dohuk's capital city and 33 percent of the total population in the governorate.

---

[9] The territory is politically divided between the Kurdistan Democratic Party (KDP) and the Patriotic Union of Kurdistan (PUK), each of which retains its own security (Peshmerga) forces. Significant numbers of refugees from the Syrian civil war began to arrive in Dohuk in early 2012, and by 2014 there were more than 100,000. By early 2017, when Iraqi forces began to recapture Mosul, 395,000 IDPs lived in Dohuk, and the vast majority were from Mosul. See International Organization for Migration, "Iraq Mission: Displacement Tracking Matrix—DTM Round 64," webpage, February 2017.

Neighborhood Versus City Resilience

The main reason to compare neighborhood-level analysis with city-level analysis is to explore how the nature and relevance of resilience capacities vary across different scales.[10] The Baghdad study compared neighborhoods in order to understand how parts of Baghdad coped with rising sectarian violence. Prior research had established that "the social and organizational characteristics of neighborhoods explain variations in the geographical concentration of violence,"[11] and more-recent studies confirm that support for (or resilience against) extremist recruitment occurred at the neighborhood or community level.[12] Therefore, the author treated neighborhoods as units of analysis where people either supported or rejected sectarianism.

The Dohuk case examined a larger social system—a city—in order to compare resilience capacities between small and large communities. For the analysis of resilience factors in Dohuk, the author relied on focus groups and interviews conducted in January and June 2017 and on a large urban profile of Dohuk governorate published by the United Nations High Commissioner for Human Rights (UNHCR) in August 2016.[13] The author was able to combine case study data with secondary survey and focus-group data in response to inquiries about social cohesion, coexistence, and coping strategies. The following sections describe each research site in more depth.

Baghdad Neighborhoods

The earlier Baghdad study compared ten neighborhoods to examine how different variables related to people's adoption or rejection of sectarian attitudes and behaviors. The research effort differentiated neighborhoods by their ethnic composition and whether they permitted or rejected sectarian militias. Thus, neighborhoods were placed in one of the six categories indicated in Table 5.1. Four neighborhoods (Al-Karadah,

---

[10] L. J. Kirmayer, M. Sehdev, R. Whitley, S. F. Dandeneau, and C. Isaac, "Community Resilience: Models, Metaphors and Measure," *Journal of Aboriginal Health*, Vol. 5, No. 1, 2009.

[11] Robert J. Sampson, Stephen W. Raudenbush, and Felton Earls, "Neighborhoods and Violent Crime: A Multilevel Study of Collective Efficacy," *Science*, Vol. 277, No. 5328, 1997.

[12] See Steven E. Finkel, Daniel Wallace, and John F. McCauley, "Contextual Violence and Support for Violent Extremism: Evidence from the Sahel," unpublished manuscript, U.S. Agency for International Development, 2016; Stevan Weine and Osman Ahmed, "Building Resilience to Violent Extremism Among Somali-Americans in Minneapolis-St. Paul," College Park, Md.: National Consortium for the Study of Terrorism and Responses to Terrorism, 2012; Van Metre, 2016; Shira Fishman, *Community-Level Indicators of Radicalization: A Data and Methods Task Force*, College Park, Md.: National Consortium for the Study of Terrorism and Responses to Terrorism, 2009; Carpenter, 2016; and Carpenter, 2012.

[13] The Dohuk Statistics Office conducted a survey in May 2016 of 1,205 households: 409 from the host community, 394 IDP households, and 402 refugee households. See UNHCR, *Displacement as Opportunity and Challenge: Urban Profile—Refugees, Internally Displaced Persons and Host Community, Duhok Governorate, Kurdistan Region of Iraq*, August 2016.

Table 5.1
Research Site Selection

	Sunni Dominant	Shi'ite Dominant	Mixed
Sectarian militias permitted	Al-'Amiriyah Al-A'dhamiya Al-Doura	Sadr City Al-Za'faraniya	Al-Bayaa'
Sectarian militias rejected	Al-Dhubat	Al-Karadah Al-Kuraiaat	Palestine Street

NOTES: Sunni-dominant areas are those where Sunnis make up more than 70 percent of the neighborhood population. Likewise, Shi'ite-dominant areas are those where Shi'ites constitute more than 70 percent of the population. Mixed areas are where two or more ethno-religious groups (i.e., Sunni, Shi'ite, Mandaean, Iranian, and Christian) make up 30–70 percent of the population.

Al-Kuraiaat, Palestine Street, and Al-Dhubat) were resilient to sectarian conflict and protected life and property during the civil war.

Al-Karadah and Al-Kuraiaat were Shi'a-dominant areas. Al-Karadah neighborhood is located in Al-Karadah district, a relatively large area on the east bank of the Tigris River, where militias operated. It was home to Sunnis and Christians, many of whom had high levels of education, and moderate-to-high socioeconomic status. Baghdad University is in close proximity, and the region was home to many businesses and NGOs. On the same (east) side of the Tigris River is historic Al-Kuraiaat, a smaller area famous for its restaurants and bordered by Al-A'dhamiya. Diversity in socioeconomic classes was reported in Al-Kuraiaat, meaning that wealthy residents intermixed with poorer residents, who also tended to have a lower standard of education.

Palestine Street is an administrative division of Sadr City, but it differs from the latter in significant ways. It is a well-known commercial area like Al-Karadah and is home to Baghdad's second-largest university, Al-Mustansiriya. Many residents had middle- to upper-level income and were highly educated. Buildings were in good condition, and home sizes were generally large. Despite being bounded by Sadr City regions, Palestine Street did not experience the same influence by the Mahdi Army and remained relatively safe.[14] Interviews and focus groups were conducted in these areas.

Al-Dhubat was the only nonviolent Sunni-dominant area where Shi'a and Christian residents also live that could be identified by the field research team. Al-Dhubat, which means "The Officers," is located within the otherwise violent Zayouna district, a residential area in Baghdad whose residents earn above-average income. Residents of Zayouna, and of Al-Dhubat in particular, include a large percentage of high-ranking Iraqi army officers.

A key point is that proximity to violent areas did not predict the spread of sectarian attitudes and behaviors. For example, both Al-Za'faraniya (where the Mahdi Army

---

[14] Interview with a YouGov facilitator, September 2011.

and AQI operated) and Al-Karadah, where they were not permitted to operate, are located within the larger Al-Karadah district. Palestine Street is a subdivision of Sadr City, the birthplace of Mahdi Army, and is plagued by attacks and counterattacks. Al-Dhubat neighborhood is in Zayouna district, which was an extremely violent area of Baghdad. There is no doubt that the proximity of violent actors increases the risk of sectarianism, but whether that risk becomes a reality depends on how it is managed by local actors.

Dohuk City

Dohuk governorate consists of four districts,[15] two of which—Dohuk and Semel—were the subject of this analysis. This research treated Semel and Dohuk as a single urban area. Semel is a suburb of Dohuk City, and each has a higher population density than other parts of the governorate. More importantly, together they host the highest percentage of refugees and IDPs in Dohuk governorate (50 percent). Virtually all IDP households are from Nineveh governorate: 54 percent from Mosul City; 39 percent from Sinjar; and 7 percent from Tal Kayf, Hamdaniya, and Tal Afar.[16] The majority of IDPs live outside camps and are mingled in with the host communities, which causes tension. "No one expected this huge number of IDPs coming to our city; everything became a mess. There was no plan to take care of the IDPs and, honestly, they should all be in camps instead of staying in the urban areas."[17]

Social fissures and safety concerns were influenced by "the war next door" and the presence of IS militants in Dohuk. Although uncommon (and absent in the official record), IS's capacity to operate in Dohuk included kidnapping[18] and recruitment.[19] Tensions and grievances were particularly high between Dohuk's host community and Sunni Arab IDPs, who "tend to live in isolation from other groups and from the host community because of their alleged role in Iraq's conflict."[20] The more-widespread and deeply felt pressures were caused by a pervasive financial crisis. A severe economic shock caused by a crash in world oil prices struck Dohuk in early 2012 at the same time that significant numbers of refugees from the Syrian civil war began to arrive.

---

[15] These districts are Amedi, Dohuk, Semel, and Zakho.

[16] UNHCR, 2016, p. 13.

[17] UNHCR, 2016, p. 19.

[18] Focus group member, June 8, 2017.

[19] Official and unofficial estimates of recruitment differ significantly. Official estimates placed the total number of Kurdish IS members at around 1,000 (see Rebecca Collard, "Kurdish ISIS Recruits Threaten Identity and Security of Kurdish State," *TIME*, January 23, 2015). An unofficial estimate by a credible source placed the number of young men recruited from religious schools in rural areas at about ten per month, per school.

[20] UNHCR, 2016, p. 25.

The economic crisis was exacerbated by fallout from serious political conflicts between the Kurdistan Regional Government (KRG) and the national government.[21] The immediate result was the KRG's inability to meet its huge government payroll, which led it to cut the salaries of public-sector employees (more than half of the workforce) by 75 percent.[22] The widespread reduction in disposable income, coupled with the burden on public services, generated significant levels of perceived deprivation. A majority of host and IDP community members viewed themselves as victims of an unfair advantage conferred on the "other" in the way that humanitarian aid is allocated[23] and over competition for jobs.[24]

Despite all of these challenges, Dohuk has escaped the widespread violence and collapse of law and order experienced in neighboring Nineveh governorate.[25] The remainder of this chapter explains how and why actors and institutions coped, adapted, and ultimately self-organized to safeguard their social infrastructure.

Social Capital

Social capital is built on trust embedded within social relationships. The structure of social relationships varies across two dimensions. The *horizontal* dimension connects people of different identity groups (e.g., Sunni, Shi'a) in the same community. The *vertical* dimension connects community members to their leaders and to different levels of government.[26] Considered together, these two dimensions of social capital shape how communities respond to upheaval and crisis.

Horizontal Relationships

Bridging social capital refers to formal and informal relationships connecting people of different identity groups through organizations, agencies, and institutions at mul-

---

[21] The KRI receives 17 percent of the federal budget, which the Iraqi government refused to pay in 2014. The failure of Erbil and Baghdad to implement an oil deal negotiated at the end of 2014 compounded the shortage of funds.

[22] The World Bank, *Kurdistan Region of Iraq: Reforming the Economy for Shared Prosperity and Protecting the Vulnerable—Executive Summary*, Washington, D.C., May 30, 2016.

[23] Fifty-four percent of host respondents and 58 percent of IDP respondents felt that aid was unfairly distributed, while 56 percent of host respondents and 52 percent of IDPs felt that competition for jobs was unfair. See UNHCR, 2016, p. 26.

[24] One year later, both concerns emerged as major themes in the interviews and focus groups.

[25] NGO Coordination Committee for Iraq, *Dohuk Governorate Profile*, Geneva, December 2015.

[26] Nat J. Colletta, and Michelle L. Cullen, *Violent Conflict and the Transformation of Social Capital: Lessons from Cambodia, Rwanda, Guatemala, and Somalia (English)*, Washington, D.C.: The World Bank, 2000.

tiple levels.[27] The Baghdad case study found higher levels of bridging social capital in the four resilient neighborhoods, as measured by the frequency of collective problem-solving and community action.

Residents in Al-Karadah, Palestine Street, Al-Kuraiaat, and Al-Dhubat reported a history of coordinated collective action to solve whole-neighborhood problems, including organizing trash collection and financial contributions for poor families, collecting signatures from residents on petitions, and cooperating to settle disputes. Humanitarian assistance to the needy was organized by community members and executed by wealthy families, individuals, and Imams through collections at mosques. One resident of Al-Karadah discussed this type of community organization in depth:

> Al-Karadah, Baghdad (2010): People in the neighborhood used to solve problems without returning to the state. They helped each other, particularly with regard to poor families. Members of the society informed the rich people about the presence of poor families. Rich people used to collect money to help the poor. Sometime a person dies or has to undergo an operation so the people used to cooperate to help them financially.

This account stands in sharp relief to those from Al-Za'faraniya, a Mahdi Army stronghold.[28] The following respondent's response to the same question is illustrative:

> Al-Za'faraniya, Baghdad (2010): People in my neighborhood didn't have ties with each other. Every person minded their own business. People don't meet or gather. I personally faced a problem; I needed money for an operation to my son; I wasn't comfortable about asking for help from the others; I sold something I have and I paid for the expenses of the operations. People of the neighborhood don't know each other.

Although several factors account for the difference in bridging capital between Al-Za'faraniya and Al-Karadah, the Baghdad research suggests the importance of two geographic factors: (1) availability of public spaces and (2) integrated housing versus residential enclaves. These dynamics also proved critical in the example of Bahrain (see Chapter Three). First, the availability of public spaces where people come together to socialize and connect creates opportunities for interacting. Neighborhoods without public places limit these possibilities, and Al-Za'faraniya is one such neighborhood. Respondents believed that the lack of markets, cafes, and playgrounds resulted in very low levels of interpersonal interaction and community cooperation. Second, residential enclaves (i.e., where Sunni and Shi'ite residents live in separate areas) affect interaction

---

[27] Norman Uphoff, "Understanding Social Capital: Learning from the Analysis and Experience of Participation," in Partha Dasgupta and Ismail Serageldin, eds., *Social Capital: A Multifaceted Perspective*, Washington, D.C.: The World Bank, 2000.

[28] Field interview in Al-Za'faraniya, November 11, 2010.

and communication between sects in mixed neighborhoods. Al-Bayaaʻ and Palestine Street differed on this variable. Palestine Street is characterized by mixed neighborhoods and proved resilient to sectarian conflict.

The configuration of physical space also mattered in Dohuk. As one respondent explained, "From its founding, Duhok was a small city; there are Christian communities inside the city, Muslims, there are Jews, and most tribes are neighbors to each other."[29] Some respondents emphasized that tensions are managed because of the strong relationship between Dohuk's tribes and religious groups. Others described tribal affiliation itself as an important form of bridging social capital, linking members of both major political parties. One person cited the Iraqi Kurdish civil war between 1994 and 1997 (which pitted KDP and PUK supporters against each other) to argue that Dohuk experienced less violence than other areas because belonging to the same tribe was more important than identification with a political party:[30]

> Dohuk City, KRI (2017): It was not easy for people to kill each other because of political issues. For example, if me and you [are] from the Doski tribe, but I am PUK and you are KDP, we don't kill each other because we are from same tribe.

As in Baghdad, Dohuk and Semel residents also reported a history of coordinated collective action between different religious groups. In line with earlier research in the disaster recovery literature, residents cited the importance of informal ties to individuals from different socioeconomic backgrounds—i.e., those who would not be accessible through bonding capital alone—and also through connections to organizations that could provide support through institutional channels:

> Dohuk City, KRI (2017): When someone has a health problem, or needs a funeral, or needs to go to the hospital and doesn't have money, people give donations. They also do this when there is a wedding but a family is not rich.

> Semel, KRI (2017): In 2010, there was a Kurdish city called Wan on the Turkish side that suffered a big earthquake, and the people of Duhok did a big campaign for the people of Wan. Nobody told us to do it—you would just see collection boxes outside so many stores or mosques, you put whatever you can donate into the box, and then that organization would send it.

Bridging capital in Dohuk City was also evident in strong economic support networks. "Very poor doesn't exist here," said another respondent, adding, "I don't know anyone who doesn't have enough food for a day." Chen and colleagues have suggested that such "informal arrangements for sharing economic gains with friends and neigh-

---

[29] Interview with a local NGO director in Dohuk, June 12, 2017.

[30] An important piece of this dynamic is the greater salience of tribal identity to Dohuk residents over political affiliation. An exploration of these dynamics is unfortunately outside the scope of this research.

bors in need may lessen relative deprivation."[31] These informal networks might have lessened the perceived unfair distribution of humanitarian aid and job opportunities discussed earlier.

Neighborhoods whose residents interacted frequently before 2003 on shared neighborhood problems were also more successful in organizing and executing actions critical to maintaining safety and security during periods of sectarian conflict. This is because prior cooperation helped build a sense of trust and community within neighborhoods and helped residents develop shared expectations about their respective roles in addressing problems and how best to coordinate their actions:[32]

> Al-Dhubat, Baghdad (2010): People self-organized to protect Yaqin mosque that was inside of the neighborhood and no one was able to reach it. They were not organized; they just wanted to protect the mosque from any enemy. There was no leader.
>
> Al-Karadah, Baghdad (2010): The good relationship between the people that was built in the previous years was sufficient to face [sectarian] tensions.
>
> Al-Kuraiaat, Baghdad (2010): Sunnis and Shi'ites had good relations with each other and they worked and cooperated to main[tain] security in the neighborhood. The people respect and value the old relationship.

Dohuk residents also attributed their successes to established relationships. When IS kidnapped a Yezidi family from Semel, local leaders were able to quickly organize their rescue by pulling together men from different tribes and villages into an ad hoc rescue team. "They were able to do it because we had worked together in the past, and we knew each other."[33]

Vertical (Linking) Relationships

Vertical relationships connect people in a community with institutions and authorities that are often (but not always) *external* to that community.[34] Vertical relationships

---

[31] A.C. Chen, V. M. Keith, K. J. Leong, C. Airriess, W. Li, K. Y. Chung, and C. C. Lee, "Hurricane Katrina: Prior Trauma, Poverty and Health Among Vietnamese-American Survivors," *International Nursing Review*, Vol. 54, No. 4, 2007.

[32] This phenomenon is also referred to as a *mental model*. Shared mental models allow people to "anticipate one another's actions and to coordinate their behaviors, especially when time and circumstances do not permit overt and lengthy communication and strategizing among team members" (Beng-Chong Lim and Katherine J. Klein, "Team Mental Models and Team Performance: A Field Study of the Effects of Team Mental Model Similarity and Accuracy," *Journal of Organizational Behaviour*, Vol. 27, 2006, p. 405).

[33] Focus group in Dohuk, June 8, 2017.

[34] Glenn A. Bowen, "Social Capital, Social Funds and Poor Communities: An Exploratory Analysis," *Social Policy and Administration*, Vol. 43, No. 3, 2009; Ichiro Kawachi, Daniel Kim, Adam Coutts, and S. V. Subrama-

connect individuals and communities to the government and financial markets. However, both systems were in flux during Iraq's sectarian civil war. Despite this fact, Al-Karadah, Al-Kuraiaat, and Palestine Street had strong links to markets because they had been centers of commerce prior to the U.S. invasion. This had two effects. First, their relatively high socioeconomic status reduced residents' vulnerability to sectarian recruitment efforts. Although both Al-Kuraiaat and Al-Karadah were Shi'ite-majority neighborhoods and Palestine Street bordered Sadr City, the Mahdi Army was not able to gain a foothold in these areas. "The middle class viewed Mahdi Army as a challenge," a resident of Al-Karadah explained. A resident of Al-Kuraiaat noted succinctly, "businessmen know full well that violence is bad for profit."

The second effect for centers of commerce like Al-Karadah and Al-Kuraiaat was that new officials and visitors set up residence there after Saddam's regime fell. "Al-Karadah became a center for the residence of the officials and [the security forces that] were protecting themselves and the people," noted one respondent. Their residences required additional security presence by Coalition and Iraqi Army forces:

> Al-Kuraiaat, Baghdad (2010): As the state grew stronger . . . the army began to deploy checkpoints and this saved the people from kidnapping.

Better security in Al-Karadah and Al-Kuraiaat helped prevent large numbers of its residents from fleeing, thereby preventing the negative effects of dislocation. In other areas, wealthy residents who could afford to leave did so as sectarian tension mounted, leaving behind poor residents who were preyed on more easily. "Many Sunnis and rich people left their houses for Syria and Jordan," recounted a resident of Al-Bayaa'. "Only poor people remained and many of them were forced to serve the terrorists. People had to cook for them and harbor them in their houses."

Residents in Al-Dhubat, the Sunni-majority neighborhood in the otherwise violent Zayouna district, also achieved a high level of security through vertical ties. Because Al-Dhubat is a small residential area, the links were contained in the close relationships that connected ordinary residents to the neighborhood's founding Haj Raad Tabra family, rather than through a cooperative relationship with the Iraqi Army.[35] The Tabra family provided the whole neighborhood (not just its own residences) with a sophisticated border-monitoring system, including surveillance equipment, cameras, civilian checkpoints, and electricity generators.

---

nian, "Commentary: Reconciling the Three Accounts of Social Capital," *International Journal of Epidemiology*, Vol. 33, No. 4, 2004; Janaina Macke and Eliete Kunrath Dilly, "Social Capital Dimensions in Collaborative Networks: The Role of Linking Social Capital," *International Journal of Social Inquiry*, Vol. 3, No. 2, 2010; and Jenny Muir, "Bridging and Linking in a Divided Society: A Social Capital Case Study from Northern Ireland," *Urban Studies*, Vol. 48, No. 5, 2011.

[35] The Iraqi Army, reconstituted after "de-Ba'thification," largely abandoned Sunni-dominant areas, leaving them vulnerable to AQI.

A second factor in Al-Dhubat's resilience was the continuity of vertical ties to government institutions that was lacking in other Sunni-dominant areas during de-Ba'thification. Many of Al-Dhubat's elder residents were former high-ranking military officers. They had served "during the 1958 revolution that overthrew the Hashemite monarchy, . . . are not pro-Ba'thists, [and] hold different views from the other Sunni areas, not only of the sect but [a] different view of the politics."[36] In other words, they did not feel aggrieved or threatened by the changes taking place.

It must be noted that the combination of vertical and *overlapping* links[37] between local leaders in Baghdad and external tribal authorities in Al-Anbar had a negative impact on community resilience. The Baghdad case study found that the Ba'thist elites and former government officials who lived in Al-'Amiriyah were situated within a complex tribal network that connected members of Saddam's Al-Bu Nasir tribe to the Dulaimi tribes in Al-Anbar, where AQI had been operating with tribal support since 2004.[38] AQI leveraged the tribal networks (via smuggling and trade routes) to enter Al-A'dhamiya and Al-'Amiriyah neighborhoods; it also entered Al-Doura from nearby rural Arab Jabur on the boundaries of Baghdad City.[39]

Thus, resilience sometimes depends on being able to disconnect from a larger network with potential negative impacts. Palestine Street, Al-Dhubat, Al-Kuraiaat, and Al-Karadah were more insulated from the external interference of tribal support for various militias because tribal leaders did not figure as prominently in local governance as "old Baghdadis,"[40] or descendants of prominent families involved in Ottoman gov-

---

[36] Email correspondence with a YouGov research coordinator, January 12, 2011.

[37] Overlapping links bond members of a subgroup to other members of the same subgroup in other locations. Tribal affiliation falls into this category of social capital.

[38] Austin Long, "The Anbar Awakening," *Survival*, Vol. 50, No. 2, 2008, p. 74. Al-Anbar is the largest province in Iraq and its residents are entirely Sunni and from the Dulaim tribe, whose membership extends into Syria, Saudi Arabia, and Jordan (Al-Zarqawi's birthplace). These links dated back to the Iran–Iraq war. As more party members (especially members of the Ba'th militia, known as the Popular Army) were sent to the front, the presence of loyal Ba'thists in tribal areas was thinned. This forced increasing reliance on tribal loyalty, and Hussein widened the circle of tribes he relied on, drawing heavily on the large Dulaimi confederation in Al-Anbar.

[39] In fact, both Sunni and Shi'a tribes controlled smuggling and trade networks into particular parts of the city, and with their blessing, AQI and the Mahdi Army used those networks to facilitate movement of people and guns.

[40] Although tribal authorities were not entirely absent, respondents described old families as the *legitimate* local leaders and reported a greater reliance on these respected old families for solving problems and resolving conflicts. For example, in Al-Dhubat, problems were reportedly resolved through the help of "trusted old families," as well as neighbors and friends. Respondents from the two other resilient Shi'a neighborhoods (Al-Kuraiaat and Al-Karadah) reported that Sheikhs were present but were more ambivalent about their influence on neighborhood affairs and stated that they were needed only for tribal disputes, and that not everyone went to them.

ernance.⁴¹ Leaders from these trusted old families made decisions based on the security of the neighborhood, not the sectarian agenda of external tribal authorities.

Local leaders also figured prominently in Dohuk. Dohuk residents were more likely to trust and seek help from informal leaders than from elected officials or the justice system. Policing and security were achieved cooperatively via strong vertical relationships between state authorities and informal tribal leaders (aghas) and religious leaders (mullahs). Each relied on the other for judicial administration. "The court will sometimes ask the Agha [tribal leader] or the Mullah [religious leader] to get involved in particular cases" to help enforce its verdict.⁴²

Likewise, tribal leaders told Dohuk police when and where they conducted mediations, because tribal customs permit revenge acts of violence in cases where dialogue fails. In such cases, police intervened by arresting the alleged perpetrator (as much for protection as for due process), protecting their extended family, and issuing warnings to aggrieved parties on both sides.⁴³ The result was an interlocking security structure involving "a great deal of cooperation between the police and courts and the informal leaders" to manage local disputes.⁴⁴

Dohuk also is connected to regional, national, and international systems that bolstered its resilience. Regional cooperation between Kurdish defense forces and the large Shammar tribe played a key role in the ability to keep IS out of the Kurdistan region.⁴⁵ KDP leaders also worked with "paramilitary forces affiliated with Turkey . . . and the National Mobilization (Al-Hashd Al-Watani) forces of Athil Al-Nujaifi, the former

---

⁴¹ Notable families are a typical social formation throughout the Arab lands of the former Ottoman Empire. They were a social class of urban elites who had served as intermediaries between the Ottoman state and the larger Iraqi population.

⁴² Focus group in Dohuk, June 8, 2017.

⁴³ Focus group in Dohuk, June 8, 2017.

⁴⁴ Focus group in Dohuk, June 9, 2017.

⁴⁵ Vertical social capital facilitates adaptive capacity but does not guarantee it. Achieving the formal alliance that resulted in a major military victory in Rabia required a three-month negotiation between tribal leadership and KRI President Masoud Barzani. The immediacy of the threat posed by IS in Shammar territory created incentives for cooperation. However, perceived and real grievances stemmed from "the rise of Kurdish influence, and Shammar claim [that] the KDP has taken steps to marginalize their political, economic and social power" around Rabia and the greater province. The recent alliance between the KRG and the Shammar tribe was made possible by (1) the Shammar tribe's "long-established tribal policy of building relations with the dominant adjacent power"; (2) the immediacy of the threat posed by IS in Shammar territory; and (3) a more recent context of cooperation between large Sunni tribes and the Kurds relating to mutually beneficial oil contracts between the KRG and international oil companies, which benefit the tribes. See Christine van den Toorn and Ahmed Ali, "Challenges and Opportunities in Post-ISIS Territories: The Case of Rabia," Institute of Regional and International Studies, IRIS Iraq Report, August 3, 2015.

governor of Ninevah Province, who has been living in Erbil since being displaced from Mosul in summer 2014."[46]

Transgovernmental humanitarian aid agreements have enabled large resource flows critical to Dohuk's local response capacity. Aside from the benefit of emergency assistance, NGOs serving the displaced created a secondary labor market for English-speaking Kurds, helping many supplement their reduced public-sector salaries. City officials are connected to regional and international actors through the KRG's Joint Crisis Coordination Center (JCC).[47] JCC is a humanitarian-government coordination platform that works closely with its counterpart in Baghdad (the Joint Coordination and Monitoring Centre) and with hundreds of aid organizations. JCC's integrative potential is high but is severely curtailed by the fraught relationship between Erbil and Baghdad. However, one positive local impact, achieved through information-sharing at monthly meetings, was the identification and banning of sectarian relief organizations that were distributing aid to Christian and Sunni families and excluding Shi'a households.[48]

Military coordination is another aspect of vertical linkage. The military agreement among Erbil, Baghdad, and the U.S.-led coalition resulted in Combined Joint Task Force—Operation Inherent Resolve (CJTF-OIR), which coordinated military operations between the Iraqi Army, Shi'ite militias (Hashd al-Shaabi or Popular Mobilization Units), and different Peshmerga forces. CJTF-OIR also has been a platform for mediating tensions between Erbil and Baghdad over the KDP policy of laying claim to contested territories during the offensive against IS. High-ranking coalition officers have facilitated negotiations between KRG and the government of Iraq over shared land use,[49] the distribution of oil revenue from Kirkuk,[50] and the provision of security in the disputed territories.[51] These instrumental agreements are not sustainable in the

---

[46] Renad Mansour, "Mosul After the Islamic State: The Kurdistan Region's Strategy," Carnegie Middle East Center, May 20, 2016.

[47] The KRG established JCC in 2014 "as a lead institution for coordination and management of all phases of crisis and disaster, such as risk assessment and mitigation, early warning and preparedness, response, and management, including preparedness, mitigation, response, and recovery to the current humanitarian crisis and all future man-made and natural disasters and crises as well as new emergencies." The center is led by a director general under the Minister of Interior. See Kurdistan Regional Government of Iraq, Ministry of Interior, "Joint Crisis Coordination Centre," webpage, undated.

[48] Interview with Hoshang Mohamed, JCC Director General, in Erbil, June 17, 2017.

[49] U.S. Department of Defense, *Assessment of U.S. and Coalition Forces to Train, Advise, Assist, and Equip the Kurdish Security Forces in Iraq*, Washington, D.C.: Office of the Inspector General, DODIG-2017-033, December 16, 2016, p. 8.

[50] Stephen Kalin and Dmitry Zhdannikov, "U.S. Helped Clinch Iraq Oil Deal to Keep Mosul Battle on Track," Reuters, October 3, 2016.

[51] Laurie Mylroie, "U.S.-Led Coalition Supports Continuing Talks Between Erbil and Baghdad," Kurdistan 24, November 15, 2017

long term. However, KRG officials refer to these examples to emphasize that third-party assistance in future political negotiations was a key component of "the kind of cooperation that is needed and that works."⁵²

So far, this chapter has argued that communities with strong horizontal relationships between religious and ethnic groups (bridging ties) and vertical relationships to centers of power (linking ties) were better equipped to deal positively and proactively with rising sectarianism, along with the violence and displacement it caused. The following section explains how these communities did so.

Translating Trust to Action

Cooperative relationships between different groups are based on interactions that fluctuate over time. Relationships are never static, and the incentives for cooperation versus conflict can shift dramatically during political or social uncertainty. Even where pre-existing cross-cutting relationships *do* exist, they tend to deteriorate rapidly in crisis environments without concerted efforts to nurture, protect, and strengthen them. In times of uncertainty and crisis, fears can grow quickly about the "other," and people's behavior deteriorates to match their assumptions about how the other is likely to act. Three strategies sustained and strengthened intergroup relations in Baghdad neighborhoods and Dohuk City: conflict resolution processes, leadership advocacy, and border monitoring. In different but complementary ways, each helped prevent the spread of sectarian attitudes and behavior.

Conflict-Resolution Processes

Conflict-resolution processes are critical to sustain high levels of trust between groups. In Baghdad neighborhoods, people engaged in spontaneous behavior intended to manage rising tensions associated with the violence surrounding them. People played the role of informal "street" mediators in order to counter sectarian mobilization. Discussions of political or religious issues were taboo under Hussein's regime, but the new coalition government encouraged "open and free debate of ideas":

> Al-A'dhamiya, Baghdad (2010): Young people started to gather at the street corners because of the unemployment. They had many discussions and debates among themselves. They divided into Shi'ite and Sunni groups with the spread of sectarianism. Friends of different sects stopped greeting each other after that. They avoided mixing because they would only talk about Omar and Ali.

Self-organized intervention in those street conversations was a conflict-resolution intervention strategy reported in all four Baghdad neighborhoods:

---

[52] Interview with a representative from the JCC, Erbil, June 15, 2017.

Al-Kuraiaat, Baghdad (2010): There were heated arguments between Sunnis and Shi'ites; they started calling each other names and accus[ing] each other of being sectarian but no killing; people from both communities would intervene to settle those arguments.

Al-Dhubat, Baghdad (2010): I don't mean they never talked about such things; I meant that they don't talk about Sunnis or Shi'ites in a degrading way. When arguments started, people tried to calm things down while other guys [in other areas] make things worse.

Informal mediation is extremely effective in reducing conflict escalation in small communities.[53] When people participate in small-group discussions like the ones described above, they are more likely to express extreme positions and advocate riskier actions than they did before.[54] Between high-prejudice individuals, such discussion can increase and intensify preexisting attitudes, worsening group polarization.[55] Street mediation helped prevent these psychological changes from taking root and spreading.

At the Dohuk City level, conflict-resolution processes were embedded in formal networks, organizations, and structures. Although informal conflict-resolution processes existed,[56] respondents believed that the most impactful initiatives were embedded in formal programs and organizations. Each initiative described was also intentionally designed to pass peacebuilding and conflict-resolution skills from person to person. These and similar programs were designed to create horizontal and vertical connections—no doubt because many of them originated in organizations with experience in peacebuilding theory and practice.

Between 2009 and 2010, Mercy Corps' Governance Promotion through Conflict Management in Iraq program "supported a nationwide network of 87 Iraqi leaders who are committed to promoting good governance and reconciliation through consensus-based negotiation." The Network of Iraqi Facilitators (NIF) was trained in negotiation, mediation, coaching, and mentoring skills. They subsequently "worked together across regional, political, and sectarian lines of division to resolve almost 130 major disputes, including tribal conflicts over land, tensions between citizens and government over services, disputes over elections, and clashes between rival factions of the Iraqi army and police." In the KRI, NIF "brought together Sunnis and Shi'ites, Arabs

---

[53] William Ury, *The Third Side: Why We Fight and How We Can Stop*, London: Penguin Books, 2003.

[54] D. J. Isenberg, "Group Polarization: A Critical Review and Meta-Analysis," *Journal of Personality and Social Psychology*, Vol. 50, No. 6, 1986.

[55] David G. Myers and G. D. Bishop, "Discussion Effects on Racial Attitude," *Science*, Vol 169, No. 3947, 1970.

[56] For example, two police officers recently decided to start using mediation to settle car accidents so that parties did not escalate tensions by involving tribes (Focus group, June 8, 2017).

and Kurds, and members from the rival Kurdish political parties" and helped resolve disputes between the PUK and KDP over control of labor unions in Dohuk.[57]

Three other initiatives that originated in Dohuk are local Peace Education workshops, Peace Journalism trainings, and Interfaith Dialogues. The community Peace Education workshops teach a three-day curriculum of techniques and strategies for resolving conflicts peacefully. They were organized by the University of Dohuk, which has KRI's first and only degree program in peace and conflict resolution. Like the Mercy Corps project, the workshops aimed to create a multiplier effect by "creating ambassadors of peace in schools, youth centers, and IDP and refugee camps."[58] In fact, local NGOs have adapted the curriculum in the work they do around the governorate. "I now use 80 percent of what I learned in the workshops I conduct for [Dak Organization for Yazidi Women's Development]. The women I have trained have welcomed the idea. They have always lived in peace with other religious groups."[59]

Peace Journalism trainings aim to produce the same positive impacts at the level of public discourse. Attendees are selected for their positions in various media outlets, which enable them to impact discourse, and for their commitment to "activist journalism" by writing stories that incorporate principles of ethnic reconciliation.[60] In one such training, participants focused on how the current conflict has influenced minorities in Sinjar, Nineveh, Tal Afar, and Mosul.[61] Participants were instructed to identify and describe major problems in each area and their impacts on Yezidis, Chaldeans, Assyrians, Turkmen, and Shabak communities. Feedback from the trainer was illustrative of the training's intended impact:

> Dohuk, KRI (2017): The way you are describing these problems is as though you are politicians, or religious leaders. Yes, fundamentalism is increasing, but what should these communities *do* about that? This is the job of the journalist: You must write about this in a different way—it must have some sort of message regarding reconciliation.

---

[57] Mercy Corps–Iraq, *Governance Promotion Through Conflict Management in Iraq (GPCMI): Final Evaluation—Results, Lessons Learned, and Recommendations for Future Programming*, January 2009–December 2010.

[58] Interview with Joutyar M. R. Sedeeq, Director of the University of Dohuk Center for Peace and Conflict Resolution Studies, January 20, 2017. High school students who attended the Peace Education workshops founded more than a dozen "youth peace clubs" that reproduced the conflict-resolution trainings (and created new adaptations through theater) to engage displaced youth in high schools and IDP or refugee camps around Dohuk governorate.

[59] Muftah, "Ambassadors of Peace in Northern Iraq," webpage, undated.

[60] Interview with Khider Domle, June 7, 2017. Dohuk trainings are organized by Domle, who is a well-known Yazidi journalist, activist, and recent author of *The Black Death*, a book about the kidnapping and sexual enslavement of Yazidi women and girls.

[61] The author observed this training during field research. Journalists from newspapers, news agencies, magazines, NGOs, and social media news websites (Kurdish news agency, Azaman and Ainkawa news agency, and a Syrian news agency) were in attendance.

By the end of the training, each journalist had developed a media story for dissemination later that week.

Interfaith Dialogue projects use a similar logic of targeting key stakeholders and have been conducted at all levels of society in Dohuk governorate.[62] The University of Dohuk has organized Interfaith Conflict Resolution Meetings between Muslim, Yazidi, Assyrian, and Chaldean leaders for five years. Participants stated that these dialogues had promoted tolerance and increased their trust of other members over time.[63] Participants in the January 2017 dialogue gave unanimous affirmative feedback to this question and further requested that the university extend the dialogue model downward into communities:[64]

> Dohuk, KRI (2017): I have learned so much about other religions coming here, and that kind of awareness needs to extend down into the community. Can the university assist in facilitating these kinds of meetings at the community level?

> Dohuk, KRI (2017): The audience here believes in peace. We are not reaching the clergy who believe in and are fomenting violence. How can we reach the clergy who don't believe in peace and non-violence?

Newer initiatives have built on the same methods of conflict-resolution training and intervention. Community-based mediation structures, called peace committees, have been actively intervening in IS-cleared areas since 2016. The peace committees were set up as part of the Nineveh Paths Project, which was funded by the United Nations Development Program and run by the Department of Peace Operations and a local NGO partner, Un Ponte Per. The goal of the peace committees was to prevent youth recruitment and improve intercommunity relations "using dialogue, mediation and restorative justice practices customized for local context, culture, and ownership."[65] The project's original funding cycle ran from October 2015 to March 2016, but at the

---

[62] At the grassroots level, for example, the priest at Our Lady Monastery in Al-Quosh has been convening regular dialogues with Christian, Yezidi, and Muslim leaders.

[63] This feedback was given during the January 2017 Interfaith Dialogue, "Peace and Conflict Resolution After ISIS," 5th Annual Dialogue, University of Duhok's Center for Peace and Conflict Resolution, Duhok, Iraq, 2017.

[64] For a history of this project and others organized by the Center for Peace and Conflict Resolution Studies, see University of Duhok, "Peace and Conflict Resolution Studies Center," webpage, undated.

[65] Peace, Action, Training, and Research Institute of Romania, "Ninevah Paths to Social Cohesion, Coexistence, and Peace," webpage, undated. The initiatives include "public awareness raising campaigns and programs to address and prevent youth recruitment and improve inter-community relations; direct interventions by community-based mediation structures (local peace committees), institutional peace councils, community measures for transitional justice and women's and youth peace teams." Kai Brand-Jacobsen, *Ninevah Paths Towards Just and Lasting Peace*, Duhok, Iraq: Un Ponte Per and Peace, Action, Training, and Research Institute of Romania, April 2016.

time of this writing, the project has been extended to support new community-based interventions and monitor and evaluate their impact more rigorously.

Leadership Advocacy for Coexistence

Credible leaders who promote a narrative of peaceful coexistence can reduce tensions. Advocacy by local religious leaders in Baghdad neighborhoods had a tremendous impact on the adoption or rejection of sectarian attitudes and behaviors. In the four resilient neighborhoods, and consistent with other studies, religious leaders articulated core values and traditions to advocate for nonviolence. In Al-Karadah, a prominent local Imam explicitly forbade young people from attacking Sunni mosques, and in Al-Kuraiaat, Al-Karadah, and Palestine Street, religious leaders spoke out regularly against sectarianism. Religious leaders in Dohuk conveyed a similar message and on a regular basis; multiple respondents reported that "the mullahs used every Friday sermon to encourage us to go out and help the refugees."

Leadership advocacy at the Dohuk City level also included messaging by the political elite. Kurdish leaders across the political spectrum have successfully propagated a strong cultural narrative of the KRI as a place of tolerance and coexistence in order to garner support from the wider international community. "The Kurdish leadership spoke the language of pluralism, human rights, and international norms in the effort to acquire international recognition and legitimacy."[66] However, this narrative also reflects how the majority of Kurds see themselves, and political leaders used it to shape public opinion as the humanitarian crisis grew. In 2015, for example, Erbil's governor responded to rising fears over IS infiltration of refugee and IDP camps in Dohuk. He issued an authoritative statement that reinforced the government's prevailing narrative that refugees and IDPs were victims requiring assistance and sympathy, not security threats.[67] President Barzani also gave several formal televised statements regarding the welcoming of IDPs. Interviewees believed that Barzani's messaging in particular had reduced tensions as newcomers began streaming into the region, because it impacted leadership structures at municipal and local levels:

> Dohuk, KRI (2017): There was a statement by Barzani to receive the IDPs and treat them very well. The tribal and religious leaders received this statement and worked on it . . . and the media especially in Duhok did good work to receive these people. And then it had an impact on the host communities and on the IDPs and refugees also. Because the IDPs were also afraid of the host community—how were they going to treat them? There was a big tension between the two.

---

[66] Ranj Alaaldin, "Kurdistan's Political Landscape and the Path Towards Independence," in Sasha Toperich, Tea Ivanovic, and Nahro Zagros, eds., *Iraqi Kurdistan Region: A Path Forward*, Baltimore, Md.: Johns Hopkins University Center for Transatlantic Relations, 2017, p. 51.

[67] Kurdistan Regional Government of Iraq, "Erbil Governor: 'IDPs Pose No Security Threat,'" webpage, September 18, 2015.

Dohuk, KRI (2017): Barzani's statement was picked up by local religious leaders and repeated every Friday.

As recounted by a leading member of the Yezidi religious community, the role of the Islamic clergy was important in the days when people fled Sinjar. "They told people, you have to provide help, open the doors of the mosques, provide safety. The real worship of God is to provide help to people." It was not inevitable that local religious leaders would pick up and share Barzani's message. Local clergy are ideologically heterogeneous, belong to different Islamic political parties, and often have complicated relationships with KDP leadership. Historically however, disaster has had a unifying effect on Islamist and secular leaders in Kurdistan, and even Islamists were largely united in condemning (and distancing themselves from) the atrocities committed by IS.[68] Whatever their reasons, the clergy's persistent messaging was critical in shaping how people responded to aiding the "other" in the context of crisis.[69]

Border Monitoring

Restricting a militia's access to a particular area is a short-term solution, with an important long-term impact: protecting people from exposure to violence. The credible threat and enactment of violence not only creates a fear-induced conformity that limits residents' responses to active or tacit cooperation but also makes people more likely to express support for violent religious extremism.[70] Thus, a defining feature of community resilience in Baghdad neighborhoods and in Dohuk was the ability to prevent the physical entry of sectarian militias and their recruiters.

The Baghdad neighborhoods did this by setting up local defense groups to defend boundaries and existing populations regardless of religion, rather than by driving out certain residents or carrying out attacks in other places:[71]

Palestine Street, Baghdad (2010): Some alleys formed self-protection groups, only for a limited period of time . . . [in] the beginning, when they faced the extremists. They were all our friends. The people had good relationships with them. They didn't make problems with the people. They prevented the entry of extremists to the neighborhood and they didn't misuse their power.

---

[68] Rebaz Ali, "Kurdistan and the Challenge of Islamism: A Conversation with Dr. Hadi Ali, Former Chairman of Kurdistan Islamic Union's Political Bureau," Washington, D.C.: Hudson Institute, August 14, 2015.

[69] Nathan C. Funk and Abdul Aziz Said, "Islam and the West: Narratives of Conflict and Conflict Transformation," *International Journal of Peace Studies*, Vol. 9, No. 1, 2004.

[70] Finkel et al., 2016.

[71] Both Anderson and Wallace (2012) and Carpenter (2016) identified this as an important factor in successful resistance strategies.

> Al-Kuraiaat, Baghdad (2010): Some good people in the neighborhood donated their rifles and trusted the young people of the neighborhood to protect [them] . . . Nobody paid them. They didn't misuse their authorities and had a good relationship with the people. They didn't belong to any party.

KDP peshmerga forces guarded the border areas proximate to Dohuk City[72] and were largely successful in preventing IS from entering the city. However, Peshmerga forces were spread thin during IS's offensive into nearby Sinjar, and IS militants were sometimes able to enter Dohuk. In these cases, residents pulled together in ad hoc defense groups:

> Semel, KRI (2017): Sometimes when daesh came near this area, people formed volunteer groups to protect themselves because the police and Peshmerga were fighting somewhere else, so people had to protect themselves.

Discussion

Social capital is a critical ingredient in the ability of communities to withstand internal and external shocks that heighten the risk of sectarian conflict. In the context of Iraq, the physical layout of urban centers—especially integrated housing and public spaces for different religious groups to interact and socialize—increased social capital. In addition, the ability of local governance structures (tribal, religious, and familial) to provide public services incentivized further cross-sectarian cooperation.[73] Repeated interactions over time built a durable type of bridging trust based on personal observation and knowledge about the dependability of others.[74] Where bridging social trust between groups was lacking, as in Al-Za'faraniya and Al-Bayaa', residents instead organized by sect. Those neighborhoods ended up with separate local militias or were ultimately "occupied" by either AQI or the Mahdi Army.

Working together on public service projects had two additional effects. First, as people worked together, they shared knowledge and learned from each other, which led

---

[72] Peshmerga forces were spread thin during IS's offensive into nearby Sinjar. However, IS also might have been able to exploit coordination problems between KDP and PUK, each of which controlled part of the governorate's larger border. Dohuk was guarded by three KDP peshmerga units (Asayish, or secret police; 80 Unit; and Zerevani forces). Policies and operational practices differed between KDP and PUK units. See Mario Fumerton and Wladimir van Wilgenburg, "Kurdistan's Political Armies: The Challenge of Unifying the Peshmerga Forces," Carnegie Middle East Center, December 16, 2015.

[73] This is also called *task cohesion*, or shared commitment among members to achieve a goal that requires the collective efforts of a group.

[74] See Margaret Levi, "When Good Defenses Make Good Neighbors," in Claude Menard, ed., *Institutions, Contracts, and Organizations: Perspectives from New Institutional Economics*, Chichester, U.K.: Edward Elgar, 2000.

to the construction of shared expectations of the task at hand (e.g., trash cleanup), working relationships (e.g., who does what), task strategies, and how to solve potential problems.[75] This enabled people to coordinate and anticipate others' needs and responses, building a capacity that could be drawn on in times of crisis. Second, working together helped communities develop a sense of their own agency. People's shared belief in their ability to achieve results catalyzed local actors to organize and execute actions critical to their safety and security. The community's actual responses—conflict resolution, leadership behaviors, and security strategies—all helped prevent the spread of sectarian attitudes and behavior, buffering communities from the potential spillover effect of sectarian conflict in neighboring areas.

The local capacity of communities to remain resilient in the face of sectarian conflict varied across the cases considered. Resilience in Baghdad neighborhoods depended less on the presence of international security and development organizations and more on local actors, social networks, ad hoc organizations, and community leaders. Resilience in Dohuk depended heavily on those international security and development organizations that helped mitigate the humanitarian crisis, create a new job market, partner with security forces, and mediate tensions between Erbil and Baghdad.

In Baghdad neighborhoods, conflict resolution was self-organized and informal. Spontaneous third-party interventions or "street mediation" successfully de-escalated public arguments, positively affecting sectarian relations. At the city level, conflict resolution processes were embedded in formal networks, organizations, and structures; moreover, many processes were designed to have an impact on a broader scale. For example, the NIF has shifted away from "small domestic or criminal disputes (e.g., car accidents between individuals or family disputes over housing) to larger, more complex, multi-stakeholder disputes involving issues such as tribal competition over land or political disputes."[76]

Advocacy by local religious leaders had a positive impact on the rejection of sectarian attitudes and behaviors at both scales (neighborhood and city). At the city level, however, advocacy necessarily included messaging by the political elite. Border monitoring at both scales was largely defensive, oriented toward defending boundaries and existing populations. However, this resilience factor does not scale as well from small to large areas. Border monitoring is easier in small areas, where people can recognize strangers who do not belong to the community. In a large area like Dohuk, the process of recognizing strange faces has become a region-wide policy of withholding access to the area not just by potential IS members but also by Arab Iraqis in general. Although Dohuk has provided refuge, security details, and housing for displaced Sunni Arab

---

[75] Janis A. Cannon-Bowers, Eduardo Salas, and Sharolyn Converse, "Shared Mental Models in Expert Team Decision Making," in N. John Castellan, ed., *Individual and Group Decision Making*, Hillsdale, N.J.: Lawrence Erlbaum Associates, 1993.

[76] Mercy Corps–Iraq, January 2009–December 2010.

leaders from Mosul (people they believe they can trust, like politicians, sheikhs, academics, and clerics), the official policy bars entry of Arabs to the governorate without the explicit permission of the asayish (Kurdish police forces).

Conclusion

Such crises as the U.S. invasion of Iraq in 2003 or IS's invasion of Mosul in 2014 do not, in and of themselves, cause ordinary people to take up arms against each other. The escalation of sectarian conflict proceeds in stages that only eventually lead to the demonization of the "other" and widespread violence. Sectarian actors encourage this transformation; most communities work against it. This chapter has argued that communities with strong horizontal relationships between religious and ethnic groups (bridging ties) and vertical relationships to centers of power (linking ties) are more likely to remain resilient to sectarian conflict.

CHAPTER SIX

Lessons and Policy Recommendations for Countering Sectarianism

Jeffrey Martini and Dalia Dassa Kaye
RAND Corporation

There is no denying that sectarianism has become a defining feature of the modern Middle East. Whether driven by political elites as regime-survival strategies or by major powers as part of power plays for regional influence, the conflicts and politics of the region have made these identities real over time in ways that will be difficult to reverse. This does not mean, however, that we should accept that sectarianism and sectarian violence cannot be prevented, or at least reduced. Indeed, at least at the local level, this study has demonstrated that communities can resist the slide toward sectarianism, bucking broader regional trends toward sectarian framing and manipulation of conflicts.

Contrary to common policy debates that paint the Middle East as a hopeless bastion of sectarian conflict, even countries that have experienced deadly sectarian civil wars have demonstrated levels of resilience in countering sectarian forces. Identifying resilience in sectarian contexts does not suggest that we ignore the real sectarian identities that continue to exist across the region. In all four cases considered in this report, some segment of the population adheres to religious identity in ways that are exclusionary of outsiders. But it is possible to reduce the salience of sectarianism, even in highly sectarian settings.

For this reason, we chose to focus on cases with mixed sectarian populations and histories of sectarian tension or conflict; in other words, the challenging cases. By identifying resilience among communities in even these difficult cases—Lebanon, Bahrain, Syria, and Iraq—we can draw broader lessons and policy recommendations for bolstering resilience in the Middle East with the aim to prevent—or at least minimize—the intensity of violent conflict.

This final chapter summarizes the main arguments advanced in the four case studies, identifies common themes and lessons, and concludes with a discussion of policy implications for the United States and international partners. This chapter should help readers understand the factors that account for resilience to sectarianism and what policymakers can do to support a community's resilience, or, at a minimum, avoid actions that undermine it.

Summary of Case Study Findings

In Chapter Two of this report, Amanda Rizkallah analyzes municipal politics for clues about what accounts for the Lebanese public's resilience to sectarian identity mobilization. Beginning with the observation that Lebanese voters have shown different levels of support for identity-based voting over time, the author investigates explanations for this variation. Rizkallah contrasts the impressive showing of a cross-sectarian coalition, Beirut Madinati (Beirut, My City), in the 2016 municipal elections with the straight-line sectarian voting on display in the 2010 election cycle. This temporal comparison provides a basis for investigating what factors account for the cross-sectarian voting of 2016 relative to the sectarian hue of the 2010 contest.

Rizkallah argues that two main factors explain this difference. The first is that the declining legitimacy of traditional elites, who are closely associated with sectarian constituencies, created a window of opportunity for a cross-sectarian coalition in 2016. The author further argues that the growing capacity of the challengers, which developed through civil society and professional networks, positioned the leaders of Beirut Madinati to take advantage of this opening in local politics. Thus, Rizkallah attributes the relative resilience of the public in 2016 to a combination of the political opportunity structure and decades of accumulated experience gained by activists and professionals with ambitions to steer Lebanon toward more-technocratic governance.

As to whether Beirut Madinati can grow as a movement and sustain the development of a cross-sectarian political culture, Rizkallah sees some signs for optimism. Internal schisms are one of the principal threats to new political groups, and the movement she profiles has largely succeeded in avoiding these fractures. Moreover, building on the momentum generated by its second-place finish in the 2016 municipal contest, the group subsequently was able to win important leadership positions in professional syndicate elections. Perhaps most importantly, changes to the electoral process—including the introduction of proportional representation at the national level—should clear the path to representation that was blocked by the winner-take-all format of the municipal vote. Finally, generational changes appear to support the growth of this movement and others like it as younger Lebanese cohorts poll as less wedded to traditional elites and less susceptible to sectarian identity mobilization.

Although Beirut Madinati represents promise in Lebanon's political development and speaks to societal resilience to sectarianism despite the scars of the past, the author identifies several challenges to sustaining the momentum generated in 2016. One challenge is that, despite a favorable political environment in 2016 to challenge traditional elites (particularly in the city of Beirut, which was suffering through a trash crisis), Beirut Madinati ultimately finished as the runner-up in the election, revealing the staying power of traditional elites even in an anti-incumbent season. Another factor working against movements like Beirut Madinati is the strategy of external actors who have an interest in hardening, not softening, sectarian identities. Local politicians have to compete against patronage networks financed by external players, principally Saudi Arabia and Iran, which have sought to use sectarian identity to project regional influence. Although the sectarian-oriented efforts of external players can backfire, such as Saudi Arabia's 2018 effort to force the resignation of Prime Minister Saad al-Hariri, external backers still exercise considerable influence and are critical to sustaining the patronage networks that have defined modern Lebanese politics. Finally, nonsectarian movements might struggle to make inroads into Lebanon's lower socioeconomic classes. The cross-sectarian message of Beirut Madinati is decidedly cosmopolitan and privileges technical competence over other forms of legitimacy, attributes that thus far have shown less resonance outside urban settings like Beirut.

In Chapter Three, Justin Gengler examines resilience to sectarianism in Bahrain. Like Rizkallah, Gengler focuses on an urban setting—in this case, different neighborhoods in the sprawling townships outside the capital. A second similarity between the cases is that, although both countries suffer from sharp sectarian tensions and Lebanon has recent historical experience with a sectarian conflict, neither country is experiencing an active civil war. On the other hand, there are several differences in the cases. Gengler focuses on housing choices—as opposed to voting preferences—as a signal of openness to cross-sectarian mixing. In contrast to Rizkallah, who relies on a temporal comparison, Gengler employs a cross-sectional comparison, analyzing two communities to discern what accounts for community resilience to sectarianism. Specifically, he profiles the situations of Bahrainis living in 'Isa Town, a mixed Sunni-Shi'a settlement, with those inhabiting Hamad Town, a virtual sectarian enclave.

Gengler begins from the hypothesis that residential integration (i.e., mixed Sunni-Shi'a neighborhoods) is an important component of resilience to sectarianism. To test this hypothesis, Gengler relies on a combination of neighborhood-level survey data and qualitative observation of local responses to the 2011 uprising. The demographic data show that 'Isa Town is a genuinely mixed area. Of the five districts within 'Isa Town for which the author has detailed demographic information, four reflect a sectarian mix of 60 percent Shi'a to 40 percent Sunni, mirroring the country's broader demographics.[1] Moreover, each district within 'Isa Town shows significant sectarian mixing—no district contains a larger margin than a two-thirds majority for one sect—suggesting that 'Isa Town is integrated at the neighborhood level. Hamad Town presents the opposite situation. Of the ten districts in Hamad Town for which the author has detailed demographic data, five are communally segregated, with at least three-quarters of the population of those districts belonging to a single sect.

This demographic composition is the backdrop for the author's examination of local grievances. Gengler finds strong evidence that government employment, access to public services, and perceptions of economic well-being are all highly contingent

---

[1] Although many authors cite Bahrain's sectarian composition as 65–70 percent Shi'a majority, Gengler's household survey research shows that the Shi'a majority may be a more modest 55–60 percent.

on sect. Bahraini Sunnis—the minority sect but the religious identity of the ruling family—fare better on all of these metrics, whereas Bahraini Shi'a are less likely to reap state benefits (e.g., government employment, social services) and hold worse perceptions of their economic well-being. The trends are more pronounced for those living in communally segregated environments insofar as Sunnis living in more-monolithic Sunni communities fare much better, whereas Shi'a living in more-monolithic Shi'a neighborhoods fare much worse.

Comparing the experiences of 'Isa Town and Hamad Town during the 2011 uprising provides Gengler a window on whether these realities better equipped one area or another to resist the slide into sectarianism that accompanied the aftermath of the 2011 uprising. He found that 'Isa Town—where residents have frequent exposure to sectarian mixing and where the stark divides between Sunni and Shi'a are mitigated by the mixed nature of the community—was less prone to sectarian violence and Sunni reprisals against the Shi'a during the uprising. Lacking the same basis for community resilience, Hamad Town featured violent clashes and retribution. The violence in Hamad Town also had a strong sectarian hue, with Sunni militias cropping up to defend group interests against a neighboring Shi'a village.

The different experiences of 'Isa Town and Hamad Town during the uprising confirm Gengler's hypothesis, suggesting that residential integration acts as a brake on violent conflict during periods of tension. The author attributes this to three mechanisms. First, residential integration implies shared physical space that encourages interactions among sectarian groups, habituating each group to the "other," which can mitigate escalation when tensions do arise between religious communities. Second, mixed neighborhoods thwart regime efforts to target resources to co-sectarians only, a practice that cements sectarian loyalties and works against a Bahraini identity that transcends sect. Third, the existence of integrated communities provides an outlet for inclusive-minded Bahrainis to live out their nonsectarian values, keeping alive their vision of a less sectarian future.

In Chapter Four, Kathleen Reedy analyzes Syria, adding a second case study on resilience in the midst of a civil war. Like two of the other contributors, Reedy employs a cross-sectional comparison, contrasting the strength of sectarian militias in Idlib and Dara'a governorates. Reedy's strategy is to compare Idlib as an example of an area that has fallen prey to sectarian actors with the situation in Dara'a, which has largely proven resilient to the inroads of Sunni sectarian actors. The relative resilience of Dara'a is all the more worthy of examination because it has endured despite a conflict that has generally empowered more sectarian actors among the Sunni Arab armed opposition groups.

The author begins her analysis by considering a series of potential explanations for why Idlib succumbed to Sunni sectarian militias while Dara'a did not. Reedy finds that several of the key variables that might explain the outcome are common between the two areas and thus cannot account for the variation. For instance, both governorates are overwhelmingly Sunni, both are underdeveloped compared with Syria's large urban centers (Damascus and Aleppo) or areas that benefited from sectarian ties to the 'Alawi-led regime (e.g., Latakia), both had similar representation in the Ba'th Party, and neither possesses a strong tribal culture in the present period.

Having considered these variables, Reedy argues that the key distinction between the two governorates is the approach of foreign actors on the governorate borders with neighboring states. Northern Idlib abuts Turkey and contains one of the key crossing points and resupply routes (Bab al-Hawa) for opposition forces in the governorate. As for Dara'a, it abuts Jordan, which provides sanctuary for some elements of the opposition and is an area from which the United States exercises a degree of control via conditions-based assistance. The key difference, Reedy argues, is in the approach of these foreign states.

Reedy sees Turkey as abetting sectarian actors in the service of broader national security objectives. Early on in the war, Turkey's overriding objective was the overthrow of the Assad regime, which Turkey saw as an impediment to stability on its southern border. Over time, that objective has evolved into checking Kurdish autonomy, for which the Sunni-Arab opposition forces are a useful partner. Although Turkey could have chosen to limit its assistance to the "moderate opposition," it appears to have pursued an "all of the above" strategy that has aided such sectarian-tinged groups as Jabhat al-Nusra and Ahrar al-Sham. Those groups have moved closer to Turkey's border to best exploit sanctuary and resupply.

In contrast to Turkey, the Hashemite Kingdom and the United States have taken a much stricter approach to the opposition that operates on the Jordanian border. These external efforts seek to use sanctuary and other forms of assistance to keep opposition units within a more moderate frame of reference. Specifically, the external backers have placed limits on the type of operations these units undertake, policed their relationships with jihadi groups in the area, and attempted to shift their focus to counter ISIS and the provision of local security versus offensives targeting the regime. Reedy argues that this approach accounts for the weak position of sectarian actors in Dara'a governorate, in contrast with the more inviting territory of Idlib.

Finally, in Chapter Five, Ami Carpenter explores one of the two case studies in the volume that address countries in civil war. Carpenter executes two cross-sectional comparisons in Iraq to analyze community resilience during the conflicts that ensued after the 2003 invasion of Iraq. The first component of Carpenter's analysis juxtaposes the experiences of different neighborhoods in Baghdad in 2010, while her second examines four districts within Dohuk governorate (KRI) during the rise of the Islamic State. In both instances, Carpenter relies on in-country fieldwork, and her treatment of two comparisons within her case should increase confidence in the robustness of her findings.

The author's analysis of Baghdad in 2010 focuses on the variation in the presence of sectarian militias and levels of violence perpetrated across neighborhoods. With the overall high level of conflict, Carpenter seeks to explain how some Baghdad neighborhoods (Al-Karadah, Al-Kuraiaat, Palestine Street, and Al-Dhubat) escape the worst violence. Drawing on the conclusions from the Baghdad component of the study, Carpenter then investigates whether these factors are at play in explaining the resilience of Dohuk to identity conflict. Dohuk represents an interesting case because of its stability in the face of an influx of internally displaced Iraqis after the Islamic State seized nearby Mosul, Iraq's second-most–populous city just 50 miles to the south.

Carpenter finds that the factors explaining resilience across these two cross-sectional comparisons are the preexistence of social capital and the formation of adaptive strategies during crises. The specific forms of social capital that Carpenter finds most salient are levels of trust, norms around community participation and cooperation, and social networks that bridge identity groups. The adaptations that are most impactful are the activation of conflict-resolution processes, the efforts of leaders to advocate for peaceful coexistence, and the creation of border-monitoring mechanisms that protect communities from the threat posed by violent sectarians operating in adjacent communities. Carpenter further argues that the presence of both factors—preexisting social capital and adaptive strategies—is necessary to create a strong buffer against sectarian conflict.

Common Themes and Lessons

The rich empirical exploration in all four cases of why some communities are able to counter sectarianism offers a variety of explanatory factors, none of which can be reduced to a single overriding argument for how to account for resilience. All the cases demonstrate a complex interplay of external and domestic factors, offering initial insights that can serve as building blocks for future research on how to stem sectarianism in divided societies.

The cases also highlight a variety of challenges to curtailing sectarian tension and conflict in the region, including the staying power of traditional elites hostile to cross-sectarian cooperation; external actors and regional powers seeking to intensify sectarianism through patronage networks; and socioeconomic gaps that create grievances, making communities more prone to sectarian manipulation. That said, the case study analyses still offer important lessons for how resilience might emerge in even highly sectarian contexts. Although the following list is not exhaustive, it offers an important starting point for future research.

Geography Matters

Borders were a critical factor in several cases in determining whether certain communities became more vulnerable to sectarian actors, often from outside the country. In the Syrian case, the ability of sectarian actors to cross over from Turkey into Idlib was a key driver for higher levels of sectarian violence than in communities on the Jordanian border, like Dara'a, which was better protected and did not face the same types of sectarian-driven actors supported by states. Similarly, in Iraq, the ability to prevent the physical entry of sectarian militias into some neighborhoods helped explain the variation in the levels of sectarian violence in different local communities. In a workshop for the study, one of the experts referred to sectarianism fostered from external sources as some of the most virulent in the region, labeling it "weapons-grade sectarianism." Although borders cannot always prevent sectarian mobilization (such as when sectarian narratives are promoted by media channels that transcend national boundaries), physical borders still matter in local settings. This is particularly the case in active war zones, where the ability of sectarian militia groups to easily traverse borders can fuel conflicts that otherwise might not turn violent.

Political Elites Can Both Foster and Impede Sectarianism

The role of political leaders proved critical in all cases, in both positive and negative ways. Political elites with patronage systems, particularly from external sources, can foster sectarianism and stymie cross-sectarian cooperation. However, when such elites lose legitimacy and are unable to deliver for their constituencies, as we saw in the Lebanon case, windows of opportunity can emerge for alternative leaders and movements with nonsectarian agendas. The Iraq case study also demonstrated that credible local leaders promoting coexistence can counter sectarian pressures. Generational change might also boost the cultivation of political elites with nonsectarian agendas over time.

Civil-Society Development Is Critical

It is difficult to capitalize on windows of opportunity if there are no alternative political leaders or movements to seize the moment with nonsectarian agendas. This requires some opening of political space, at least at the local level, for movements to form around issues that transcend sectarian identities, such as economic development, education reform, female empowerment, or environmental challenges. In the case of Lebanon's Beirut Madinati movement, the trash crisis created a focal point for grassroots organization and political mobilization across sectarian lines. In Syria, local administrative councils have tried to buffer communities from militias, although many councils lack the capacity to prevent armed groups from controlling decisionmaking in their areas.

Cross-Sectarian Interaction Can Serve as a Buffer to Sectarianism

Communities with existing cross-sectarian interaction, particularly in urban areas, possess what Carpenter calls "social capital," which can boost resilience in the face of sectarian challenges, as occurred in some communities in Iraq even at the height of armed conflict. The stronger the level of trust and social connections among community members across sectarian lines, the stronger the social capital that can better equip communities from sliding into sectarianism when conflict emerges. Conversely, when communities are built to segregate citizens along sectarian lines and create economic disparities, as occurred in Hamad Town in the Bahrain case, the prospects for sectarian division and conflict increase. Cross-sectarian interaction can be increased by the development of physical infrastructure that encourages walkability and emphasizes public spaces.

Less Pronounced Socioeconomic Gaps Improve a Community's Ability to Resist Sectarianism

The 'Isa Town example from the Bahrain case study demonstrates that the narrower the socioeconomic gaps between Sunni and Shi'a residents (in large part because, in mixed cities, it is more difficult to discriminate against a particular sect), the less likely we are to see sectarian grievances and violence emerge. But in neighborhoods where economic grievances and discrimination are greater, we are more likely to see communities vulnerable to sectarian violence. One related area that might merit further research is whether communities suffering greater negative economic impacts from climate change might be more susceptible to sectarian conflict, with countries like Iran as possible case studies for such analysis.

Policy Recommendations

Clearly, some of the most critical factors that can reduce the salience of sectarianism in the Middle East would be the reduction of conflict and narrowing of socioeconomic gaps that fuel grievances and make populations susceptible to sectarian-based elites and regional powers who are serving their own narrow interests. But ending conflict and socioeconomic disparity in the region is a long-term and ambitious goal, and unfortunately not one that policymakers can easily or quickly implement. However, we can draw more-achievable policy lessons from the case studies, particularly at the community level. Some preliminary policy recommendations that might guide decisionmakers both within and outside the region who seek to minimize sectarian conflict in the Middle East over time are as follows:

- *Improve the control of borders.* Cutting off the resources, supplies, and fighters coming from foreign sources is critical, as is pressing border countries to stop these flows, particularly in conflict zones like Syria and Iraq. Communities that are better walled off from external sectarian influence exhibit higher levels of resilience and lower levels of violence. The international community can support improved border control through programs that focus on physical infrastructure, capacity-building of partners' border security forces, and leveraging of technology (e.g., biometrics) relevant to these challenges. As the Iraq case study demonstrates, not all border security is provided by formal state institutions. In these cases, the international community might need new types of programming that empower localities over the typical state-based approaches.
- *Limit foreign funding of sectarian leaders and parties.* The fueling of sectarian conflict from external sources, and the patronage systems that sustain this, is one of the most significant drivers of sectarian tension and violence in the region. Exerting leverage on regional governments (in particular, Iran and Saudi Arabia)

to curtail such activities is critical. Preventing sectarian conflicts that have negative spillover effects across the region should create a common incentive among external powers to limit the influence of sectarian actors, even if the external powers are at odds on broader policy goals. The international community can use financial leverage to crack down on state funding to groups designated as foreign terrorist organizations. The challenge is that some of the individuals and groups purveying sectarianism are not designated terrorists, and many do not qualify for designation because they are not necessarily advocating for violence. In these cases, the international community will need to convince funders that the net effect of their support runs counter to their interests. Pointing to instances of "blow back" (i.e., when sectarian actors turn on their patrons after receiving foreign funding) is one potential argument.

- *Encourage civil-society development.* Pressing for freedom of expression and association in bilateral dialogues with regional partners is crucial. This does not mean insisting on elections or backing specific opposition leaders or parties. Rather, the focus should be on opening up space at the local level for civic engagement as a peaceful channel for expressing grievances and discussing policy challenges that cut across sectarian agendas. Civil-society movements can help cultivate new cadres of leaders and form an important alternative to sectarian-driven elites. This requires creating more spaces for dialogue. Even non-democratic governments recognize the need for release valves, and most national leaders in the region say that they are seeking to build national identities that transcend sect. Opening up more space for greater cross-sectarian cooperation at the community level would be a good way to test that resolve.

- *Focus on governance.* It is important to help regional leaders focus on domestic governance agendas, particularly in terms of the ability to better deliver public services through institutional capacity-building and skills development among their youthful populations. Highlighting leaders who are dependent on patronage and corrupt practices and who are not delivering basic services to their people can open up opportunities for alternative leaders. Cultivating leaders who support domestic reform programs aimed to benefit the broader public—not just a particular group or tribe—will be critical for reducing sectarianism and solving day-to-day public policy challenges. The reputation of regional leaders among the international community is an important currency. Just ask former Iraqi Prime Minister Nouri al-Maliki, who was removed via joint pressure from the United States and Iran after they concluded that his sectarian orientation had contributed to the rise of ISIL. The international community could do more in this area before the onset of a crisis. By praising leaders who prioritize public services and refrain from engaging in divisive identity politics, the international community can bolster incentives for inclusive politics.

- *Take urban planning seriously.* How cities are designed in the Middle East matters, not only for sustainable development but also for social and political stability. Urban areas designed to better integrate different sectors of society and increase economic opportunities and social interaction through public spaces are more likely to remain stable and peaceful when societal tensions increase. Although it will be difficult to redesign villages and urban areas already based on segregated models where interaction across tribal or sectarian affiliations is limited, post-conflict areas provide an opportunity to rebuild in ways that could foster greater integration and reduce intercommunal tension in the future. Many countries have rich experience in urban renewal, and the challenges of climate change are bringing greater attention to cities and bolstering their resilience to natural catastrophe. These global trends can create new opportunities to improve infrastructure in Middle Eastern cities and create more public spaces to enhance economic development and attract intercommunal mixing.
- *Promote local media.* Regional media outlets on both sides of the sectarian divide are increasingly promoting sectarian agendas. This mobilizes sectarian leaders and movements and increases the prospects for conflict in communities with high levels of socioeconomic grievance and low levels of cross-sectarian interaction and trust. More support for local media could help counter such trends, increasing coverage of technocratic municipal issues that transcend sectarian difference, such as water challenges, trash collection, youth unemployment, or education gaps. The international community has invested significant resources in creating a message against violent extremism. Because narrow identity politics is a major source of regional instability, the same donors have a parallel interest in promoting more-inclusive groupings that transcend sect. A palatable approach to achieving this aim is to support media coverage with nonsectarian agendas.

The aim of this research effort is not to solve the problem of sectarianism in the Middle East or to pretend it does not exist. Rather, this effort seeks to fill important gaps in our understanding of how resilience might already be at work and the factors that might boost or undermine it. Although research has already illuminated what might be driving sectarianism in the region, we have far less understanding about how we might counter it. Identifying resilience at local community levels in highly divided societies in the Middle East is a step in that direction, but it is only the beginning in tackling a complex challenge that is likely to stay with the region for years to come.

References

'Abd al-Jabar, Falah, "al-Mushkila al-Ṭā'ifiya fī al-Watan al-'Arabī [The Sectarianism Problem in the Arab Nation]," *Al-Mustaqbal al-'Arabī Journal*, Vol. 408, January/February 2013.

a-Noufal, Waleed Khaled, and Dan Wilkofsky, "On the Defensive in Dara'a, Reported Islamic State Affiliates Deploy 'Unheard of' Suicide Bombings," Syria Direct, April 5, 2016. As of April 20, 2018:
https://syriadirect.org/news/on-the-defensive-in-daraa-reported-islamic-state-affiliates-deploy-'unheard-of'-suicide-bombings

Abdo, Geneive, "The New Sectarianism: The Arab Uprisings and the Rebirth of the Shi'a–Sunni Divide," Washington, D.C.: Brookings Institution, Saban Center for Middle East Policy, Analysis Paper No. 29, April 2013.

Abu-Rish, Ziad, "Municipal Politics in Lebanon," *Middle East Report*, Vol. 46, 2016.

Ajroudi, Asma, "Unpicking the Results of Lebanon's Elections," *Al-Jazeera*, May 10, 2018. As of November 12, 2018:
https://www.aljazeera.com/news/2018/05/unpicking-results-lebanon-elections-180510171253490.html

al-A'ali, Mohammed, "Clashes Spark Plea for Calm," *Gulf Daily News*, December 4, 2011.

Al-Arabiya, "In an Interview Today, Mohammed bin Salman to Tackle Saudi, Regional Issues," May 1, 2017. As of November 9, 2018:
http://english.alarabiya.net/en/media/television-and-radio/2017/05/02/Saudi-Deputy-Crown-Prince-to-appear-on-MBC-.html

al-Assil, Ibrahim, "Al-Qaeda Affiliate and Ahrar al-Sham Compete for Control in Idlib," Middle East Institute, March 7, 2017. As of April 20, 2018:
http://www.google.com/url?sa=t&rct=j&q=&esrc=s&source=web&cd=3&cad=rja&uact=8&ved=2ahUKEwjNxsqstN7eAhXE11MKHTEnByIQFjACegQIBhAC&url=http%3A%2F%2Fen.omrandirasat.org%2Fpublications%2Freports%2Fdownload%2F53_5d83efe1fcfd9f8eb921291eb94d83d2.html&usg=AOvVaw2FpWtrfGEXAkZd4oXNt48T

al-Khalidi, Suleiman, "Rebels Capture Last Syrian Town in Idlib Province," Reuters, May 28, 2015. As of April 20, 2018:
http://www.reuters.com/article/us-mideast-crisis-syria-ariha-idUSKBN0OD2LK20150529

———, "Syrian Army and Allies Step Up Bombing of Rebels in Deraa City," Reuters, June 11, 2017a. As of April 20, 2018:
http://www.reuters.com/article/us-mideast-crisis-syria-deraa-idUSKBN19305V

———, "Syrian Rebels Re-Open Main Border Crossing with Turkey," Reuters, July 27, 2017b. As of April 20, 2018:
https://www.reuters.com/article/us-mideast-crisis-syria-crossing/syrian-rebels-reopen-main-border-crossing-with-turkey-idUSKBN1AC2PD

Al-Nakib, Farah, "Revisiting Ḥaḍar and Badū in Kuwait: Citizenship, Housing, and the Construction of a Dichotomy," *International Journal of Middle East Studies*, Vol. 46, No. 1, 2014, pp. 5–30.

Al-Tamimi, Aymenn Jawad, "The Massacre of Druze Villagers in Qalb Lawza, Idlib Province," Syria Comment, June 15, 2015. As of April 20, 2018:
https://www.joshualandis.com/blog/the-massacre-of-druze-villagers-in-qalb-lawza-idlib-province

———, "'Reconciliation' in Syria: The Case of Al-Sanamayn," Middle East Forum, April 27, 2017. As of April 20, 2018:
http://www.meforum.org/6671/reconciliation-in-syria-the-case-of-al-sanamayn

Alaaldin, Ranj, "Kurdistan's Political Landscape and the Path Towards Independence," in Sasha Toperich, Tea Ivanovic, and Nahro Zagros, eds., *Iraqi Kurdistan Region: A Path Forward*, Baltimore, Md.: Johns Hopkins University Center for Transatlantic Relations, 2017, pp. 33–44.

Alami, Mona, "What's Keeping Syria's Rebel Forces from Consolidating Their Power?" *Al-Monitor*, September 26, 2016. As of April 23, 2018:
https://www.al-monitor.com/pulse/originals/2016/09/syria-north-south-opposition-groups.html

Aldrich, Daniel P., and Michelle A. Meyer, "Social Capital and Community Resilience," *American Behavioral Scientist*, Vol. 59, No. 2, 2015, pp. 254–269.

Alfarooqmli, "ميليشيا الفاروق تقتحم كرزكان و تمسح الإساءات [The Faruq Militia Storms Karzakan and Wipes Out Graffiti]," YouTube, August 10, 2011. As of April 20, 2018:
https://www.youtube.com/watch?v=cCANLKvjuCA

Alhasan, Hasan T., "The Role of Iran in the Failed Coup of 1981: The IFLB in Bahrain," *Middle East Journal*, Vol. 65, No. 4. 2011, pp. 603–617.

Ali, Rebaz, "Kurdistan and the Challenge of Islamism: A Conversation with Dr. Hadi Ali, Former Chairman of Kurdistan Islamic Union's Political Bureau," Washington, D.C.: Hudson Institute, August 14, 2015. As of November 15, 2018:
https://www.hudson.org/research/11528-kurdistan-and-the-challenge-of-islamism

American Federation of Labor and Congress of Industrial Organizations, "Public Submission to the Office of Trade and Labor Affairs Under Chapter 15 of the U.S.-Bahrain Free Trade Agreement: Concerning the Failure of the Government of Bahrain to Comply with Its Commitments Under Article 15.1 of the U.S.-Bahrain Free Trade Agreement," April 21, 2011.

Amnesty International, *"Torture Was My Punishment": Abductions, Torture, and Summary Killings Under Armed Group Rule in Aleppo and Idlib, Syria*, London, July 2016. As of November 16, 2018:
https://www.amnesty.org/download/Documents/MDE2442272016ENGLISH.PDF

Anderson, Mary B., and Marshall Wallace, *Opting Out of War: Strategies to Prevent Violent Conflict*, Boulder, Colo.: Lynne Rienner Publishers, 2012.

Associated Press, "Aid Groups: Jordan Deports Thousands of Syrian Refugees," Voice of America, May 12, 2017. As of April 20, 2018:
https://www.voanews.com/a/aid-groups-jordan-deports-thousands-of-syrian-refugees/3849003.html

Atallah, Sami, and Diana Kallas, "The Role of Regional Administrations in the Context of Decentralization," Lebanese Center for Policy Studies, Roundtable Report Series, August 2012.

Bahrain Independent Commission of Inquiry, *Report of the Bahrain Independent Commission of Inquiry*, final revision, December 10, 2011.

Barnard, Anne, and Maria Abi-Habib, "Why Saad Hariri Had That Strange Sojourn in Saudi Arabia," *New York Times*, December 24, 2017.

Batatu, Hanna, *Syria's Peasantry, the Descendants of Its Less Rural Notables, and Their Politics*, Princeton, N.J.: Princeton University Press, 1999.

BBC News, "Iran FM: Sectarian Strife Is Worst Threat in World," November 11, 2013. As of April 19, 2018:
http://www.bbc.com/news/world-middle-east-24893808

Beirut Madinati, *Municipal Program 2016–2022*, Beirut, Lebanon, archival copy, 2016.

BICI—*See* Bahrain Independent Commission of Inquiry.

Bonnano, George, "Loss, Trauma, and Human Resilience: Have We Underestimated the Human Capacity to Thrive After Extremely Aversive Events?" *American Psychologist*, Vol. 59, No. 1, January 2004, pp. 20–28.

Bonnano, George, and Anthony Mancini, "Beyond Resilience and PTSD: Mapping the Heterogeneity of Responses to Potential Trauma," *Psychological Trauma: Theory, Research, Practice, and Policy*, Vol. 4, No. 1, 2012, pp. 74–83.

Boudreau, Thomas E., "When the Killing Begins: An Epistemic Inquiry into Violent Human Conflict, Contested Truths, and Multiplex Methodology," in T. Maytók, J. Senehi, and S. Bryne, eds., *Critical Issues in Peace and Conflict Studies: Theory, Practice, and Pedagogy*, Lanham, Md.: Lexington Books, 2012, pp. 19–42.

Bowen, Glenn A., "Social Capital, Social Funds and Poor Communities: An Exploratory Analysis," *Social Policy and Administration*, Vol. 43, No. 3, 2009, pp. 245–269.

Brand-Jacobsen, Kai, *Ninevah Paths Towards Just and Lasting Peace*, Duhok, Iraq: Un Ponte Per and Peace, Action, Training, and Research Institute of Romania, April 2016. As of November 19, 2018:
https://www.unponteper.it/wp-content/uploads/2015/10/Nineveh_Paths_Brief_EN.pdf

Brumberg, Daniel, "Transforming the Arab World's Protection-Racket Politics," *Journal of Democracy*, Vol. 24, No. 3, 2013, pp. 88–103.

Cambanis, Thanassis, "People Power and Its Limits: Lessons from Lebanon's Anti-Sectarian Reform Movement," in Thanassis Cambanis and Michael Wahid Hanna, eds., *Arab Politics Beyond the Uprisings: Experiments in an Era of Resurgent Authoritarianism*, Washington, D.C.: Century Foundation Press, March 2017.

Cammett, Melani, *Compassionate Communalism: Welfare and Sectarianism in Lebanon*, Ithaca, N.Y.: Cornell University Press, 2014.

Cannon-Bowers, Janis A., Eduardo Salas, and Sharolyn Converse, "Shared Mental Models in Expert Team Decision Making," in N. John Castellan, ed., *Individual and Group Decision Making*, Hillsdale, N.J.: Lawrence Erlbaum Associates, 1993, pp. 221–245.

Carpenter, Ami C., "Havens in a Firestorm: Perspectives from Baghdad on Resilience to Sectarian Violence," *Civil Wars Journal*, Vol. 14, No. 2, 2012.

———, *Community Resilience to Sectarian Violence in Baghdad*, New York: Springer-Verlag, 2016.

The Carter Center, "Syria: Pro-Government Paramilitary Forces," November 5, 2013. As of November 12, 2018:
https://www.cartercenter.org/resources/pdfs/peace/conflict_resolution/syria-conflict/pro-governmentparamilitaryforces.pdf

Centre for Human Dialogue, *Local Administration Structures in Opposition-Held Areas in Syria*, Geneva, April 2014.

Chaaban, Jad, Diala Haidar, Rayan Ismail, Rana Khoury, and Mirna Shidrawi, "Beirut's Municipal Elections: Did Beirut Madinati Permanently Change Lebanon's Electoral Scene?" Arab Center for Research and Policy Studies, September 2016.

Chen, A. C., V. M. Keith, K. J. Leong, C. Airriess, W. Li, K. Y. Chung, and C. C. Lee, "Hurricane Katrina: Prior Trauma, Poverty and Health Among Vietnamese-American Survivors," *International Nursing Review*, Vol. 54, No. 4, 2007, pp. 324–331.

Chulov, Martin, "Iran Repopulates Syria with Shia Muslims to Help Tighten Regime's Control," *The Guardian*, January 13, 2017. As of April 20, 2018:
https://www.theguardian.com/world/2017/jan/13/irans-syria-project-pushing-population-shifts-to-increase-influence

Clarke, Hilary, "Blast Kills Fighters After Jihadists Take Control of Syria's Idlib," CNN, July 24, 2017. As of April 20, 2018:
http://www.cnn.com/2017/07/24/middleeast/syria-idlib-control-hts/

Cockburn, Patrick, "Syrian Civil War: Jabhat al-Nusra's Massacre of Druze Villagers Shows They're Just as Nasty as Isis," *The Independent*, June 14, 2015. As of April 20, 2018:
http://www.independent.co.uk/voices/commentators/syrian-civil-war-jabhat-al-nusras-massacre-of-druze-villagers-shows-the-group-is-just-as-nasty-as-10318348.html

Collard, Rebecca, "Kurdish ISIS Recruits Threaten Identity and Security of Kurdish State," *TIME*, January 23, 2015. As of April 23, 2018:
http://time.com/3679970/kurds-isis-recruits/

Colletta, Nat J., and Michelle L. Cullen, *Violent Conflict and the Transformation of Social Capital: Lessons from Cambodia, Rwanda, Guatemala, and Somalia (English)*, Washington, D.C.: The World Bank, 2000.

Corstange, Daniel, "Vote Trafficking in Lebanon," *International Journal of Middle East Studies*, Vol. 44, No. 3, 2012, pp. 483–505.

Daily Star, "Jad Tabet Wins Beirut Order of Engineers Polls," April 8, 2017. As of November 7, 2018:
http://www.dailystar.com.lb/News/Lebanon-News/2017/Apr-08/401164-polls-open-for-beirut-order-of-engineers-council.ashx

"Dara'a Council," Facebook page, undated.

Davison, John, "Death Toll from Aleppo Bus Convoy Bomb Attack at Least 126: Observatory," Reuters, April 15, 2017. As of April 20, 2018:
https://www.reuters.com/article/us-mideast-crisis-syria-idUSKBN17H04Y

The Day After, *Sectarianism in Syria: Survey Study*, Istanbul, 2016. As of April 20, 2018:
https://scm.bz/en/fifth-estate/sectarianism-in-syria-survey-study

Dearden, Lizzie, "Syria: Bombing Hits Bus Convoy," *The Independent*, April 15, 2017. As of April 20, 2018:
http://www.independent.co.uk/news/world/middle-east/syria-bombing-explosion-attack-buses-convoy-aleppo-rebels-assad-regime-madaya-kefraya-foua-a7685186.html

Dukhan, Haian, "Tribes and Tribalism in the Syrian Uprising," conference paper, St. Andrews University, Scotland, 2014.

e14feb, " زعيم البلطجية السعيدي يجيش المليشيات المسلحة [*Baltajiya* Headman al-Saʿidi Enlists Armed Militias]," YouTube, March 13, 2011. As of April 20, 2018:
https://www.youtube.com/watch?v=6i_zIUr7f1E

The Economist, "Drawing in the Neighbours," July 2, 2015. As of April 20, 2018:
https://www.economist.com/news/middle-east-and-africa/
21656692-turkey-and-jordan-are-considering-setting-up-buffer-zones-war-scorched

Ekman, Mikael, ed., *ILAC Rule of Law Assessment Report: Syria 2017*, Enskede, Sweden: International Legal Assistance Consortium, 2017. As of November 15, 2018:
http://www.ilacnet.org/wp-content/uploads/2017/04/Syria2017.pdf

Ersan, Mohammad, "Extremist Expansion in Southern Syria Puts Jordan on Guard," *Al-Monitor*, March 13, 2017. As of April 23, 2018:
https://www.al-monitor.com/pulse/originals/2017/03/
syria-southern-front-islamist-factions-threat-jordan.html

Eskaf, Mahmoud, "Syria: Tahrir al-Sham Adopts Damascus Twin Bombings," *Middle East Observer*, March 13, 2017. As of April 20, 2018:
https://www.middleeastobserver.org/2017/03/13/syria-2/

Evans, Tom, "Bosnian Leader: 'Ethnic Cleansing' Continues 15 Years After the War," CNN, March 1, 2010. As of April 23, 2018:
http://www.cnn.com/2010/WORLD/europe/03/01/bosnia.herzegovina/index.html

Favier, Agnes, "Local Governance Dynamics in Opposition-Controlled Areas in Syria," in Luigi Narbone, Agnes Favier, and Virginie Collombier, eds., *Inside Wars: Local Dynamics of Conflict in Syria and Libya*, San Domenico di Fiesole, Italy: European University Institute, 2016, pp. 6–15.

Fearon, James, and David Laitin, "Bahrain," unpublished manuscript, June 15, 2005. As of April 18, 2018:
https://web.stanford.edu/group/ethnic/Random%20Narratives/BahrainRN1.1.pdf

Fearon, James D., and David D. Laitin, "Violence and the Social Construction of Ethnic Identity," *International Organization*, Vol. 54, No. 4, 2000, pp. 845–877.

Femia, Francesco, and Caitlin Werrell, "Syria: Climate Changes, Drought and Social Unrest," Center for Climate and Security, February 29, 2012. As of April 20, 2018:
https://climateandsecurity.org/2012/02/29/syria-climate-change-drought-and-social-unrest/

Fildis, Ayse Tekdal, "Roots of Alawite-Sunni Rivalry in Syria," *Middle East Policy*, Vol. 19, No. 2, 2012, pp. 148–156.

Finkel, Steven E., Daniel Wallace, and John F. McCauley, "Contextual Violence and Support for Violent Extremism: Evidence from the Sahel," unpublished manuscript, U.S. Agency for International Development, 2016.

Fishman, Shira, *Community-Level Indicators of Radicalization: A Data and Methods Task Force*, College Park, Md.: National Consortium for the Study of Terrorism and Responses to Terrorism, 2009.

Fisk, Robert, "Syria Civil War: The Untold Story of the Siege of Two Small Shia Villages—And How the World Turned a Blind Eye," *The Independent*, February 22, 2016. As of April 20, 2018:
http://www.independent.co.uk/news/world/middle-east/nubl-zahra-a6889921.html

Friedman, Brandon, and Uzi Rabi, "Sectarianism and War in Iraq and Syria," Foreign Policy Research Institute, January 5, 2017. As of April 20, 2018:
http://www.fpri.org/article/2017/01/sectarianism-war-iraq-syria/

Fuccaro, Nelida, *Histories of City and State in the Persian Gulf: Manama Since 1800*, Cambridge, U.K.: Cambridge University Press, 2009.

Fumerton, Mario, and Wladimir van Wilgenburg, "Kurdistan's Political Armies: The Challenge of Unifying the Peshmerga Forces," Carnegie Middle East Center, December 16, 2015. As of November 16, 2018:
https://carnegieendowment.org/2015/12/16/kurdistan-s-political-armies-challenge-of-unifying-peshmerga-forces-pub-61917

Funk, Nathan C., and Abdul Aziz Said, "Islam and the West: Narratives of Conflict and Conflict Transformation," *International Journal of Peace Studies*, Vol. 9, No. 1, 2004, pp. 1–28.

Gause, F. Gregory III, *Beyond Sectarianism: The New Middle East Cold War*, Washington, D.C.: Brookings Institution, Doha Center, Analysis Paper No. 11, July 2014.

Gengler, Justin, "How About That Police Reform," Religion and Politics in Bahrain, blog post, January 8, 2012. As of April 20, 2018:
http://bahrainipolitics.blogspot.com/2012/01/how-about-that-police-reform.html

———, "Royal Factionalism, the Khawalid, and the Securitization of 'the Shī'a Problem' in Bahrain," *Journal of Arabian Studies*, Vol. 3, No. 1, 2013, pp. 53–79.

———, "Understanding Sectarianism in the Persian Gulf," in Lawrence Potter, ed., *Sectarianism in the Persian Gulf*, New York: Oxford University Press, 2014, pp. 31–66.

———, *Group Conflict and Political Mobilization in Bahrain and the Arab Gulf: Rethinking the Rentier State*, Bloomington, Ind.: Indiana University Press, 2015.

Ghattas, Kim, "Syria War: Southern Rebels See US as Key to Success," BBC News, December 9, 2014. As of April 20, 2018:
http://www.bbc.com/news/world-middle-east-30374581

———, "Beirut's Lovable Losers," *Foreign Policy*, May 2016. As of November 7, 2018:
https://foreignpolicy.com/2016/05/26/beiruts-loveable-losers/

Goldberg, Jeffrey, "The Obama Doctrine," *The Atlantic*, April 2016. As of November 7, 2018:
https://www.theatlantic.com/magazine/archive/2016/04/the-obama-doctrine/471525/

Gubler, Joshua R., and Joel Sawat Selway, "Horizontal Inequality, Crosscutting Cleavages, and Civil War," *Journal of Conflict Resolution*, Vol. 56, No. 2, 2012, pp. 206–232.

Haddad, Bassam, *Business Networks in Syria: The Political Economy of Authoritarian Resilience*, Stanford, Calif.: Stanford University Press, 2011.

Haddad, Fanar, "Sectarian Relations in Arab Iraq: Contextualising the Civil War of 2006–2007," *British Journal of Middle Eastern Studies*, Vol. 40, No. 2, 2013, pp. 115–138.

Hajjar, Bahjat, Corinne von Burg, Leila Hilal, Martina Santschi, Mazen Gharibah, and Mazhar Sharbaji, *Perceptions of Governance: The Experience of Local Administrative Councils in Opposition-Held Syria*, Bern, Switzerland: Swiss Peace, 2017.

Harb, Mona, *Cities and Political Change: How Young Activists in Beirut Bred an Urban Social Movement*, Rome, Power 2 Youth, Istituto Affari Internazionali, Working Paper No. 20, September 2016.

Harris, Katie, David Keen, and Tom Mitchell, *When Disasters and Conflict Collide: Improving Links Between Disaster Resilience and Conflict Prevention*, London: Overseas Development Institute, 2013.

Heller, Sam, "Keeping the Lights on in Rebel Idlib," The Century Foundation, November 29, 2016. As of April 20, 2018:
https://tcf.org/content/report/keeping-lights-rebel-idlib/

Heras, Nicholas A., "A Profile of Syria's Strategic Darʻa Province," *CTC Sentinel*, Vol. 7, No. 6, June 2014, pp. 20–23. As of April 20, 2018:
https://ctc.usma.edu/posts/a-profile-of-syrias-strategic-dara-province

Heydemann, Steven, "Syria's Uprising: Sectarianism, Regionalization, and State Order in the Levant," FRIDE Working Paper, No. 119, 2013.

Holes, Clive, "Dialect and National Identity: The Cultural Politics of Self-Representation in Bahraini Musalsalāt," in Paul Dresch and James Piscatori, eds., *Monarchies and Nations: Globalization and Identity in the Arab States of the Gulf*, London: I. B. Tauris, 2005, pp. 52–72.

Hubbard, Ben, and Hwaida Saad, "Lebanon's Vanishing Prime Minister Is Back at Work. Now What?" *New York Times*, November 25, 2017.

Huesmann, L. Rowell, and Lucnya Kirwil, "Why Observing Violence Increases the Risk of Violent Behavior in the Observer," in D. J. Flannery, A. T. Vazsonyi, and I. D. Waldman, eds., *The Cambridge Handbook of Violent Behavior and Aggression*, Cambridge, U.K.: Cambridge University Press, 2007, pp. 545–570.

Human Rights Watch, "Syria: Attacks on Religious Sites Raise Tensions," webpage, January 23, 2013. As of April 20, 2018:
https://www.hrw.org/news/2013/01/23/syria-attacks-religious-sites-raise-tensions

Institute for War & Peace Reporting, *Local Governance Inside Syria: Challenges, Opportunities, and Recommendations*, Washington, D.C., 2014.

Interfaith Dialogue, "Peace and Conflict Resolution After ISIS," 5th Annual Dialogue, University of Duhok's Center for Peace and Conflict Resolution, Duhok, Iraq, 2017.

International Organization for Migration, "Iraq Mission: Displacement Tracking Matrix—DTM Round 64," webpage, February 2017. As of April 23, 2018:
http://iraqdtm.iom.int/

Isenberg, D. J., "Group Polarization: A Critical Review and Meta-Analysis," *Journal of Personality and Social Psychology*, Vol. 50, No. 6, 1986, pp. 1141–1151.

Johnson, Todd M., and Brian J. Grim, eds. *World Religion Database*, Boston, Mass.: Brill, 2015. As of November 9, 2018:
https://www.worldreligiondatabase.org/

Kalin, Stephen, and Dmitry Zhdannikov, "U.S. Helped Clinch Iraq Oil Deal to Keep Mosul Battle on Track," Reuters, October 3, 2016. As of November 16, 2018:
https://www.reuters.com/article/us-mideast-crisis-usa-mosul-exclusive-idUSKCN12314Z

Karasapan, Omer, "The Internally Displaced in the Middle East and North Africa: Harbingers of Future Conflict?" Brookings Institution, July 5, 2017. As of April 20, 2018:
https://www.brookings.edu/blog/future-development/2017/07/05/the-internally-displaced-in-the-middle-east-and-north-africa-harbingers-of-future-conflict

Kawachi, Ichiro, Daniel Kim, Adam Coutts, and S. V. Subramanian, "Commentary: Reconciling the Three Accounts of Social Capital," *International Journal of Epidemiology*, Vol. 33, No. 4, 2004, pp. 682–690.

Keatinge, Tom, "The Importance of Financing in Enabling and Sustaining the Conflict in Syria (and Beyond)," *Perspectives on Terrorism*, Vol. 8, No. 4, August 2014, pp. 53–61.

Kelley, Michael B., "Damascus Is 'Totally Exposed from the South' After Rebels Take Key Towns," Business Insider, March 29, 2013.

Kelly, Sarah, "The Psychological Consequences to Adolescents of Exposure to Gang Violence in the Community: An Integrated Review of the Literature," *Journal of Child and Adolescent Psychiatric Nursing*, Vol. 23, No. 2, May 2010, pp. 61–73.

Khalaf, Abdulhadi, "The New Amir of Bahrain: Marching Sideways," *Civil Society*, Vol. 9, No. 100, 2000, pp. 6–13.

Khalaf, Samir, *Civil and Uncivil Violence in Lebanon: A History of the Internationalization of Communal Conflict*, New York: Columbia University Press, 2002.

Khuri, Fuad I., *Tribe and State in Bahrain: The Transformation of Social and Political Authority in an Arab State*, Chicago: University of Chicago Press, 1981.

Kingston, Paul W. T., *Reproducing Sectarianism: Advocacy Networks and the Politics of Civil Society in Post-War Lebanon*, Albany, N.Y.: State University of New York Press, 2014.

Kinninmont, Jane, *Bahrain: Beyond the Impasse*, London: Chatham House/Royal Institute of International Affairs, 2012.

Kirmayer, L. J., M. Sehdev, R. Whitley, S. F. Dandeneau, and C. Isaac, "Community Resilience: Models, Metaphors and Measure," *Journal of Aboriginal Health*, Vol. 5, No. 1, 2009, pp. 62–117.

Kurdistan Regional Government of Iraq, "Erbil Governor: 'IDPs Pose No Security Threat,'" webpage, September 18, 2015. As of April 23, 2018:
http://krg-iran.com/english/index.php/kr/item/762-erbil-governor-idps-pose-no-security-threat

Kurdistan Regional Government of Iraq, Ministry of Interior, "Joint Crisis Coordination Centre," webpage, undated. As of November 16, 2018:
http://jcc.gov.krd/en/article/read/216

Landau, Simha F., and Danny Pfeffermann, "A Time-Series Analysis of Violent Crime and Its Relation to Prolonged States of Warfare—The Israeli Case," *Criminology*, Vol. 26, No. 3, August 1988, pp. 489–504.

Landis, Joshua, "Islamic Education in Syria: Undoing Secularism," Minority Rights Group International World Directory of Minorities, 2011a. As of April 20, 2018:
http://www.ou.edu/content/dam/International/IPHome/Bios/landisdoc/IslamicEduinSyria.pdf

———, "Syria: Background," Minority Rights Group International World Directory of Minorities, 2011b. As of April 20, 2018:
https://minorityrights.org/country/syria/

Levi, Margaret, "When Good Defenses Make Good Neighbors," in Claude Menard, ed., *Institutions, Contracts, and Organizations: Perspectives from New Institutional Economics*, Chichester, U.K.: Edward Elgar, 2000, pp. 137–157.

Lewis, Norman N., "The Frontier of Settlement in Syria, 1800–1950," *International Affairs*, Vol. 31, No. 1, 1955, pp. 48–60.

Lim, Beng-Chong, and Katherine J. Klein, "Team Mental Models and Team Performance: A Field Study of the Effects of Team Mental Model Similarity and Accuracy," *Journal of Organizational Behaviour*, Vol. 27, 2006, pp. 403–418.

Lister, Charles, *Profiling Jabhat al-Nusra*, Washington, D.C.: Brookings Institution, Project on U.S. Relations with the Islamic World, Analysis Paper No. 24, 2016.

Long, Austin, "The Anbar Awakening," *Survival*, Vol. 50, No. 2, 2008, pp. 67–94.

Louër, Laurence, *Transnational Shia Politics*, New York: Columbia University Press, 2008.

———, *Shiism and Politics in the Middle East*, New York: Columbia University Press, 2012.

———, "Sectarianism and Coup-Proofing Strategies in Bahrain," *Journal of Strategic Studies*, Vol. 36, No. 2, 2013, pp. 245–260.

Lund, Aron, "Showdown at Bab al-Hawa," Carnegie Middle East Center, December 12, 2013. As of April 20, 2018:
http://carnegie-mec.org/diwan/53896?lang=en

———, "Does the 'Southern Front' Exist?" Carnegie Middle East Center, March 21, 2014. As of April 20, 2018:
http://carnegie-mec.org/diwan/55054

———, "Syria's Bedouin Tribes: An Interview with Dawn Chatty," Carnegie Middle East Center, July 2, 2015. As of April 20, 2018:
http://carnegie-mec.org/diwan/60264

———, "Assad's Broken Base: The Case of Idlib," The Century Foundation, July 14, 2016. As of April 20, 2018:
https://tcf.org/content/report/assads-broken-base-case-idlib/

Macke, Janaina, and Eliete Kunrath Dilly, "Social Capital Dimensions in Collaborative Networks: The Role of Linking Social Capital," *International Journal of Social Inquiry*, Vol. 3, No. 2, 2010, pp. 121–136.

Makdisi, Ussama, "After 1860: Debating Religion, Reform, and Nationalism in the Ottoman Empire," *International Journal of Middle East Studies*, Vol. 34, No. 4, 2002, pp. 601–617.

———, "The Problem of Sectarianism in the Middle East in an Age of Western Hegemony," in Nader Hashemi and Danny Postel, eds., *Sectarianization: Mapping the New Politics of the Middle East*, New York: Oxford University Press, 2017, pp. 23–34.

Mansour, Renad, "Mosul After the Islamic State: The Kurdistan Region's Strategy," Carnegie Middle East Center, May 20, 2016. As of April 23, 2018:
http://carnegie-mec.org/2016/05/20/mosul-after-islamic-state-kurdistan-region-s-strategy-pub-63615

Mapping Militant Organizations, "Ahrar al-Sham," Stanford University, August 5, 2017a. As of April 23, 2018:
http://web.stanford.edu/group/mappingmilitants/cgi-bin/groups/view/523

———, "Hay'at Tahrir al-Sham (Formerly Jabhat al-Nusra)," Stanford University, August 14, 2017b. As of April 23, 2018:
http://web.stanford.edu/group/mappingmilitants/cgi-bin/groups/view/493

Matthiesen, Toby, *Sectarian Gulf: Bahrain, Saudi Arabia, and the Arab Spring That Wasn't*, Stanford, Calif.: Stanford University Press, 2013.

———, "Sectarianization as Securitization: Identity Politics and Counter Revolution in Bahrain," in Nader Hashemi and Danny Postel, eds., *Sectarianization: Mapping the New Politics of the Middle East*, New York: Oxford University Press, 2017, pp. 199–214.

McDonnell, Patrick J., and Nabih Bulos, "Syrian Military and Druze Allies Join Forces to Fend Off 'Terrorists,'" *Los Angeles Times*, June 21, 2015. As of November 15, 2018:
http://www.latimes.com/world/middleeast/la-fg-syria-south-20150621-story.html

Menkhaus, Ken, "Making Sense of Resilience in Peacebuilding Contexts: Approaches, Applications, Implications," Geneva Peacebuilding Platform, Paper No. 6, 2013.

Mercy Corps–Iraq, *Governance Promotion Through Conflict Management in Iraq (GPCMI): Final Evaluation—Results, Lessons Learned, and Recommendations for Future Programming*, January 2009–December 2010. As of April 23, 2018:
https://www.mercycorps.org/sites/default/files/
mercy_corps_iraq_gpcmi_final_evaluation_2011-06-02_2.pdf

Miller, Greg, and Karen DeYoung, "Secret CIA Effort in Syria Faces Large Funding Cut," *Washington Post*, June 12, 2015. As of April 20, 2018:
https://www.washingtonpost.com/world/national-security/
lawmakers-move-to-curb-1-billion-cia-program-to-train-syrian-rebels/2015/06/12/
b0f45a9e-1114-11e5-adec-e82f8395c032_story.html?utm_term=.bb5e59cd0cbb

Milliken, Jennifer, "Resilience: From Metaphor to an Action Plan for Use in the Peacebuilding Field," Geneva Peacebuilding Platform, Paper No. 7, 2013.

Mitchell, Jocelyn Sage, "Beyond Allocation: The Politics of Legitimacy in Qatar," Ph.D. thesis, Georgetown University, Washington, D.C., 2013.

Moaddel, Mansoor, Jean Kors, and Johan Gärde, *Sectarianism and Counter-Sectarianism in Lebanon*, Ann Arbor, Mich.: University of Michigan Population Studies Center, Report 12-757, 2012.

Moritz-Rabson, Daniel, "In Wartime Syria, Local Councils and Civil Institutions Fill a Gap," PBS Newshour, July 31, 2016. As of April 20, 2018:
http://www.pbs.org/newshour/updates/civil-society-emerges-syria-war/

Morris, Loveday, "Battling on Two Fronts, Moderate Syrian Rebels Struggle for Funding, Lost Fighters," *Washington Post*, October 18, 2013. As of April 23, 2018:
https://www.washingtonpost.com/world/middle_east/
battling-on-two-fronts-moderate-syrian-rebels-struggle-for-funding-lose-fighters/2013/10/17/
fa9232e6-359e-11e3-89db-8002ba99b894_story.html?utm_term=.0a0f8cf1431e

Muftah, "Ambassadors of Peace in Northern Iraq," webpage, undated. As of April 23, 2018:
https://muftah.org/ambassadors-peace-northern-iraq/

Muir, Jenny, "Bridging and Linking in a Divided Society: A Social Capital Case Study from Northern Ireland," *Urban Studies*, Vol. 48, No. 5, 2011, pp. 959–976.

Myers, David G., and G. D. Bishop, "Discussion Effects on Racial Attitude," *Science*, Vol. 169, No. 3947, 1970, pp. 778–779.

Mylroie, Laurie, "U.S.-Led Coalition Supports Continuing Talks Between Erbil and Baghdad," Kurdistan 24, November 15, 2017. As of November 16, 2018:
http://www.kurdistan24.net/en/news/0e02d665-f0ef-489d-b4b6-bbb370cef8f2

Nashed, Mat, "Militants Stifle Civil Society in Syria's Idlib," *Al-Monitor*, July 26, 2017. As of April 20, 2018:
http://www.al-monitor.com/pulse/originals/2017/07/syria-idlib-militants-civil-society.html

Nasr, Vali, *The Shia Revival*, New York: Norton, 2006.

———, "The War for Islam," *Foreign Policy*, January 22, 2016. As of April 18, 2018:
http://foreignpolicy.com/2016/01/22/the-war-for-islam-sunni-shiite-iraq-syria

National Consortium for the Study of Terrorism and Responses to Terrorism, "Global Terrorism Database," data file, 2017. As of April 20, 2018:
https://www.start.umd.edu/gtd

Naylor, Hugh, "Moderate Rebels Take Key Southern Base in Syria, Dealing Blow to Assad," *Washington Post*, June 9, 2015. As of April 20, 2018:
https://www.washingtonpost.com/world/middle_east/
moderate-rebels-take-key-southern-base-in-syria-dealing-blow-to-assad/2015/06/09/
9d6ff9c2-0ea5-11e5-a0fe-dccfea4653ee_story.html?utm_term=.b71fd2d824c3

New York Times Archives, "The Syrian Outbreak: Details of the Damascus Massacre, Foreign Intervention in Syria," digitized version of an article from August 13, 1860. As of April 20, 2018:
http://www.nytimes.com/1860/08/13/news/
syrian-outbreak-details-damascus-massacre-foreign-intervention-syria.html

NGO Coordination Committee for Iraq, *Dohuk Governorate Profile*, Geneva, December 2015. As of June 17, 2017:
http://www.ncciraq.org/images/infobygov/NCCI_Dohuk_Governorate_Profile.pdf

Nordland, Rod, "Al Qaeda Taking Deadly New Role in Syria's Conflict," *New York Times*, July 24, 2012. As of April 20, 2018:
http://www.nytimes.com/2012/07/25/world/middleeast/
al-qaeda-insinuating-its-way-into-syrias-conflict.html

Obeid, Ghinwa, "Doing the Numbers: Ministers Break Down Expat Vote," *Daily Star*, April 19, 2018. As of November 12, 2018:
http://www.dailystar.com.lb/News/Lebanon-News/2018/Apr-19/
445853-doing-the-numbers-ministers-break-down-expat-vote.ashx

Opall-Rome, Barbara, "Jordan Proves Heavyweight in Fight Against ISIS," Defense News, May 9, 2016.

Parasiliti, Andrew, Kathleen Reedy, and Becca Wasser, *Preventing State Collapse in Syria*, Santa Monica, Calif.: RAND Corporation, PE-219-OSD, 2017. As of November 16, 2018:
https://www.rand.org/pubs/perspectives/PE219.html

Parrish, Karen, "Official: Stopping Foreign Fighter Flow to ISIS Requires Collaboration," U.S. Department of Defense, April 5, 2017. As of April 20, 2018:
https://www.defense.gov/News/Article/Article/1141615/
stopping-flow-of-foreign-fighters-to-isis-will-take-years-official-says/

Patai, Raphael, *The Arab Mind*, rev. ed., New York: Scribner, 2002.

Peace, Action, Training, and Research Institute of Romania, "Ninevah Paths to Social Cohesion, Coexistence, and Peace," webpage, undated. As of November 19, 2018:
http://patrir.ro/en/activitatea-noastra/dpo/past-projects/
nineveh-paths-social-cohesion-coexistence-peace/

Perry-Castañeda Library Map Collection, "Syria Maps: Syria (Political) 1976," University of Texas, 2017.

Pettigrew, Thomas F., "Intergroup Contact Theory," *Annual Review of Psychology*, Vol. 49, No. 1, 1998, pp. 65–85.

Pfefferbaum, Betty, Rose L. Pfefferbaum, and Richard L. Van Horn, "Community Resilience Interventions: Participatory, Assessment-Based, Action-Oriented Processes," *American Behavioral Scientist*, Vol. 59, No. 2, 2015, pp. 238–253.

Phillips, Christopher, "Sectarianism and Conflict in Syria," *Third World Quarterly*, Vol. 36, No. 2, March 2015, pp. 357–376.

Potter, Laurence, ed., *Sectarianism in the Persian Gulf*, New York: Oxford University Press, 2014.

Rahnema, Ali, ed., *Pioneers of Islamic Revival*, London: Zed Books, 1994.

Rashid, Madawi, "Sectarianism as Counter-Revolution: Saudi Responses to the Arab Spring," *Studies in Ethnicity and Nationalism*, Vol. 11, No. 3, 2011, pp. 513–526.

Rizkallah, Amanda, "Beirut's Election Was Surprisingly Competitive. Could It Shake Up Lebanese Politics?" *Washington Post*, May 11, 2016. As of November 7, 2018:
https://www.washingtonpost.com/news/monkey-cage/wp/2016/05/11/beiruts-election-was-surprisingly-competitive-could-it-shake-up-lebanese-politics/?utm_term=.f74434fcfc23

Robinson, Heather M., Ben Connable, David E. Thaler, and Ali G. Scotten, *Sectarianism in the Middle East: Implications for the United States*, Santa Monica, Calif.: RAND Corporation, RR-1681-A, 2018. As of November 9, 2018:
https://www.rand.org/pubs/research_reports/RR1681.html

Sampson, Robert J., Stephen W. Raudenbush, and Felton Earls, "Neighborhoods and Violent Crime: A Multilevel Study of Collective Efficacy," *Science*, Vol. 277, No. 5328, 1997, pp. 918–924.

Serwer, Daniel, "Yes, Mr. Obama, There Is a Syrian Opposition," Middle East Institute, October 23, 2015. As of April 20, 2018:
http://www.mei.edu/content/at/yes-mr-obama-there-syrian-opposition

Shaheen, Kareem, "UN Calls for Access to Syrians Stranded in Desert After Deraa's Fall," *The Guardian*, July 13, 2018. As of December 11, 2018:
https://www.theguardian.com/world/2018/jul/12/assads-forces-retake-daraa-birthplace-of-syrias-uprising

Shawki, Ammar, and Roy Gutman, "A Letter from Rebel-Controlled Idlib, Syria," *The Nation*, December 1, 2016. As of November 15, 2018:
https://www.thenation.com/article/letter-from-rebel-controlled-idlib-syria/

Slutkin, Gary, "Violence Is a Contagious Disease," in *Contagion of Violence: Workshop Summary*, Washington, D.C.: Forum on Global Violence Prevention, National Academies Press, 2013, pp. 94–111.

Smith, Hannah Lucinda, "Jihadists' Tour Guide Shuttles Foreign Fighters into Syria," Vice News, February 3, 2014. As of April 20, 2018:
https://news.vice.com/article/tour-guide-shuttles-foreign-fighters-into-syria

Stark, Rodney, and William Sims Bainbridge, *A Theory of Religion*, New Brunswick, N.J.: Rutgers University Press, 1996.

START—*See* National Consortium for the Study of Terrorism and Responses to Terrorism.

Sterling, Joe, "Daraa: The Spark That Lit the Syrian Flame," CNN, March 1, 2012. As of April 20, 2018:
http://www.cnn.com/2012/03/01/world/meast/syria-crisis-beginnings/index.html

"Syria: Amid Rebel Buildup, Fear of New War," UPI, March 28, 2013. As of April 20, 2018:
http://www.upi.com/Top_News/Special/2013/03/28/Syria-Amid-rebel-buildup-fear-of-new-war/UPI-99421364503255/

Syria Direct, "Airstrike Destroys Church in Idlib, Where Christians Once 'Happily Coexisted,'" August 11, 2016. As of April 20, 2018:
http://syriadirect.org/news/airstrike-destroys-only-church-in-idlib-city-where-christians-once-%E2%80%98happily-coexisted%E2%80%99

Syrian Central Bureau of Statistics, "Basic Education Schools (1st & 2nd Cycle) by Ownership of School and Sex of Pupils 2005–2009, and Distribution of Schools by Governorate for 2009," webpage, 2011a. As of April 20, 2018:
http://www.cbssyr.sy/yearbook/2010/Data-Chapter11/TAB-2-11-2010.htm

———, "Pupils of Basic Education (1st Cycle) by School Governorate and Sex 2005–2009, and Distribution of Schools by Governorate for 2009," webpage, 2011b. As of April 20, 2018:
http://www.cbssyr.sy/yearbook/2010/Data-Chapter11/TAB-5-11-2010.htm

———, "Rate Unemployment by Governorate and Labor Force," webpage, 2011c. As of April 20, 2018:
http://www.cbssyr.sy/work/2011/TAB20.htm

———, "The Medical Professional, 2005–2010, and Distribution by Governorate, 2010," webpage, 2011d. As of April 20, 2018:
http://www.cbssyr.sy/yearbook/2011/Data-Chapter12/TAB-2-12-2011.htm

Taleb, Julia, "Syrians Roll Back Extremism in Idlib Without Military Intervention," Waging Nonviolence, May 23, 2017. As of April 20, 2018:
https://wagingnonviolence.org/feature/syrians-roll-back-extremism-idlib

Tastekin, Fehim, "Syria's Idlib Emerges as Achilles Heel in Russia-Turkey Partnership," *Al-Monitor*, July 30, 2018. As of November 15, 2018:
https://www.al-monitor.com/pulse/originals/2018/07/turkey-russia-syria-astana-on-verge-of-collapse-due-to-idlib.html

UNHCR—*See* United Nations High Commissioner for Refugees.

United Nations Educational, Scientific and Cultural Organization, World Heritage Centre, "Manama, City of Trade, Multiculturalism and Religious Coexistence," webpage, July 20, 2018. As of December 19, 2018:
http://whc.unesco.org/en/tentativelists/6354/

United Nations High Commissioner for Refugees, *Displacement as Opportunity and Challenge: Urban Profile—Refugees, Internally Displaced Persons and Host Community, Duhok Governorate, Kurdistan Region of Iraq*, August 2016. As of November 16, 2018:
https://data2.unhcr.org/en/documents/details/52297

United Nations Human Rights Council, "'I lost My Dignity': Sexual and Gender-Based Violence in the Syrian Arab Republic," Independent International Commission of Inquiry on the Syrian Arab Republic, A/HRC/37/CRP.3, March 2018. As of November 15, 2018:
https://giwps.georgetown.edu/resource/i-lost-my-dignity-sexual-and-gender-based-violence-in-the-syrian-arab-republic/

United Nations Office for the Coordination of Humanitarian Affairs, *2016 Humanitarian Needs Overview*, Brussels, October 2015. As of April 20, 2018:
https://reliefweb.int/report/syrian-arab-republic/2016-humanitarian-needs-overview-syrian-arab-republic

United States Institute of Peace, "Resilience as a Peacebuilding Practice: To Realism from Idealism," webpage, undated. As of April 20, 2018:
https://www.usip.org/insights-newsletter/resilience-peacebuilding-practice-realism-idealism

University of Duhok, "Peace and Conflict Resolution Studies Center," webpage, undated. As of November 15, 2018:
http://web.uod.ac/about/president-university/peace-and-conflict-resolution-studies-center

Uphoff, Norman, "Understanding Social Capital: Learning from the Analysis and Experience of Participation," in Partha Dasgupta and Ismail Serageldin, eds., *Social Capital: A Multifaceted Perspective*, Washington, D.C.: The World Bank, 2000, pp. 215–252.

Uppsala Conflict Data Program, "Armed Conflict Dataset," Uppsala, Sweden: Uppsala University, Department of Peace and Conflict Research, 2016. As of November 9, 2018:
http://ucdp.uu.se/

Ury, William, *The Third Side: Why We Fight and How We Can Stop*, London: Penguin Books, 2003.

U.S. Agency for International Development, *Conflict Assessment Framework, Version 2.0*, Washington, D.C., June 2012.

U.S. Department of Defense, *Assessment of U.S. and Coalition Forces to Train, Advise, Assist, and Equip the Kurdish Security Forces in Iraq*, Washington, D.C.: Office of the Inspector General, DODIG-2017-033, December 16, 2016.

U.S. Department of State, "Bahrain," from Bureau of Democracy, Human Rights, and Labor, *July–December 2010 International Religious Freedom Report*, September 13, 2011. As of April 20, 2018: https://www.state.gov/j/drl/rls/irf/2010_5/168261.htm

Valeri, Marc, "Oman's Mediatory Efforts in Regional Crises," Norwegian Peacebuilding Resource Centre, March 2014.

van den Toorn, Christine, and Ahmed Ali, "Challenges and Opportunities in Post-ISIS Territories: The Case of Rabia," Institute of Regional and International Studies, IRIS Iraq Report, August 3, 2015. As of April 23, 2018: http://auis.edu.krd/iris/sites/default/files/IIR%20Report.pdf

Van Metre, Lauren, "Fragility and Resilience," Fragility Study Group, Policy Brief No. 2, September 2016.

Verdeil, Éric, "Les Services Urbains à Beyrouth: Entre Crise Infrastructurelle et Réformes Contestées," *Géosphères*, 2013, pp. 33–58.

Warner, John, "Questioning Sectarianism in Bahrain and Beyond: An Interview with Justin Gengler," Jadaliyya, April 17, 2013. As of November 7, 2018: http://www.jadaliyya.com/Details/28458/Questioning-Sectarianism-in-Bahrain-and-Beyond-An-Interview-with-Justin-Gengler

Wehrey, Frederic, *Sectarian Politics in the Gulf*, New York: Columbia University Press, 2014.

Weine, Stevan, and Osman Ahmed, "Building Resilience to Violent Extremism Among Somali-Americans in Minneapolis-St. Paul," College Park, Md.: National Consortium for the Study of Terrorism and Responses to Terrorism, 2012.

The White House, *National Security Strategy*, Washington, D.C., February 2015.

———, *National Security Strategy of the United States of America*, Washington, D.C., December 2017.

The World Bank, *Kurdistan Region of Iraq: Reforming the Economy for Shared Prosperity and Protecting the Vulnerable—Executive Summary*, Washington, D.C., May 30, 2016. As of April 23, 2018: http://documents.worldbank.org/curated/en/708441468196727918/pdf/106132-WP-P159972-PUBLIC-EXECUTIVE-SUMMARY-of-KRG-Economic-Reform-Roadmap-post-Decision-Review-5-30-2016.pdf

Yosif, Yaman, and James Bowker, "After 'Marginalizing' the East, Dara'a's New Electoral System Aims for Equity," Syria Direct, November 10, 2015.

Zenn, Jacob, "Al-Qaeda-Aligned Central Asian Militants in Syria Separate from Islamic State–Aligned IMU in Afghanistan," The Jamestown Foundation, May 29, 2015. As of April 20, 2018: https://jamestown.org/program/al-qaeda-aligned-central-asian-militants-in-syria-separate-from-islamic-state-aligned-imu-in-afghanistan

Lightning Source UK Ltd.
Milton Keynes UK
UKHW050310230721
387619UK00002B/24